CONTENTS AT A GLANCE

Introduction 1

I Your Marketing Message

1 Your iPhone and iPad App Marketing Strategy: Grand
   Slam or Base Hits? 9
2 What Makes a Winning iPhone/iPad App? 25
3 Identifying Your App's Unique Value 37
4 Identifying Your Target Audience 55
5 Building Your App's Total Message 67

II Delivering Your Message

6 Electronic Word of Mouth 89
7 Using Social Media in Your App Marketing 111
8 Timing Your Marketing Activities 125
9 Getting the Word Out About Your App 135

III Pricing Your iPhone/iPad App

10 Pricing Your App 153
11 Conducting an App Pricing Analysis 167
12 Selling Value over Price 179
13 Breaking into the App Store Top 100 189
14 Level the Playing Field with a Free App 201
15 The App Pricing Roller Coaster 215
16 App Promotions and Cross-Selling 223
17 Using iPhone/iPad Analytics 235

IV Implement a Marketing Plan/Launch Your App

18 Why Have a Marketing Plan? 249
19 Components of an App Marketing Plan 257
20 Marketing Essentials and the Right Mix 269
21 25 Essential iPhone/iPad Marketing Activities 275
22 Implementing Your Plan 287
23 iPhone/iPad Apps for Corporate Marketing 295

TABLE OF CONTENTS

Introduction 1

I Your Marketing Message

1   Your iPhone and iPad App Marketing Strategy: Grand
    Slam or Base Hits? 9
       We've Seen This Movie Before 10
       The Big Win—Grand Slam 14
       The Steady Win—Base Hits 18
       The No Win—Strikeout 20
       Benefits/Drawbacks of the Big Win and
          Steady Win Strategies 21
       Summary 23
2   What Makes a Winning iPhone/iPad App? 25
       Build Something Unique 26
       Deliver New Features 28
       Tie Your App into Trends and News 30
       Tie Into Seasons and Holidays 32
       Tie Your App to Part of a Wider Solution 32
       Apps Created from Other Platforms 33
       Winning Game Apps 35
       Summary 35
3   Identifying Your App's Unique Value 37
       The Four Questions 39
       Who Are Your Competitors? 40
       Identifying Your Competition 42
       Learning from Your Competition 45
       What Are the Key Features of Your iPhone/iPad App? 47
       What Are the Benefits of Your iPhone/iPad App? 48
       What's Unique About Your App? 50
       Summary 51
       Competitive Worksheet 52
4   Identifying Your Target Audience 55
       Refining Your Audience 57
       Segmenting Your Market 57
       Picking Your Market Segment 62
       Targeting Your Market 63
       Summary 65
5   Building Your App's Total Message 67
       Choose an Effective App Name 70
       App Store Text: Lighten It Up 77
       Make Graphics Your Focal Point 79
       Make Your App's Icon Jump 80
       Build a Simple, Clean Product Website 82

Strive for Immediate Positive Reviews 85
Summary 86

II Delivering Your Message

6   Electronic Word of Mouth 89
Positive External Reviews 92
Coordinated Marketing Effort 94
Generating Demand 95
Reaching Interested Buyers 96
Choosing the Right Delivery Methods 96
Three Key Areas 97
Direct Marketing for Your App 97
Summary 109

7   Using Social Media in Your App Marketing 111
Selecting Your Social Media Tools 114
Using Facebook 115
Tweeting 118
Using Blogs 120
Using LinkedIn 121
Using YouTube 123
Summary 124

8   Timing Your Marketing Activities 125
App Buying Cycles 126
Winning Marketing Activities 129
Timing the Launch of Your App 130
Summary 132

9   Getting the Word Out About Your App 135
When to Write a Press Release 136
Do You Have What It Takes? 138
Writing Your Press Release 139
Embedded Links 145
Attaching Multimedia to Your Press Release 146
Press Release Signature 147
Publishing and Distributing Your Press Release 148
Summary 150

III Pricing Your iPhone/iPad App

10   Pricing Your App 153
Competing Against Free Apps 155
Some Pricing Misconceptions 158
Offer a Free Version of Your App 160
Setting Your App's Price 160
Summary 166

11   Conducting an App Pricing Analysis 167
Cost/Benefit Analysis 168
Breakeven Analysis 175
Summary 177

12   Selling Value over Price 179
     Selling Value 182
     Additional Thoughts on Selling Value 186
     Summary 188
13   Breaking into the App Store Top 100 189
     Develop a Great App 190
     Beat Up Your App...Mercilessly 192
     Have Friends in High Places 192
     Cross-Promote 194
     Keep the Size Under 20MB 194
     Price It Right 195
     Integrate Your App with Other Apps 195
     Optimize Your Web and App Store Copy 196
     Develop Your Brand and Promote It Like Crazy 196
     Reach Out to Apple 198
     Summary 199
14   Level the Playing Field with a Free App 201
     Build a Paid App—Standalone 203
     Build a Free App, Build a Following 204
     Build a Paid App and a Free App at the Same Time 206
     Free Apps with Ads 209
     Can iAds Help You to Monetize Your App? 211
     Summary 213
15   The App Pricing Roller Coaster 215
     Raising Your Price 217
     Lowering Your Price 218
     Temporary Price Drops 220
     Value-Add Sales 221
     Launch Your App Free for a Limited Time 222
     Summary 222
16   App Promotions and Cross-Selling 223
     Promotional Marketing for iPhone/iPad Apps 224
     Cross-Selling 227
     Summary 233
17   Using iPhone/iPad Analytics 235
     Analytics Components 236
     Utilize Paid Ad Campaigns 240
     Top Analytics Vendors 240
     Analytics and Privacy 244
     Summary 245

IV Implement a Marketing Plan/Launch Your App
18   Why Have a Marketing Plan? 249
     Top 10 Reasons Why You Should Have
          an App Marketing Plan 250
     Summary 256

19   Components of an App Marketing Plan 257
        Marketing Goals and Objectives 259
        Market Analysis 260
        Business Environment 261
        Strengths, Weaknesses, Opportunities,
            and Threats Analysis 262
        Marketing Focus 264
        Financial Information 265
        Marketing Calendar 265
        Summary 268
20   Marketing Essentials and the Right Mix 269
        Keep Your App Store Content New and Exciting 270
        How Much Should I Spend? 270
        Striking a Balance 271
        Summary 274
21   25 Essential iPhone/iPad Marketing Activities 275
        Delivering Your iPhone/iPad App to the World 276
        iPhone/iPad Pricing and Promotions 279
        App Product Website 280
        Social Media Marketing 281
        Other App Marketing Activities 283
        Summary 285
22   Implementing Your Plan 287
        Determine Goals for the Marketing
            Campaign—What Results
            Do You Hope to Achieve? 288
        Establish Measurement Criteria 289
        Gather Prospects to Target for Campaign 290
        Tracking Results—Measuring Marketing ROI 290
        Managing Your App Marketing Activities 291
        Summary 293
23   iPhone/iPad Apps for Corporate Marketing 295
        Is an iPhone/iPad App Right for Your Company? 297
        Build an App to Extend/Reignite the Brand 298
        Apps to Extend a Web-based Product's Use 301
        Summary 305

About the Author

Jeffrey Hughes is the creator and lead instructor for Xcelme's (www.xcelme.com) iPhone and iPad App Marketing course, which has helped hundreds of independent developers market their iPhone and iPad apps effectively in a very competitive market. He has two decades of experience as a marketer, publisher, and speaker, working with high tech companies including McAfee, Blue Coat, and Novell.

Jeffrey consults and gives seminars around the world to developers, corporations, and universities on how to position their apps, improve their marketing approach, and win new customers. Hughes is the author of 13 books including *Android Apps Marketing: Secrets to Selling Your Android App*. Hughes has a B.S. degree in marketing and a minor in computer science from Brigham Young University. He resides in Scottsdale, Arizona.

Dedication

This book is dedicated to my daughters Laurin and Mckenna who inspire and encourage me each day. May your dreams come true.

Acknowledgments

I would like to acknowledge senior acquisitions editor Katherine Bull whose guidance and support over the past several years has been unwavering. She is one of the best in the business and always finds time to encourage and remove obstacles along the sometimes bumpy path of publishing. Moving words around the computer screen can be hard work, and nobody understands this better than Katherine as she provided gentle reminders of upcoming deadlines.

I would also like to thank Romny French for her amazing editing and organizational skills. She was able to pull this project together to meet critical deadlines and keep the project on track. I also want to thank Samantha Sinkhorn for her speedy production of the book into its final form. She has worked tirelessly under very tight deadlines and does incredible work.

Finally, I want to thank the many developers who have contributed to this book with their marketing suggestions and ideas, app photos, and other support. This is a remarkable industry with incredible growth similar to the early years of the Internet. It is exciting to be a part of this growth and help many developers achieve success with their apps.

We Want to Hear from You!

As the reader of this book, you are our most important critic and commentator. We value your opinion and want to know what we're doing right, what we could do better, what areas you'd like to see us publish in, and any other words of wisdom you're willing to pass our way.

As an associate publisher for Que Publishing, I welcome your comments. You can email or write me directly to let me know what you did or didn't like about this book—as well as what we can do to make our books better.

Please note that I cannot help you with technical problems related to the topic of this book. We do have a User Services group, however, where I will forward specific technical questions related to the book.

When you write, please be sure to include this book's title and author as well as your name, email address, and phone number. I will carefully review your comments and share them with the author and editors who worked on the book.

Email: feedback@quepublishing.com

Mail: Greg Wiegand
Editor-in-Chief
Que Publishing
800 East 96th Street
Indianapolis, IN 46240 USA

Reader Services

Visit our website and register this book at quepublishing.com/register for convenient access to any updates, downloads, or errata that might be available for this book.

Introduction

Over the past three years, I have witnessed something remarkable as iPhone and iPad developers have created and posted apps to Apple's App Store at a breathtaking pace. The App Store has swelled to more than 400,000 apps and still shows no signs of abating. The gold rush to sell iPhone and iPad apps is still on, and you've created (or want to create) the next blockbuster iPhone/iPad app. Each time another Tiny Wings reaches the pinnacle of success, you see dollar signs and want to be a part of this explosive business opportunity. So do 135,000 of your friends—all toiling late nights and weekends to strike it rich. Large development companies also want a piece of the action and have teams of programmers cranking out apps as quickly as they can bring them to market. The accelerated pace of technology is compounding the problem of getting noticed. We have moved beyond "Internet time"—referring to the incredible speed at which technology advances—to "mobile time," where technology is deployed almost instantly to anyone with a mobile device. This means that consumers have an avalanche of choices when it comes to the technology and content they consume.

What we are seeing on the App Store, however, is not a new phenomenon. Amazon boasts hundreds of thousands of book titles, most selling perhaps a few copies a month. Only the most publicized and best books make Amazon's Top 100 list on its home page. The fact that the top 100 selling books are on the list helps them sell even more copies. It's self-perpetuating, so every author aspires to be on that list. In a similar fashion, every iPhone/iPad app developer aspires to make it on Apple's Top 100 or Top 10 or on the New and Noteworthy or Staff Picks lists. They know that making it on those lists will catapult them into realizing dramatic sales, for a time at least.

Beyond posting your app on Apple's App Store, you may be wondering what else is needed to successfully market your iPhone/iPad app. In short, lots! The days of simply posting your app on the App Store and achieving instant success are long gone. Sure, some developers have hit pay dirt, and, just like the next Vegas jackpot winner, everyone loves to read those stories. It's not impossible, but the odds of hitting the jackpot have gone up dramatically. So many apps have been introduced so quickly that it's impossible for any casual observer to keep track of the 600+ apps delivered to the App Store each day. Customers are faced with the challenge of reviewing scores of similar apps and trying to figure out the best ones to download. It's a tall order for any app buyer.

How does an independent developer stand out in a sea of apps? How can someone beat the odds in this high-stakes game? The answer is (sort of) simple. Build a great (and I mean great) iPhone/iPad app and devise a stellar marketing plan to capture the hearts and minds of thousands of people so they will download your app. The execution of these two strategies, however, is not so simple. Many developers rush their apps to market and think the momentum of the App Store will carry them forward. They think a little luck will be on their side and that they'll get a positive review or get noticed by Apple's staff with a mention. But often they end up with a mediocre app, no reviews, and maybe 3–4 downloads a day. Then they consider marketing...as an afterthought.

Not doing any marketing is a surefire way *not* to get noticed. Marketing in some form or another is going to raise your chances of success. All apps that have achieved dramatic success have done so through marketing, either intentionally or unintentionally. Successful apps have managed to attract the attention of reviewers and capture the imaginations of thousands through positive word of mouth.

If you have aspirations to make more than a little spending money from your app, then you must follow tried-and-true marketing (and some offbeat) principles to get your app noticed. As a developer you need to think about the key areas of marketing before, during, and after your app is created and launched. You need to build your app with a clear objective and have a clearly identified audience who will be interested in your solution. You also need to think about pricing and promotions, sales and support, and creating buzz for your app. This is not easy work but absolutely necessary to achieve the results you want to see with your app.

The good news is that the marketing process for iPhone/iPad apps is really no different than marketing any other product; it's just highly compressed in terms of the buying process. The principles are the same, even though some of the marketing tools have expanded dramatically in recent years, especially in the area of mass communication and social media. The steps are also still the same: You develop an app that customers need and want, create a solid marketing message, deliver the message to the right audience, build a following, and develop new apps and upgrades to retain existing customers. Remember that marketing is a *process*, not a one-time event. Marketing also takes hard work and effort. It is not a spectator sport.

When you understand that marketing is a continuum that incorporates these fundamental steps, you will be able to plan and implement them to increase sales success for your iPhone app. This book will assist you in understanding the necessary marketing steps to increase exposure for your iPhone/iPad app(s), whether you are a first-time developer or have created and posted a number of apps for sale. This book assumes you want to move beyond being a casual developer and seller of iPhone apps to a successful marketer of your own best-selling apps and brand. The following illustrates the broad steps in the marketing process.

Part I: Your Marketing Message

Everything from naming your app to the text you place on the App Store (and many other components) contributes to your marketing message. What sets your iPhone/iPad app apart from all your competitors? How can you convey that unique message to your buyers? Let's face it: There are lots of competitors with similar apps. In Part I, you review steps to help you create a unique message that will help distinguish your app from the competition. You'll do this by examining positioning, target audience, competition, and other market conditions. The following chapters are included in this part:

- **Chapter 1, "Your iPhone and iPad App Marketing Strategy: Grand Slam or Base Hits?"**—Learn how messaging works and understand how iPhone messaging is similar and, in some cases, very different from marketing for other products.

- **Chapter 2, "What Makes a Winning iPhone/iPad App?"**—What are the key selling points of your app? Can you identify key strengths and competitive advantages to highlight your app? Learn how to distill this essential information.

- **Chapter 3, "Identifying Your App's Unique Value"**—Let's zero in on what matters and create a crisp message that meets some basic criteria and is easy to remember.

- **Chapter 4, "Identifying Your Target Audience"**—The best results from your marketing message come when you have targeted a specific audience with a clear message. Learn how to find your target audience.

- **Chapter 5, "Building Your App's Total Message"**—An effective app name, a crisp App Store message, and a clear website all contribute to your overall marketing message. Choosing not to do some of these things may not impact your sales. Not doing any of them will.

Part II: Delivering Your Message

With a carefully crafted message, you are now ready to deliver your message to the right audience and through the right means for maximum exposure and effectiveness. Part II provides an overview of the various methods available to reach different audiences and create demand for your iPhone/iPad apps. Demand is created when you help prospective customers see that you have a solution to their problem or you pique their curiosity with a challenging game or puzzle. The demand for most products is already there; it's just a matter of creating a message that resonates with that audience and gets them to notice your app. The following chapters are included in this part:

- **Chapter 6, "Electronic Word of Mouth"**—Word of mouth is one of the most powerful means of increasing sales of your iPhone/iPad app. Learn how to go about getting people to talk about your app.

- **Chapter 7, "Using Social Media in Your App Marketing"**—Create a following for your brand and your apps using Facebook, Twitter, Blogs, and YouTube. You can use these newer social media tools to achieve greater exposure for your app.

- **Chapter 8, "Timing Your Marketing Activities"**—When do you want to communicate your message? Often, timing plays a role in how well your marketing message is received. Learn how to coordinate the delivery of your marketing message for maximum impact and results.

- **Chapter 9, "Getting the Word Out About Your App"**—A press release can be a very powerful tool to spread the word about your app, but it has to be written professionally and adhere to very specific guidelines to attract the attention of your audience. Learn the tricks of the trade.

Part III: Pricing Your iPhone/iPad App

A key aspect of marketing your iPhone/iPad app is to carefully set your price. Setting your price is not a trivial matter. This Part walks you through pricing considerations and helps you understand the buyer's mentality and their decision-making process. You learn how to create promotions and cross-sell your app where possible, another important aspect of pricing. The following chapters are included in this part:

- **Chapter 10, "Pricing Your App"**—Perhaps one of the biggest challenges of developing an iPhone/iPad app is pricing. In this chapter, you learn how and where to begin to price your app for maximum success.

- **Chapter 11, "Conducting an App Pricing Analysis"**—A pricing analysis will help you calculate your breakeven: how many apps you need to sell to cover your costs and start to make a profit.

- **Chapter 12, "Selling Value over Price"**—Some apps will be priced higher than the usual $0.99 or $1.99. Learn how to convey the value of your apps and get the price that you're entitled to for your hard work.

- **Chapter 13, "Breaking into the App Store Top 100"**—You can do a number of things in an effort to get your app into the Top 100. Learn the best tips to reach maximum success in the App Store.

- **Chapter 14, "Level the Playing Field with a Free App"**—Learn the pros and cons of creating a free version of your app or how to use the in-app purchase capability to expand your sales. In-app purchases are the trend of the future for iPhone/iPad applications.

- **Chapter 15, "The App Pricing Roller Coaster"**—Raising and lowering your price can have an impact on sales, but there is a cost, and you'll learn all about it here.

- **Chapter 16, "App Promotions and Cross-Selling"**—Promotions aren't just for your local car dealership. Some promotions can work to sell your iPhone/iPad app. Cross-selling can also work in certain circumstances. Learn about pay per install and app recommender campaigns.

- **Chapter 17, "Using iPhone/iPad Analytics"**—Now's the time to let math be your friend. These kinds of app analytics help you sell more of your apps. Learn the tools available for iPhone/iPad developers and how to interpret the results to your benefit.

Part IV: Implement a Marketing Plan/Launch Your App

With the right message and the right audience, combined with the right marketing tools and methods, you can create extremely effective marketing campaigns. This part walks you through the steps of implementing a marketing campaign and provides a fully developed sample campaign ready for you to implement. The following chapters are included in this part:

- **Chapter 18, "Why Have a Marketing Plan?"**—When developers hear about a marketing plan, they usually run the other way. This marketing plan is short, to the point, and effective. You need to have a plan to guide your app to sales success.

- **Chapter 19, "Components of an App Marketing Plan"**—Learn the basic components of an iPhone app marketing plan and how they can be used to help you stay on track during development and launch.

- **Chapter 20, "Marketing Essentials"**—Not all marketing plans are designed the same. Learn which types of apps need a certain plan. Learn what to do if you've already posted your app and you're not seeing great sales.

- **Chapter 21, "25 Essential iPhone/iPad Marketing Activities"**—Learn the top 25 marketing activities that will help your app achieve maximum exposure and success.

- **Chapter 22, "Implementing Your Plan"**—If you have planned for it, your app launch should be an exciting and exhilarating experience. Learn how to get ready for the launch of your iPhone app.

- **Chapter 23, "iPhone/iPad Apps for Corporate Marketing"**—If you are working for a large corporation, you want to read this chapter on how to develop apps that help your company with branding. Lots of companies have built apps for name recognition and brand value alone, whereas others charge for them.

So there you have it. Who thought so much could be said about marketing an iPhone/iPad app? Apple has created an incredible opportunity for developers around the world to achieve success on the App Store. Although not without its flaws and complaints, the App Store has created a tremendous opportunity for individual developers and companies to build and sell mobile technology for the masses. Here's to your success.

Your Marketing Message

1 Your iPhone and iPad App Marketing Strategy: Grand Slam or Base Hits? 9

2 What Makes a Winning iPhone/iPad App? 25

3 Identifying Your App's Unique Value 37

4 Identifying Your Target Audience 55

5 Building Your App's Total Message 67

1

Your iPhone and iPad App Marketing Strategy: Grand Slam or Base Hits?

As an iPhone or iPad app developer you may be hoping to strike it rich selling your app to millions of customers, or at least tens of thousands of customers, to make your hard work pay off. Other equally ambitious developers hope to achieve a steady income writing apps and leave their other full-time jobs behind. Although these goals are possible, it is very difficult to make it onto to the top 25 best selling or most downloaded apps categories.

There are several reasons why it's hard to make it big. First, the sheer number of apps for sale on the App Store has made it much more difficult to stand out from the crowd. Instead of just a few similar apps in your category, there are likely hundreds, even thousands if you are selling a game, vying for the buyer's attention.

Secondly, the intense pricing pressure causes many developers to start off at a low price or quickly drop their prices to $0.99, a figure that makes it extremely difficult to break even much less make any profit. According to the website 148 Apps (www.148apps.biz), almost 42% of all apps (games included) are priced at $0.99. Figure 1.1 shows a range of apps, from free to $9.99, and their percentage totals on the App Store. You'll notice that 77% of all apps sold are at $1.99 or lower.

Application Price Distribution

This page shows a table showing the number of apps and games in each price category.

App Price	Count By Price - Active Apps			
	# Apps	# Games	Total	% of Total
Free	114,878	20,089	134,967	(36.35%)
0.99	86,431	23,225	109,656	(29.54%)
1.99	40,243	6,824	47,067	(12.68%)
2.99	20,383	2,549	22,932	(6.18%)
3.99	11,797	663	12,460	(3.36%)
4.99	12,392	1,014	13,406	(3.61%)
5.99	4,344	103	4,447	(1.20%)
6.99	2,656	163	2,819	(0.76%)
7.99	4,712	61	4,773	(1.29%)
8.99	1,271	17	1,288	(0.35%)
9.99	7,326	126	7,452	(2.01%)

Source: www.148apps.biz

Figure 1.1   iPhone app prices tend to be bunched around the $.99 and $1.99 level and lower.

The large number of competing apps may seem daunting; however, these statistics are not presented to be discouraging. Rather, this chapter is designed to point out that the App Store has matured very quickly, and you have to develop a solid marketing strategy to realize success. The App Store is not running on Internet time—it's on mobile time! Your marketing strategy also has to be tuned to work with your buyer.

We've Seen This Movie Before

The iTunes App Store is much like your local supermarket. In the 1980s, the average supermarket carried about 7,500 items. Today, that same supermarket carries upward of 52,000 items! Every vendor is fighting for shelf space so more people will buy their products. Amazon.com is no different; booksellers are trying to stand out in a very crowded market. Not counting other items, its bookstore alone boasts well over 250,000 titles. Many authors hope to achieve fame and fortune by landing on the top 100 list on Amazon's book home page. Other authors had hoped to get their big break by being mentioned on Oprah or some other television show. The App Store has exploded from its introduction of fewer than 1,000 apps to well over 435,000 apps at the time of this writing. Just like the supermarket vendors, every app developer is vying for that eye-level virtual shelf space. They are either hoping to make it into the top 100 sales for their categories in the App Store or get a mention in the "Staff Favorites," "New and Noteworthy," or "What's Hot" sections of the App Store. Table 1.1 shows the breakout of the highest selling categories of apps available on the App Store. Approximately 500–600 apps are posted to the store each day! According to Apple, almost 7,500 apps per week are still being submitted for the approval process. Although it may take another year or so, the App Store could see over a half million apps!

Table 1.1   App Store Percentages for the Most Popular Categories on the App Store

Type of iPhone/iPad App	Percentage of Total Apps
Games	29%
Books	24%
Entertainment	22%
Travel	13%
Education	12%

Source: www.148apps.biz

As the store has grown, it has necessitated reconfiguration numerous times to further segment the apps into logical groups where buyers can more easily connect with sellers. Apple continues to improve the search capabilities of the store, adding more home page app categories such as "Made for IOS 4" and "What We're Playing" in the Games section. All of these groupings help your app to get more visibility if it's rotated in for one of those groupings. As shown in Figure 1.2, the top paid, free, and grossing apps are shown in the right column on the App Store's home page and are displayed on the home page of the App Store.

If you drill down into a category such as Lifestyles, you see that there is also a breakout of the top 10 paid apps and the top 10 free apps along with a newer category for top 10 grossing apps as shown on the right side in Figure 1.3. Notice that this particular category has 70 pages of paid apps (12569) at 150 apps displayed per page! If you add in free apps in the Lifestyle category, there are over 23,000 total apps at the time of this writing! If your app manages to sell enough copies to make it into the top 100, you will see your sales climb dramatically (as long as you stay on this coveted list.)

Figure 1.2   Top Paid Apps, Top Free Apps, and Top Grossing Apps are shown to the right of the App Store's home page.

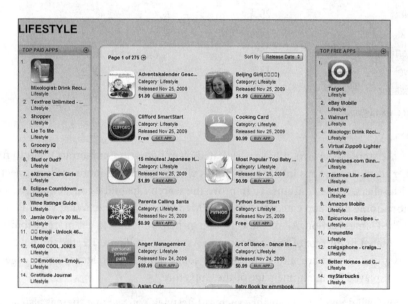

Figure 1.3   Each category on the App Store has a listing for paid and free apps.

You can also sort the apps within each category by Name (A–Z breakouts) and by Release Date and Bestsellers as shown in Figure 1.4. Searching by Name is helpful if you're searching on a particular name of an app or your best guess as to its name. Release date is the default. Searching on some of the other categories such as "What

Figure 1.4   The App Store allows you to sort by Name, Release Date, and Most Popular within each category.

Hot" allows you to search by name alphabetically or by when the app was featured. Newly featured apps are first on the list.

The App Store will continue to make improvements to help strengthen and refine the search process and showcase apps in the best way possible. In order to create a winning sales and marketing strategy for your app, it's important to understand the dynamics of the App Store and understand that there are several strategies that you can employ.

There are three pillars of your app's success as shown in Figure 1.5. Failure to address all three of these areas means the likelihood of your app succeeding in the market is slim. I know there are stories of some apps seemingly not addressing these areas and yet achieving wild success. This is true. There are always examples of people achieving success in books or movies that, for some odd reason, defy all understanding and lack of marketing. I wish that success for all of you.

The same goes for iPhone/iPad apps. But even the successful apps that achieve (perhaps) undeserving success have done at least two of these three things right. They definitely have a market for their apps, regardless of how stupid or pointless the apps might be. They may claim to have done no marketing, but word of mouth (a form of marketing) has propelled them to success.

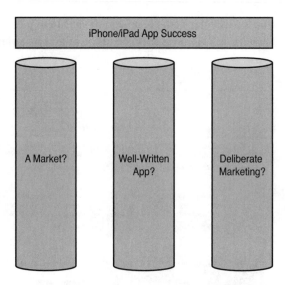

Figure 1.5   Three pillars of iPhone/iPad app success: a market, well-written app, and deliberate marketing

 Note

Someone once said (possibly Rudi Giuliani) that hope is not a strategy. Hope is also not a marketing strategy! Posting your app on the App Store and hoping for the best is not a plan and will more than likely result in mediocre sales unless it takes off virally, and we all hope that will happen for you!

Most developers are trying to knock their apps out of the park. They want the grand slam and think anything less is failure. A number of developers give up, thinking there's only two possible outcomes to selling their apps: the Big Win or No Win. But there are actually three possible outcomes: the Big Win app, the Steady Win app, and the No Win app. All apps fall into one of these three categories. Over time and without marketing or product updates, all apps will eventually slide from one category down to the next one below.

The Big Win—Grand Slam

The Big Win apps or Grand Slams are generally characterized by explosive sales from their launches. Games, by far, make up the majority of the Big Win apps. Why? Because games take advantage of the impulse buy that occurs directly from an iPhone. Games are the most likely app to be bought on impulse. The impulse buyer cares about what's hot right now and what looks like the most fun to play.

Sometimes a community of people is familiar with a particular development company and is hungry to purchase its new app. Some companies have made their apps successful by porting an already successful PC or Mac game over to the iPhone platform. But I am also seeing small up and comers making big names for themselves. Who can forget Tiny Wings (Andreas Illiger) overthrowing Angry Birds for at least a month!

Big Win apps have also been positioned by large development companies with huge followings. Their aim is to achieve quick sales on apps that are priced in the games sweet spot from $0.99 to $1.99. At this price point, the impulse buyer is looking for something to occupy her time. The longevity of this type of app may be short, lasting only several months. Then the same company releases another app and focuses its attention on that. Some winning apps are designed in such a way to bring the customer back over and over again with paid add-ons or frequent updates. One of the most popular game apps to provide frequent releases is Pocket God shown in Figure 1.6. Pocket God refers to its updates as "Episodes" and has built a very strong community of users that keep the game in the spotlight. User suggestions for new features keep the game fresh and exciting.

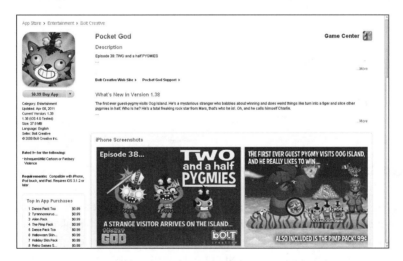

Figure 1.6   Pocket God has done a very good job keeping customers engaged with its frequent new "Episodes," or product updates.

Another common element for Big Win games is that they are usually very simplistic in their premises. The masses of iPhone users purchase games that are easy to learn. Low on learning, high on enjoyment is the rule of thumb for the quick win Big Win games. Think of Tiny Wings. It is easy to learn but challenging and incredibly addictive. The typical game buyer doesn't want to learn tons of rules to a new game. They want to understand the point of the app immediately and start playing right away.

Just when we think only big development houses can win in the iPhone/iPad game business another Tiny Wings comes along and steals the show. But the stakes are high. Think about how great the music, graphics, and game play are in Tiny Wings. It's no easy feat to do all of those things well. And it's costly to hire outside expertise to help you create the pieces of the app where you may lack experience. Larger companies have the development staff that can bring apps to market more quickly without sacrificing quality. It simply takes an independent developer longer to create a high powered, high quality game app. However, when a following is created and the app is updated frequently, you will continue to attract customers and positive reviews as shown with Tiny Wings in Figure 1.7.

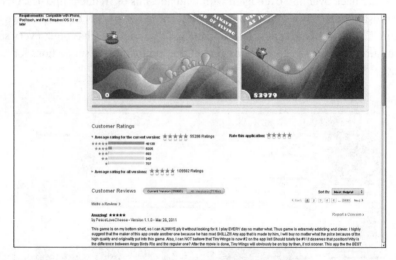

Figure 1.7   Positive reviews continue to roll in for the infamous Tiny Wings App.

The last characteristic of the Grand Slam apps is that they often get a big break from the press or large review sites as being an app to look at. Think of Touch Arcade, a very large game review site, which is a must-have review if you are to succeed with your app in a big way. You not only need to post your app on this site, but also get them to review yours. Tom Clancy achieved remarkable success with his book *The Hunt for Red October* when Ronald Reagan praised the book after he read it while on vacation. After Reagan's comments, sales of that book skyrocketed. If an iPhone/iPad app gets a lucky break from a major review site, it can serve as the catalyst to get sales moving in a big way. Word of mouth takes it from there. This is the holy grail of app marketing.

Some other apps that fall into this category are shown in Figures 1.8 and 1.9. These apps have achieved phenomenal success. Angry Birds continues to stay on the best seller list due to its amazing graphics, simple play premise, and huge following. Fruit Ninja also hit the mark with its amazing graphics and addictive game play. And who can forget Doodle Jump and its New York developers, who are brothers, that hit it big as shown in Figure 1.10.

Figure 1.8   Angry Birds has achieved Big Win success with well over 1.3 million downloads. They also offer an add-on pack for additional play, adding to their revenues.

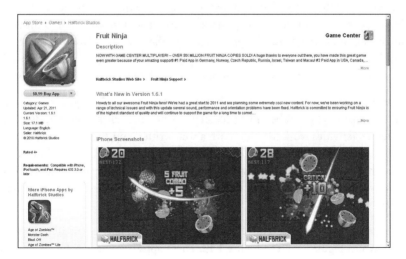

Figure 1.9   Fruit Ninja achieved early success with its incredible use of graphics and simple premise of design.

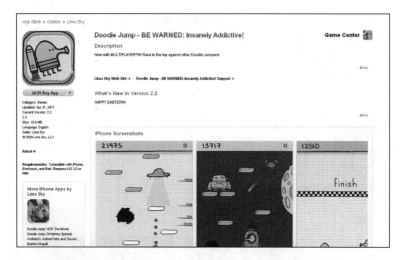

Figure 1.10   Doodle Jump is the runaway best selling game from Lima Sky, Inc. It is on Apple's Highest Grossing App list.

The Steady Win—Base Hits

The next category of iPhone/iPad apps is the Steady Win, also known as base hit apps. This category may be overlooked by some app developers who focus solely on the Big Win. The majority of new iPhone/iPad apps land in this category even if the developer has intentions of his app making it into the Big Win group. These apps rely on app reviews, positive blog posts, advertising, and making it onto the App Store's "wall of fame" where the app is placed in the "New and Noteworthy" or "Staff Picks" or "What's Hot" sections for a short period of time. These placements are definitely helpful and will boost sales noticeably while you remain on that list.

These apps also rely on good, old-fashioned, consistent marketing. The revenue with this type of app can be more predictable when the seller understands what marketing activities work for him. With a well written app, the right marketing mix, and product updates, this type of app can achieve success on the App Store. It may not be multimillion dollar success, but it can be decent. It may be enough to compel you to write multiple apps, build a brand, and truly make a business out of your efforts.

Some apps that have achieved solid success that are not necessarily iPhone games are shown in Figure 1.11 and Figure 1.12. These apps have been achieving a steady revenue stream for their developers albeit not millionaire levels. They have strong value propositions, and their products resonate with their intended audience. These apps are focused on finance, saving money, getting healthy, travel, and other topics that interest almost everyone.

Figure 1.11   Save Benjis is an app that allows you to do price comparisons. They also offer an upsell to their product, a newer app with the popular barcode scanner feature.

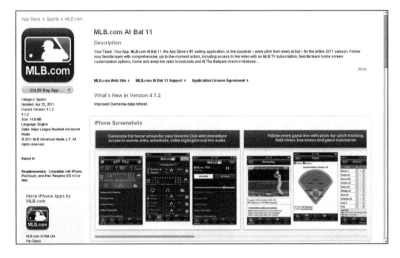

Figure 1.12   MLB.Com is a long-time selling app that provides immediate access to scores, stats, video highlights, and live audio.

Given that most apps fall into the category of Steady Win, the bulk of this book is focused on helping you achieve ongoing success through a complete marketing approach. Although with this revision we have learned considerably more about the Big Win apps and will share these tips with you throughout the book. Utility type apps (almost anything that isn't a game) generally command a higher selling price and can have more predictable revenue streams. Independent developers will most likely be playing in this category whether they realize it or not.

The No Win—Strikeout

Sadly, a large number of apps on the App Store are DOA. After working months and months or paying someone else to write your app, you post the app to the App Store and anxiously await its review and approval. After a few weeks you get the word back that your app has been approved. The app is posted within a few hours of approval, and your expectations soar! You can see the checks rolling in from Apple. You've already bought the swimming pool (remember *Christmas Vacation*). Then, you wait. You check your sales stats each day. A few sales here, a few sales there.... What has happened? Where are all the buyers? What happened to the 10,000 daily downloads? You thought people would be breaking down the doors to get this new app. You are discouraged and think you've wasted your time. You've probably thought about dropping your price. Surely there must be something wrong with the App Store to cause this.

Sometimes, even very well-written apps end up unnoticed and ignored. An app that sees 0 or 1–2 sales a day is not going to cut it to reach your break even. At the time of this writing, there are over 78,000 apps that are inactive and no longer for sale on the App Store. So what does a person do who finds himself in this predicament where his app is not doing well? It's time for a total app makeover. Ask yourself the following questions and be brutally honest:

1. Is there really a market for my app? Did you come up with your app idea while sitting around with a bunch of friends and thought you had stumbled onto something that was incredible? Or did you do some solid competitive research to see if there were similar apps already posted, especially in the Free app categories? Nothing wrong with creating a competing app if you can make it better, but it's *got* to be better! Often whenever we think we have a great idea we need to really analyze whether it's viable or not. Ask some family, friends, or coworkers if they would be willing to pay for such an app. Find out if you have a market (and its potential size) for your app before you start coding or launch into an expensive project with a developer.

2. Is your app extremely well written? A number of apps on the App Store are poorly written. They have bugs, or some of the features don't work too well. This is a surefire way to get a one-star rating on the App Store by a disgruntled buyer. Even at $0.99 people will take the time to point out that your app is crap and not worth the money on the customer reviews. One of the outcomes of competition is that prices fall and quality goes up. Customers expect an app to work just as well at $0.99 as they do at $29.99.

3. Have you done any marketing yet? As I mention time and time again in this book, marketing is not posting your app to the App Store. You've

had your app approved by Apple, and that's a great accomplishment. Now the second half of your work starts. Selling iPhone/iPad apps is not a passive activity if you intend to make money at it. A few other questions to consider: Does your app's icon convey what the app does? Icons that don't convey what the app does or at least what category the app is in are missing a marketing opportunity. Does the name of your app communicate the value of your app or help tell the story of what it does? Does your web copy match your product website in terms of crisp well-written content? All of these things combined help you to tell the story of your app and communicate its value. Figure 1.13 shows some sample icons that do a good job of communicating their value.

Figure 1.13   These icons communicate very nicely what the apps do such as a sports app a professional team may have built. This is an important part of your overall marketing.

There is always an explanation as to why an app is not successful. The answer is always there with a little digging.

If you should decide that your old app should rest in peace, at least you can have a better understanding of what you can do the next time around to help you achieve success. Don't kid yourself when you answer any of these questions. If you truly believe you have a great idea for an app and you've done your homework, then go for it. If you have written a great app and know it without a doubt, then apply some marketing and get those sales moving.

Benefits/Drawbacks of the Big Win and Steady Win Strategies

The App Store is not a perfect democratic society and never will be. No matter how many changes Apple makes to the App Store, there will always be unhappy participants. So you can whine about what's wrong with it, or you can figure out how to work the system to your best advantage. Table 1.2 illustrates the advantages and disadvantages of the Big Win strategy. The App Store is not for the faint of heart. Table 1.3 shows the advantages and disadvantages of the Steady Win strategy. Again, it's more likely you'll end up in this category than the Big Win.

Table 1.2 Big Win Advantages/Disadvantages

Advantages	Disadvantages
Make lots of money quickly.	Customers expect high quality at a crazy low price like $0.99.
Deliver apps quickly to market.	Usually requires development team to get app created quickly. Time is of the essence.
Games are extremely popular with this market strategy.	Extremely competitive, very fickle.
Charge a low price to attract customers.	Highly price-sensitive customers, promotions have limited impact, no pricing flexibility.

Table 1.3 Steady Win Advantages/Disadvantages

Advantages	Disadvantages
Make money slowly but more predictably.	Developers who get discouraged easily don't see their efforts through to success.
Apps build a customer following for add-ons.	Must build updates on a frequent basis and respond quickly to customer feedback.
Almost any app can participate in the Steady Win category.	Games are a challenge here because of their short lifespan. Developers must build in add-ons to keep the audience coming back.
Apps can achieve access into the Top 100 (or other categories) with consistent marketing.	Income drops off dramatically if steps are not taken to keep the consumer in front of the app. Marketing is a full-time job.

If you haven't started developing your iPhone/iPad app, you are at an important decision-making point. Making a strategy decision now will help you make important marketing decisions as you get closer to launch. Having clear (and realistic) expectations of where your app will be positioned on the App Store gives your app purpose and will help you avoid the No Win bucket.

Summary

iPhone and iPad apps fall into one of three categories: Big Wins, Steady Wins, and No Wins. The Big Win is what every independent developer tends to go after. However, you should also look closely at the Steady Wins category of selling as this affords the best opportunity for most developers. Good marketing can make the difference between no revenue (No Win) and steady revenue (Steady Win).

Decide now what your iPhone selling strategy is going to be, and you'll have an easier time defining a marketing plan and sticking with it. It will save you a lot of heartburn too if you look realistically at your app and its market and set realistic expectations on your success. Don't get me wrong, I want you to be wildly successful in selling your app. I hope you hit a grand slam into the parking lot, but I also want you to realize that it's hard work to get there and takes some very positive reviews from very powerful review sites. Even getting base hits is hard work but more likely, especially when you apply some marketing to it.

For those of you who think you've got an app lost in the No Win bin, it's never too late! You can resurrect your app from the No Win status to the Steady Wins status as long as your app is well written, has a strong premise, and gets some good marketing. Are you prepared to rewrite a poorly written app? Does your app really have sales appeal? If so, then roll up your sleeves, put your marketing hat on, and keep reading.

2

What Makes a Winning iPhone/iPad App?

Everyone is searching for ideas to build the next winning iPhone or iPad app. Although there is no single formula for building a successful-selling iPhone or iPad app, there are a number of things that can and must be done to achieve success. I've also learned a lot over the past year that I share here.

Without covering the basics, your app is likely to languish on the App Store with minimal sales. Good apps continue to be posted to the App Store that do not sell as well as they should usually because not much marketing has been applied to the project. Unless you stage a large event to launch your app and get it started with strong momentum or your app gets picked up by Apple on the home page of the App Store, you may find yourself in this situation.

Keep in mind that marketing is not a single event but a continuous process of aligning your message with your buyer and delivering your message over and over again so that your audience absorbs it and acts on it. Think about marketing in terms of other products you buy. How often do you see the same commercial on TV? How many times have you seen the same email ads or banner ads? Either you start out with a following, do something significant to get people's attention, or you have to get the word out methodically over a period of time.

In the next sections of this chapter, I walk through some of the key elements of a winning app. If you are just starting development of your app, then you are at a good point to evaluate if the app you are building meets this criteria. If you are mid-development or have completed your app, then use this chapter as a benchmark to assess how well you stack up in each of these areas. It's never too late to go back and retrofit your app. Updates are one of the keys to a successful app as you'll read in the following sections.

Build Something Unique

The best way to come upon a unique idea for an app is to rely on your own personal experience and identify where you see a need. This is easier said than done because most of us go along and may not think about how we could improve our lives with a new technology solution. You have to make a conscious effort to envision new ways of doing things. You can start by asking yourself the following questions:

1. What are your favorite hobbies? Is there anything about those hobbies that could be improved by applying an app solution to the problem? (Hobbies can be anything that you enjoy: gardening, stamp collecting, photography, genealogy, scrapbooking, cooking, collecting anything, antiques, and so on.)

2. What sports do you play? Is there a particular technique you have learned playing a sport that would be particularly helpful to others? (Better golf swing, ways to hit a ball better, how to be a better right fielder, how to swim faster, how to prepare for the triathlon or to be an Ironman, better tennis tips, and so on.)

3. What line of work are you in? Is there anything in your line of work that could benefit from the use of an iPhone/iPad app? (Sales tools, materials and construction calculators, financial and insurance aids, and so on.)

4. What challenges do you face in your life? Is there an app that could help someone cope with a handicap or other illness? (Think about soothing apps, mental health apps, physical health apps, stress coping apps, and so on.)

5. What are your least favorite chores? Is there an app that could help someone with bill paying, gift buying, and so on?

6. What daily activity takes you the most time to complete? Is there an app that could help people speed up that activity?

7. What childhood games did you enjoy playing? Could that game (or a variation of that game) make a great game app?

We're all trying to build a better mousetrap. With each passing day, it becomes more difficult to build a completely new and unique app. As I have mentioned before, whenever you come up with an idea for an iPhone/iPad app, the first thing you should do is a search on the App Store for that type of app. The chances are pretty good that you will find some or many apps that are close to what you have thought about building. For example, let's take a topic like the sport lacrosse. You think you've got a great idea to develop an iPhone/iPad app that helps you learn how to play lacrosse. So let's check the App Store for lacrosse apps. An example of my search is shown in Figure 2.1. There are currently 65 apps on lacrosse!

Figure 2.1   My search of lacrosse apps reveals 65 lacrosse-related apps. Who would have thought?

However, on closer inspection of the lacrosse apps, some apps help you keep score (the author doesn't really know this game too well), and some of the apps actually teach you how to play or coach lacrosse. There are several lacrosse games in the group too. So when you perform a search for your particular app idea, be sure to look more closely at the apps that you find and dissect them into separate groups to get an idea of exactly how many apps you are competing against. While it looks like 65 apps at first glance, is more like five or six that closely match your goal of teaching someone how to play lacrosse.

It's a little more difficult to do this type of analysis for game apps because there are so many similar apps with so many variations. You can do a more targeted search by using the App Store's targeted subcategory search as shown in Figure 2.2. If you are searching on card games you can select "games" as the main category and "cards" as the subcategory. This will help narrow the number of apps, but it's still a very large number to sift through.

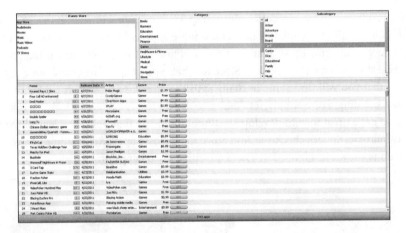

Figure 2.2   Search for similar games on the App Store using subcategories to narrow down the results.

Although you may not land on an original idea, it is possible to build an app that improves on what's already out there. The chances are very good that you will find a number of functions missing from a competitor's app. As mentioned before, if you can narrow down the top competitive apps to just a few, go ahead and spend a few dollars to download some of them and see what features they have and what they lack.

List the key features of the competitive apps as well as features that the available apps are lacking. You will start to see a pattern in terms of base features that this type of app must have to be viable in the market. Then you can look at what features you can add that will make your app a whole lot better.

Deliver New Features

Winning apps require frequent feature updates. If you don't keep the app updated, your audience will lose interest in your app and will quit using it and coming to your product website. You must look at your app as a dynamic product. It should be architected in such a way that you can easily add enhancements, new levels, and updates. Each time you make an update and the app goes through the App Store approval process, your app will see renewed sales momentum.

Some developers have adopted the idea that they will increase their sales by doing an upgrade as fast as they can push it through. Figure 2.3 shows a snapshot of the first page of a game in the Games/Action category of the App Store If you review the graphic you'll see that the publisher is this app points out in the "What's new in this version" section what has changed in this release of the app. Depending on the category, this percentage may be 30% or higher.

Figure 2.3   Some developers use frequent updates to keep their customers coming back again and to attract new customers.

Each update also helps you address customer comments/suggestions/complaints and keeps your relationship with your customers intact. You can use each update to comment on how you are addressing customer recommendations and how you are listening to your customers. This helps you build a following of loyal users because they know they are being heard by you and you are addressing their concerns and suggestions.

 Note

If you have bugs that need to be resolved, these should be fixed right away. Do not wait, or your customers may become discouraged, give you bad reviews, and comment on other blog posts that your app is not worth the money or downloading even if it's free.

Tie Your App into Trends and News

Trends are always occurring around the world; look no further than the Internet or cable news stations for ideas. Here are some trend ideas to help you get your thought process moving:

- **Going green**—Look for opportunities in this space on how someone can use an iPhone/iPad app to make a difference in the world. How about an app that helps you drive more economically or an app designed to help you reduce your cost of heating or cooling. An example of such an app is shown in Figure 2.4 and capitalizes on the very popular "green" trend. Other green areas that you could consider include how to save water, make your own cleaning supplies, composting, recycling, walking and biking instead of driving, and so on.

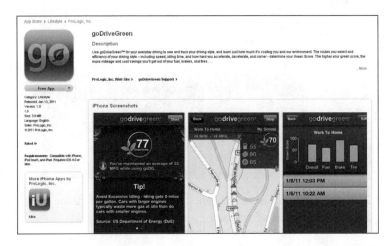

Figure 2.4   An example of a "green app" that helps drivers save gas and money by driving more efficiently

- **Eating healthy**—A lot of money is spent each year by consumers who want to eat better, feel better, and live longer. This is a long-term trend that has lots of growth opportunity. Apps to consider for this area might be meal planners, nutritional value of fruits, vegetables, and so on. Contact publishers of health books and ask if they would like to partner with you to write a healthy iPhone/iPad app to be included with every book sale for free. You could also contact health food product companies with the same idea. An example of these types of eating healthy apps is shown in Figure 2.5.

- **Fashion**—Fashion trends are always popular, and you can look to design all kinds of apps around this trend. An app idea could be one

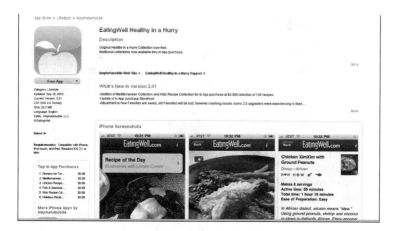

Figure 2.5   Eating healthy is a strong trend, and there are many apps that can be created for this category.

that helps someone dress with matching clothes—dare I say that men need this type of app more than women; children and teens as well. Apps that allow someone to get the latest updates in fashion trends could be successful: Are hats or boots in this year or out, for example?

- **Home Décor and Design**—This is a huge trend because people want to make their homes comfortable through quick activities and full renovations. There are tons of ideas to develop apps that help someone get organized, landscape an old rundown backyard, create a new look with paint and other inexpensive supplies, and so on. An example of home décor design app is shown in Figure 2.6.

Figure 2.6   An app that helps you design your home's interior and snap photos of samples of fabrics and flooring to include in your design

Tie Into Seasons and Holidays

Another way to come up with a winning app is to look at seasons and holidays for ideas. The only problem with seasonal apps is, well, they are seasonal. You'll see a burst of sales for apps tied to a particular holiday or season, and sales will drop off dramatically after it has passed. One strategy is to create multiple apps for different holidays so you are focusing on selling apps all year long. This means, however, that you will have to apply your marketing efforts to selling your brand with some specific holiday sales campaigns for each app during its holiday.

Seasonal apps can do better than holiday apps because a season can last for a number of months. There are apps for spring, summer, autumn, and winter as illustrated in Figure 2.7. Games, however, can transcend all seasons and do well with consistent marketing. Games such as downhill skiing shown in Figure 2.8 can do well all year long if they are fun and exciting.

Figure 2.7   Seasonal apps can be sold for longer periods of time and can sell well all year depending on the app.

Tie Your App to Part of a Wider Solution

Perhaps the most popular category of apps is the social networking-related apps. Anytime there is a powerful and well-known Internet application such as Facebook, Twitter, MySpace, LinkedIn, and so on, there is an opportunity for you to create an ancillary app to one of these (and many more) Web 2.0 technologies. Look for ways to add value to these applications, and you may be able to create a blockbuster app that people will purchase to help them use these other technologies. Figure 2.9 shows a clever app that can aid Facebook users in updating their status. Figure 2.10 is another example that helps you keep track of Facebook friends' birthdays.

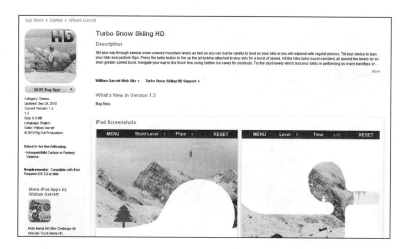

Figure 2.8 Games, even if they are seasonal, can do well all year long when marketed well.

Figure 2.9 Look for apps that you can create that add value to Web 2.0 technologies.

Apps Created from Other Platforms

Provided you have the rights to a PC or Mac application, you can develop the application for the iPhone. Many successful games were originally developed from the success of PC or Mac-based games. If you happen to like computer games, you can always check with the developer/company of that game to see if they would like to collaborate on building a similar game for the iPhone.

Figure 2.10   Facebook, Twitter, and many other social networking sites lend themselves well to creating add-on apps.

 Note

Always be careful of copyrighted games. Never duplicate an existing PC/MAC game for the iPhone without obtaining complete written permission to build the app.

An illustration of one of the most successful games in iPhone history is shown in Figure 2.11. This company already had a strong following from its successful game business, so they had a natural progression to the iPhone/iPad app.

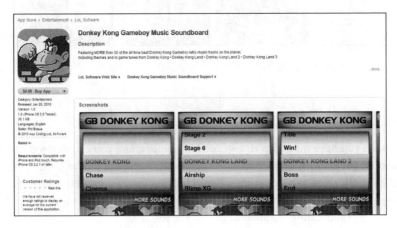

Figure 2.11   Building a game from a successful PC/MAC game can help you achieve huge success.

Winning Game Apps

I often get asked, "What makes a winning game app?" This is a very difficult question to answer since there does not seem to be any rhyme or reason to winning games. But, there are at least two things that all winning games have in common: games size and whether the game is addictive across a broad brush of users. If you look at the top 10 – 25 winning games you will find that these two characteristics are almost always present.

Keep Games Under 20MB

Because games are such an impulse buy, users tend to download them straight to their phones instead of connecting to the iTunes App Store from their Macs or PCs. There is a 20MB limit when downloading directly from an iPhone or iPad. If you check the apps in the top 10 and usually top 25 of the App Store, you will find that they are under 20MB in size. Angry Birds, Tiny Wings, and so on are all under 20MB in size.

If you already have a following for your app, then you can often exceed the 20MB limit. But anytime the user has to download from the App Store off their Macs or PCs, you run the chance that they will forget to download your app. Apps are typically downloaded on impulse, and you want to capture that impulse buy.

Your Game Must Be Addictive

This sounds like I'm stating the obvious, but if you design a game, keep the following in mind: your game must be easy to learn and difficult to master! Take a look at Tiny Wings, for example. It has been the number one and number two selling app for some time during the first part of 2011. The game is simple to learn and understand but very difficult to master. It keeps you coming back over and over again wanting to beat your last score. This game has that addictive quality that gets people talking about it and users downloading it by the millions.

Summary

A winning app requires some real planning and thinking. There is no single formula for creating a blockbuster app, but winning apps must be sufficiently unique, and you must be able to create a message that will generate huge interest. Hitting on a completely unique idea for an app is fairly difficult though not impossible. If you are having difficulty coming up with a great new idea, look to improve an existing app out there. Download some of your competition and see what features they offer and which they lack.

A successful app must also have frequent feature updates. Use the updates as an opportunity to broadcast your message to your existing audience and to new buyers. Marketing is not a single event but a series of events that persuade the buyer to take a look at your app and then buy it. Rather than looking at doing a single press release, look for opportunities to make multiple announcements to keep your app in front of your market.

3

Identifying Your App's Unique Value

In this chapter you learn the criteria and steps required to develop a unique selling proposition, including details on understanding your application's unique qualities, strengths, weaknesses, and competitive selling points. Working through these steps will provide you a messaging platform that you will use through all of your marketing programs.

What is really meant by marketing? To many developers, marketing typically means two things: advertising and selling. However, marketing is really much more. Marketing is the process by which you convert a prospect into a buying customer. In its most basic progression your buyer first learns that you understand his needs and that you have a solution to his problem.

This is accomplished through many different means of messaging that are covered throughout this book. For many nongame apps, the solution to a buyer's problem can be fairly straightforward.

If you sell a calculator app, for example, your solution is geared towards someone who wants a tool to perform calculations of some type. This buyer knows what they want and they go looking for it on the App Store. Your job as a marketer of your app is to make sure your app is among those that the buyer reviews.

If buyers are looking for a tennis game, they are going to search the App Store for tennis games (of which there are many). They will enter "tennis games" or something similar in the App Store search. A list of tennis games will then come up for review. If a buyer has no particular type of game in mind, her decision will be much more spontaneous, and your challenge to stand out from all the other games across the App Store is more complicated. Your goal is to connect with the prospective buyer at some minimal level, enough so that he or she will click your icon and read more about your app. This first step leads to a more in-depth review of your app. This whole process can take place in a split second.

After a prospect "trusts" you, you can then lead him through the steps to purchasing your app. Depending on the app type, you may lead him through these steps rather quickly, or he may spend some time trying to make a decision about several similar apps. The example in Figure 3.1 shows the buying process, which happens very fast for some buyers and slower for others.

Your App Marketing Cycle

Figure 3.1 The buying process includes awareness, connection, trust, and purchase decision. Buyers of any product, including iPhone/iPad apps, go through this decision process although usually at an accelerated pace.

To guarantee a successful marketing effort, start by taking a look at the bigger picture and analyzing your iPhone/iPad app as a whole in relation to your competition.

The (crisp and concise) answer to this question is what helps you define your app's unique value to your buying audience. You have probably heard this idea before, but your unique value has also been defined as identifying your unique competitive advantage. The terms "unique selling proposition" or "unique value proposition" are also used frequently in marketing circles. That's general marketing speak for identifying what's really cool about your product or service and conveying that to your audience in a concise, easy-to-understand message.

In the iPhone/iPad app world you have to identify the unique functionality of your app and communicate that value to your audience. The trick to creating a powerful unique selling proposition is to boil out in a few words an identifying point that embodies your app's unique value. Your unique selling proposition must answer the question as to why anyone should buy your app over all the other similar apps in the App Store that they have to choose from. This assumes that your app *has* unique value, something I talk about later.

 Note

Having a clear and concise selling proposition helps you differentiate your app from the competition. With so many competing apps on the App Store, you must do everything you can to create an edge against the competition. Your app, plain and simple, must stand out.

The Four Questions

There are four questions that you need to answer to help you define your app's unique value and create a unique selling proposition. The answers to these questions become the pillars of your marketing efforts and should be incorporated into your overall marketing plan for maximum success:

1. Who are your competitors?

2. What are the key features of your iPhone/iPad app?

3. What are the benefits of your iPhone/iPad app?

4. What is unique about your app?

Note

Your marketing message matters now more than ever. With more than 400,000 iPhone/iPad apps for sale, you must do everything you can to make a splash. Your message will be seen on your own website and on the Apple App Store description area for your app and other promotions you may create. Take a little time to do this right!

Who Are Your Competitors?

Competition in any business can be defined as "the effort of two or more parties acting independently to secure the business of a third party by offering the most favorable terms" (Wikipedia/competition/economics). Competition gives consumers greater selection and better products at better prices. It is important to understand that competition should not be viewed as a bad thing. Competition establishes a market and drives interest around your iPhone/iPad app. Although it is possible to open a new business and truly offer a niche service (meaning that you have entered a new market without any direct competitors), it rarely happens in today's business environment. The same holds true for apps on the App Store.

Understanding your competition is one of the most critical, yet misunderstood aspects of marketing and applies equally to iPhone/iPad app marketing. Even if you have not started developing your iPhone/iPad app, you should survey the App Store and look at the competition to see what you're up against. Do you think you've thought of the perfect iPhone/iPad app? Check the App Store to see what's already been built in that category. I can almost guarantee that there is a similar app to what you are building or plan to build. If not, then you may be onto something!

Chances are there are many competitors out there with the same or similar applications. This is not said to discourage you but to emphasize the point that you must take a close look at the competition. Not too many years ago Hyundai entered the U.S. car market. They no doubt surveyed the competition to determine what they were up against. They had a very large hill to climb. They built their marketing plan and executed on it and have been quite successful by any measure. You have a similar hill to climb with the App Store. A quick scan on the App Store for apps to help you name your baby, for example, reveals more than 180 apps on this topic as shown in Figure 3.2.

Figure 3.2 A search on the App Store helps you identify similar apps that may be your competition.

You can also be guaranteed that if you do create a truly unique application and your app shows signs of success, you will not be the only one offering that type of app for very long. Other people and companies emulate success. Rather than fearing the competition, learn to understand your competitors to leverage their successes and note their failures. Competitive reviews of other apps should also be viewed as an ongoing task—new competition will enter your market, and if you do not keep a watchful eye on your competitors, you will allow others to displace you.

📩 *Note*

Your competition can be leveraged to aid your marketing efforts. There's no shame in "copying" a good idea—especially if it works. You can be assured that your competitors will be watching you closely, too. The App Store is full of apps that are very similar to other best selling apps.

Meaningful differences in your iPhone/iPad app compared to that of your competitors should be created and communicated to your target buyer via multiple avenues, several of which are discussed in this book. These channels include your web messaging, features and benefits copy on the App Store, product design graphics, icon colors, advertising and other promotion mediums including marketing campaigns, and even spokespersons.

Intuitively (or based on research and/or trial and error) you believe that your app will succeed. You believe this because you are doing something different from some or all of your competitors. The first marketing test of any business, small or large, is to understand how you are unique when compared to your competitors. For example, you may be selling a financial app that offers some unique features that you think nobody else can match. So perhaps you focus your message around communicating that your app has a highly complex financial formula that is super handy to have on the iPhone or iPad. This special feature will resonate with some customers and separate you from your competitors.

Identifying Your Competition

There are two types of competitors: direct and indirect. A direct competitor could be considered anyone who offers the exact app that you provide to the same target audience. So in the previous example of applications that help you name your baby, there are at least 180 that do similar things. An indirect competitor is someone who offers a similar app but targets a different audience. So if you look at the games category on the App Store, you will see tens of thousands of games. Some are geared to younger kids while others are clearly geared to a male audience. Regardless, they may be your competitor especially if someone is just looking for any game to play. An example of a few game competitors is shown in Figure 3.3.

Figure 3.3   Indirect competition can come from a very crowed category, such as games, where your app resides on the App Store.

Identifying your direct competitors is important as you finalize your decision about your app's unique messaging. It reduces risk, time, required resources, and expense when planning a marketing strategy. It may be more profitable to carefully target a specific segment of a category where the odds of success are greatest. So posting an app in the category Lifestyle and focusing your animal-related app on residential customers that spend a lot of money on their pets can be a very good marketing approach. Figure 3.4 illustrates an iPhone/iPad app that is in the Lifestyle category and is focused on pets.

Figure 3.4   This app has been appropriately placed in the Lifestyle category, helping it be identified more easily.

Finding your competitors takes some effort. Because the number of apps is so great, the easiest way to search for your competitors is to go into the App Store and use the "Power Search" function. You can search by unique category or search all categories. Search for your app type by starting with the All category enabled. This will give you broad results of apps that might be similar to yours as illustrated in Figure 3.5.

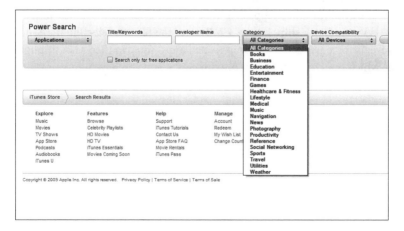

Figure 3.5   Start your competitive search by using "All Categories" and searching on the topic for your app.

The example in Figure 3.6 shows the results of doing a search on quilting-related iPhone/iPad apps by specifying in the Title/Keywords section the word "quilting." Given that the list is short relative to other apps, you can quickly see all the apps in the entire store that pertain to this topic.

Figure 3.6   Enter specific titles or keywords for the type of app you are looking for. This will help you narrow down your search.

Now let's look at a much tougher category, games. There are, of course, thousands upon thousands of games in every games subcategory on the store. So you will need to be very specific on the type of games you want to identify in your competitive exercise. In the next example we are searching for competitive battleship games. The best way to find these apps is to first select the category "Games" and then type in the keyword **battleship**. Figure 3.7 displays the results. Selecting the See All button reveals three pages of battleship related apps. You can then scan through them to see which ones most closely approximate the app you have written or intend to write.

 Note

The App Store has recently started displaying the number of pages for the app type you search on. Most of us are used to seeing "Page 1 of 10" in search results, for example. The App Store displays a "next" button along with the pages. You can view all apps or click through page by page. The apps are displayed in 5 columns by 36 deep or 180 apps per page.

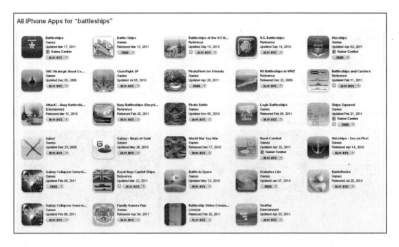

Figure 3.7   Searching for battleship games using the Games category and specific keywords

Learning from Your Competition

As soon as you've determined your key competitors, build out a small list on a spreadsheet to make some notes about their features and other noteworthy items. You can also use the list to track the competition on an ongoing basis. Table 3.1 at the end of this chapter shows a sample worksheet that can be built in Excel to help you gather your competitive data. Try to narrow your list to two or three apps that most closely resemble what your app does or will do.

Spend time reviewing the competition's written description of their apps on the App Store. Be sure to review their pictures and, most importantly, customer reviews. The customer reviews reveal a lot about an app. People tend to talk about what they liked and what they think is missing in the app or what could make it better. No reviews either means that the app is very new or it has not been downloaded too much or sold too well. You can check the date the app was made available by looking at its basic info next to the icon as shown in Figure 3.8.

Sometimes it may be necessary to purchase an app to understand its full capability and assess its features. Competitors in every product area routinely purchase each other's products to understand their strengths and weaknesses, especially in the software industry. Software companies have dedicated labs, for example, where they do nothing but test their competitor's products in an effort to improve their own product and marketing programs.

Figure 3.8 The posting date for new and updated apps is shown next to the app's icon.

 Note

> Keep in mind that I am never suggesting that you steal someone else's proprietary work. You are trying to understand how you can improve your own app and build a better app than what's currently out there. This is perfectly legal and within the bounds of ethical behavior.

When you have narrowed your list to the most likely competitors, ask yourself the following questions as you do some competitive iPhone/iPad app reconnaissance. The answers to these questions will help you make some important marketing and development decisions:

- What unique features does your competitor's app have that yours doesn't?

- How do the graphics look compared to your app?

- What claims do they make about their apps? Is it the only iPhone/iPad app to utilize such and such feature?

- Does the app appear to have multiple updates?

- Is their marketing message consistent?

- Do they have a strong, compelling offer for their prospective buyers?

- What do you like or not like about the overall presentation of their app?

- If you've installed it, how well does the app run?

- How is the game play? What makes the game or app compelling?

- Would you tell your friends about the app?

- Are their features such as Facebook or Twitter in the app that make it easy to share with friends?

Maybe you've borrowed a good app idea from some other source and are attempting to build a successful business around it. Every buyer expects multiple options in their apps, and many of the apps look very much alike. However, if you examine the more successful apps, you'll notice that they tend to emphasize and promote something special or unique. It may be better graphics or higher sound quality. If it's a game, it may be insanely addictive. Some developers undoubtedly borrowed their ideas from other companies (for instance, Electronic Arts sets a high bar with their game apps), others they've dealt with, promotions they have noticed, and so on. Successful developers always find ways to make their apps stand out from the crowd or at least stand out from the crowd in their immediate niche areas.

 Note

Even established businesses need to periodically re-evaluate their direction in relation to competition. For example, Apple has a very long history and a strong base of loyal customers. In recent years Apple has built many retail stores at great expense. Although the core "business" for Apple was very strong, the company had to very carefully decide who its retail market was and then position its stores uniquely. They have successfully created a different kind of buying experience for their products. Apple stores do not have the typical computer warehouse look. Instead they are clean and non-cluttered and very well organized, focusing the buyer's attention to each product for sale: iPhones, iPads, iPods, Macs, accessories, and so on. The strategy has been so successful that Microsoft started opening its own retail stores in late 2009.

What Are the Key Features of Your iPhone/iPad App?

Features are "descriptions" of your iPhone/iPad app (for example, touch controls, accelerometer use, multi-function, and so on). When you review your app against the competition you'll want to look at all of the quantifiable features that the other apps offer as compared to your own. You can use Table 3.1 at the end of this chapter to build a comparative list. Utility applications on the App Store, such as financial calculators and other scientific apps tend to lean toward feature points in their product descriptions. Feature descriptions on the App Store work best when they are in a bulleted list so that the buyer can quickly scan the list for what they are looking for. Keep the list short and relevant. Long lists get ignored, but a short list of features (five to ten) bullets will get read more willingly. An example of an app with a feature list is shown in Figure 3.9.

Figure 3.9   A calculator application with a feature list allows the buyer to quickly scan for functions she is looking for in a calculator.

 Note

Be sure to review the free apps in your category as well. If you are building an app that does not have any more features or functionality than a free app, the chances are slim that you will see sales success with your app. People love free but are willing to pay for value, and it's your job to convey your app's value!

When you have determined your app's key features, you want to also think in terms of the benefits those features will provide your buyer. Don't make the buyer figure it out for themselves. You can help the buyer to "connect the dots" by clearly articulating the benefits of each feature as explained in the next section.

What Are the Benefits of Your iPhone/iPad App?

Benefits are the "advantages" you receive from using your app (for example, hours of fun, feel better today, live healthier, experience less stress, lose weight faster, stay cleaner, have brighter smiles, and so on). A benefit is a powerful way to help you sell your product. Many marketers and iPhone/iPad app sellers overlook this very powerful concept when describing their apps on the App Store. When you link a benefit with a feature, you are helping the buyer see the whole story about your app. When we buy a car, for example, we go into a dealer showroom and start to look around. A particular car attracts our attention. It could be its color or its sleek or sporty look. On the window is a sticker that lists a bunch of features. The salesperson will answer your questions about all the features, but what he really wants is for you to experience the car's benefits. They want you to feel good about the car, which is why they always ask if you want to take it out for a test drive. They know that if they can get you to experience the "feel" of the car, its performance, its quiet ride, its new smell, and so on, they are more likely to get your business. Obviously buying a car is a much bigger decision than buying an iPhone/iPad app, but in this highly competitive App Store, you want to take every opportunity to reach the potential buyer of your app at both levels: features and benefits.

Notice as you read reviews of each iPhone/iPad app on the App Store that people tend to discuss their feelings about the app in terms of its benefits ("Most fun I've had in a long time!" or "This game is so addicting I can't put it down"). Notice the reviews shown in Figure 3.10. They are focused on how addictive the game is and that they love playing it. Whether the app developer has consciously intended to make this connection with his audience is in many cases coincidental, but one thing is certain: All successful apps connect with their audience through features and benefits. Therefore, if you want to increase the chances of success selling your app, you must make these connections happen with your buyer.

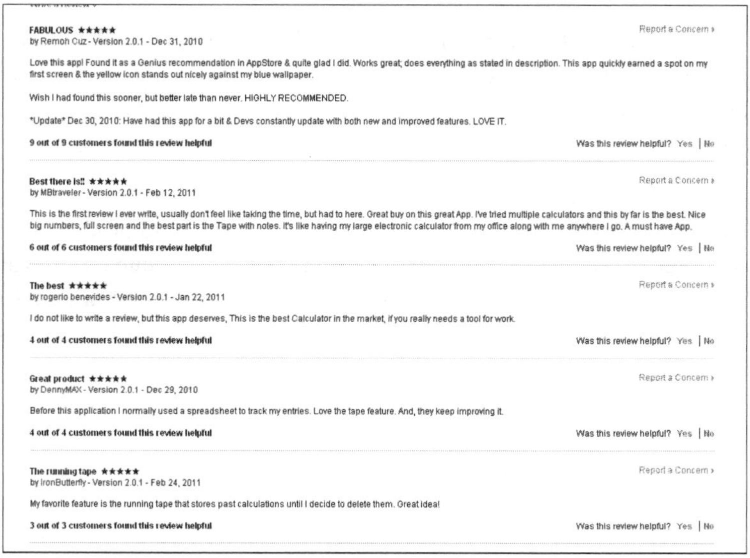

Figure 3.10   App Store product reviews tend to lean toward how the buyer feels about an app in terms of its benefits.

What's Unique About Your App?

How is your app different? Can you express it in terms of a concise statement or your graphics? This differentiator forms the basis for all your advertising, promotions, communications, and other marketing activities. Is your difference something that your buyer can appreciate so that he'll prefer or even seek out your app rather than your competitors? To successfully market his or her app, every developer needs to focus on what's special and different about his app.

To determine the unique qualities of your app, note your answers to the following questions:

1. Which words or phrases best describe what your iPhone/iPad app offers your customers (for example, educational assistance, financial problem solving, health answers, lifestyle, fitness ideas, entertainment, and so on)?

2. What qualities do you think will attract customers to your app (for example, incredible graphics, crisp sounds, amazing music, fast action, and so on)?

3. What qualities do you think will keep your customers coming back (for example, attention to detail, evolving new features, consistently challenging games, frequent updates, and so on)?

4. Did your responses to questions 2 and 3 reiterate what you had indicated initially for question 1?

If you answered no, where is the mismatch? Perhaps you don't fully understand the unique qualities of your app yet or you are you not sure about your customer's purchasing habits. Spend some time carefully working on this section until you come up with responses for questions 2 and 3 that fully support question 1.

As an example, I am going to be selling an educational app on the App Store. I am in the design stages of my app and want to make sure that I am producing an app that is unique in the market. I need to determine the app's unique qualities so that my message is strong and clear to my buyer. I have created the following responses to each of these questions. The application in my example is an education assistant geared to high school students to help them prepare for the SAT.

This is what I have come up with for my example:

1. What words or phrase best describe my app?

    Answer: Premier SAT Preparation

    In three short words I have described the quality of my app, the type of app, and my implied audience. You can do the same for your app. A basketball game app can be juiced up by calling it Blazin' Basketball

Pro. A less exciting calculator app can be brought to life by calling it Genius Calc. You get the idea.

2.   What unique characteristics will attract customers to your app?

Answer: Complete SAT Prep (Math, Science, and Writing)

The answer to question 2 supports question 1. I can call my app "Premier" because I have a complete solution. Not only do I have math and science practice tests, but I also include the newer writing component of the SAT. I provide test-taking advice, tips, and tricks.

3.   What qualities of your app will keep your customers coming back?

Answer: Download frequent updates of the latest SAT exams

The app provides frequent updates to help the high school student stay up on the latest material so they can be better prepared for their SAT.

4.   Did your responses to questions 2 and 3 reiterate what you had indicated initially for question 1?

Answer: The app's descriptions found in answers 2 and 3 support statement 1 as being a complete SAT preparation app and the fact that you can download frequent updates.

The idea of this exercise is to identify a clear statement of value about your app. When you provide solid answers to questions 2 and 3 that support question 1, you are well on your way to understanding and defining your app's unique value. This information will be tremendously valuable to you in your other marketing efforts discussed later in this book.

Summary

Successful marketing of your iPhone/iPad app requires you to determine your app's unique value and be able to boil out a clear, concise message for it. You gather this information by going to the App Store and reviewing competing apps to identify their strengths and weaknesses. How can you build a better app if you don't know what's already available? Understanding your app's unique value is the first step to building a foundation by which you can market your app.

Understanding your app's unique value will also come in very handy as you prepare to write your press release and design your web and App Store verbiage. With a clear value proposition for your app, you can confidently promote your app to communities across the Internet.

Competitive Worksheet

The worksheet in Table 3.1 will help you organize information about your local competitors. This is a good exercise for any app developer to help you have a running list of features in competing apps. A completed worksheet provides you with the following benefits:

- Gain a greater understanding of your competitors

- Understand your competitor's key messages and how you might revise yours if needed

- Identify areas of competitor strengths and weaknesses so you can more fully target your message and marketing campaigns

- Compare pricing to help you understand where you fit in the local consumer's mind

Table 3.1   Competitive Worksheet

Direct Competitors

Competing App Name	Website	Key Features	Key Messages	Target Audience	Noteworthy Reviews	Strengths	Weaknesses	Price

Indirect Competitors

Competitor Name	Website	Key Features	Key Messages	Target Audience	Noteworthy Reviews	Strengths	Weaknesses	Price

4

Identifying Your Target Audience

As you learned in the previous chapter, identifying your app's unique message is one of the keys to successful marketing. Now it's time to take a look at your target market, so you can carefully focus your message to the right audience. Some app developers think that it doesn't really matter if they identify their target market; as long as their apps are on the App Store, it will take care of itself. They think the right people will find their app regardless of what they do, especially if they get selected for a "Staff" pick or the "New and Noteworthy" category. You will definitely see a spike in sales while your app remains in one of those categories. But when your app is no longer getting top billing on the iTunes home page, your sales will drop off, and you'll be back to figuring out how to market your app. Therefore, identifying your target market does matter.

As shown in Figure 4.1, there are two ways to focus on driving awareness to your iPhone/iPad app. The first way is on the App Store itself, by specifying relevant keywords for searches and deploying other techniques to make your app stand out. The second way is by driving traffic to your own product website and then sending visitors to the App Store to buy your app. You will have more influence on driving traffic to your own site than on the App Store. Both of these areas are discussed in greater detail in other parts of this book. However, the focus of this chapter is that identifying your target audience is a vital step to achieving sales success of your app. It also saves you time and money if your marketing efforts are aligned more closely to your most likely buyer.

Two Ways to Find Your App on the App Store:

App Store Searches

- Power Search
- Keywords specified by you
- Included on one of the store's temporary areas (Staff Picks, New and Noteworthy, etc.)

Product Website Searches

- SEO activities
- Keywords specified by you
- Advertising
- Press Releases
- Blog posts
- Reviews

Figure 4.1   There are two ways to drive interest in your iPhone/iPad apps: App Store searches and product website searches (that direct you back to the App Store with an App Store link).

You have a general idea of who will buy your app simply by the type of app you develop. If you are developing an investing app, you know your market will be investors. However, there are many categories of investors. Some are risk averse, and they will be looking for an app to suit their conservative investing needs. Other investors are interested in highly risky stock options trading and will want an app to help them make options buy/sell decisions. Games, of course, have all kinds of categories of buyers. Some games are focused on children, whereas others target the male teen market. Some games may appeal to a general audience but have as their core audience a specific demographic.

Do you know precisely who your buyer is? Do you know how many apps your audience typically buys each year? These points help you identify your target buyer. What about other customers you might provide this app to? What is the lifestyle information (for example, recreational/entertainment activities, buying habits, cultural practices, and so on) for this target buyer? This type of information can help you in two important ways. First, it can help you make changes to your iPhone/iPad app to better match what your customers likely want. Secondly, it can tell you how to best reach your customers through search engine optimization, advertising, promotions, marketing campaigns, and so on.

 Note

A company that sells iPhone/iPad golf games knows that its typical customer is a golf nut. But it also knows that its buyer is a sports fan. Thus, if it can build a game realistic enough to be used by professional athletes, it will have a convincing story to tell about its quality. It can also benefit by using athletes as spokespersons in its reviews and advertising and by placing advertisements in sports magazines where its customers are likely to see them.

Refining Your Audience

How can you refine your understanding of your customer base to help with marketing planning? You should examine this question from two angles:

- **Segmenting the market**—Dividing the existing market into sections or segments that may become new niches for your iPhone/iPad app sales

- **Targeted marketing**—Identifying the heavy users of your app, so you can direct your marketing efforts more precisely to them for repeat business

Segmenting Your Market

Another way to help focus your unique value is to take some time to segment your market. This exercise allows you to understand further who you are selling to and what kind of concise message you can deliver to them. If the universe of all potential buyers is your "market," then the market can be divided into segments based on any number of factors.

For example, you might analyze your customers by age group and find that you sell (or will sell) most of your apps to people aged 18 to 34. You might segment them by family size and find that you sell most of your products to single men. You may divide them up by economic status and find that you sell most products to people with an annual income of about $30,000 to $65,000. Or you might divide them up by interests and find that you sell most of your apps to people who are avid fishermen or sports enthusiasts.

Note

Many independent developers stop after segmenting their market once, thinking they have enough information to be able to identify and communicate with their most likely customers. However, larger, more successful app development companies will attempt to push on further to find out even more information about their customers' lifestyles, values, life stage, and so on.

Let's define some terms that you will come across as you segment your iPhone/iPad app market. Obviously I could mention other segments, but these are some of the most common:

- Demographics refer to age, sex, income, education, race, marital status, size of household, geographic location, and profession. An understanding of demographics helps you define your marketing message and define a suitable marketing plan. Every app caters to at least one of these components.

- Lifestyle refers to the collective choice of hobbies, recreational pursuits, entertainment, vacations, and other nonwork-time pursuits. Some apps are strictly for fun, and so you should position your app in the appropriate category on the App Store. Other apps are health-related and therefore should be placed into this category on the App Store.

- Belief and value systems include religious, political, nationalistic, and cultural beliefs and values. These types of apps include religious topics, sermons, speeches (political and religious), and so on.

- Life stage refers to the chronological benchmarking of people's lives at different ages (for example, pre-teens, teenagers, empty-nesters, and so on). Many games can be classified in this category but also other apps such as health and fitness apps.

The App Store requires you to segment your market to some degree when you specify the category in which to place your app. Think very carefully about the category you select for your app. This can impact your sales dramatically if someone does a Power Search on the App Store by category and does not find your app where it logically should reside. Some apps and their category placement are clear cut, such as games. As a developer, you know when you post your game app to the store that you will select the Games category to post it. You can then further specify in a subcategory that the Game is a "Dice" game, as shown in Figure 4.2. Other apps are not as simple to categorize. Perhaps you have written an app that helps someone locate a friend. The app could be placed in the Navigation category, or it could be placed in the Social Networking category. Still, someone else may have developed an app that is educational as well as entertaining. That app could go in the Entertainment or Education category. The best category for your app is where you believe your buyers would most likely search on it.

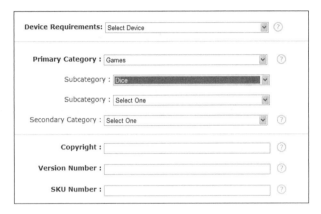

Figure 4.2   The Games category allows you to select up to two subcategories to help direct the buyer to your app.

 Note

> If you are struggling to figure out to which category to post your app, ask your friends which location they would naturally search on the App Store for your type of app. Ask 15–20 people to get a good sample. A clear trend should emerge of one category over another. If you feel that your app is in the wrong category after posting, you can change it at any time by going to iTunes Connect, logging in, and editing your app's profile information.

A list of App Store categories is shown in Figure 4.3 from the iTunes Connect website, where you will add your apps and select a primary category in which to place your app. You may also select a secondary category if needed. For example, you could select Health and Fitness as a primary category and Medical as a secondary category if you are selling an app that helps someone do cardio training, as shown in Figure 4.4. Because the Games category is so large, the App Store provides subcategories for this section. At the time of this writing, no other category allowed for more than one subcategory.

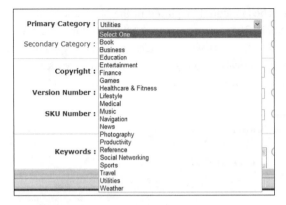

Figure 4.3   iTunes Connect website allows you to add new iPhone/iPad apps and select a primary and secondary category for your app. Selecting the right category for your app will help you to segment your market.

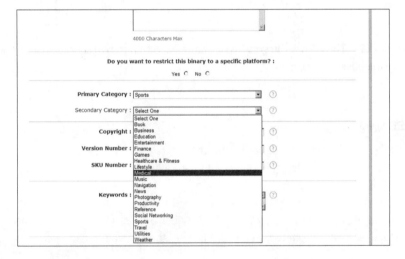

Figure 4.4   iTunes Connect also allows you to enter an optional secondary category to help further segment your market.

How can you find out more about your potential iPhone/iPad app customers? The most effective means is through some level of market research. Larger companies segment their markets by conducting extensive market research projects, consisting of several rounds of exploratory research. They do customer and product data collection. Professional researchers gather data from users of similar products on

- Number and timing of purchases

- Reasons for purchases

- Consumers' attitudes about various product attributes

- Importance of the product to the lifestyle of consumer

But how can you find out more about your app customers with budget and time constraints? What can an independent iPhone/iPad app developer do to segment her market?

Read the reviews posted on the App Store to gather valuable information on what customers like and don't like about your competitor's apps. Customer reviews are brutally honest with both praise and criticism. The comments will help you gain an understanding of how people perceive the app, its audience, and overall satisfaction. Obviously the more positive reviews than negative (based on the five-star rating) indicates the overall impression of the customer base. A predominantly high number of positive reviews and ratings indicates strong acceptance of the app. This also means that the app is resonating with a particular market segment. There will always be a few complainers who give the app a one-star rating, but if the majority of reviews are single star, then it is reason for concern. An example of an app receiving a good review is shown in Figure 4.5. The next example shows an app with a high number of negative reviews, displayed in Figure 4.6.

Figure 4.5 An example of an app with generally positive reviews. Read the customer comments of apps that are similar to yours to understand what types of customers are buying this app. This will help you segment your market and see what customers like about the app.

 Note

If an app is receiving mixed reviews, meaning the number of positive reviews is roughly equal to the number of negative reviews, you should very carefully read the reviews as they usually indicate that the app is hitting a part of their target market but leaving the other part unsatisfied. The reviews always indicate what feature or features are missing from the app.

Figure 4.6 An example of an app with poor reviews. The customers will indicate why the app is not doing well. Comments like "App is not worth the money" indicate that the app is poorly written and obviously not really resonating with any market segment.

 Note

> If you have multiple apps in your brand, you could have a different target audience based on the types of apps you have developed. For example, you may have developed game apps for children and teens, two markets that you would segment differently based on their needs. If you are selling a single app, you should look to target only one segment. Spill over into other segments is always a nice benefit, but you should focus on one market segment for best results.

Picking Your Market Segment

Picking the right market segment also means that the segment is

- Measurable in quantitative terms (how many? who are they?)—If you are developing a game app, try to figure out the potential size of your market. You can estimate your market by doing an Internet search and gathering some general statistics on its overall size. But trying to figure out your market segment size is difficult. You're better off determining who they are. For example, your game market may be young women 13–17 who are followers of the latest movie sensation.

- Substantial enough to generate planned sales volume through planned marketing activities—One thing is certain: You must have a market large enough to generate sufficient sales. If you develop an app that has a market that can be counted in just a few thousand, you may have a difficult time reaching them. The biggest reason is there is no way to know how many potential buyers in that small market own an iPhone/iPad or an iPod Touch. There must be enough target buyers on a frequent enough basis to sustain your company sales, spending, and profits from month to month.

You should also examine other important factors around targeting that could affect your app's success:

- Strength of competitors to attract your targeted buyers away from your app—How loyal are your customers? Could they be easily persuaded to switch to a competitor based on their marketing efforts (better pricing, better graphics, and so on)?

- Similarity of competitive apps in the buyers' minds—If the customer sees little difference in your app versus a competitors', you will have a problem.

- Rate of new app introductions by competitors—If innovation is the key to success in your market and you are asleep at the wheel, the competition will eventually overtake you.

Targeting Your Market

Perhaps the driving force behind targeted marketing or "segmentation" is the need to satisfy and keep those consumers who really love your apps. Even large iPhone/iPad development companies have embraced targeted marketing, continuing to refine and target their product offerings to different buyer groups.

Marketers of most products know that "20 percent of your buyers consume 80 percent of product volume." If you could identify the buyers that make up that key 20 percent and focus efforts on finding others like them, you could sell much more product with much less effort. Why? *Because you're not spending your marketing efforts convincing the buyer they need your application—your efforts are spent targeting the potential buyers that already need your application.* You just need to convince them that you are different (and better) than the competition.

 Note

Targeting existing buyers of similar apps is a great way to expand your business because they don't need to be convinced to purchase your apps. The buyer is already looking for an app like yours. Someone has already done the heavy lifting and made buyers out of them. Apple provides this help for your app automatically within the App Store. In the bottom of your product screen, there is a note that says "Customer Also Bought" as shown in Figure 4.7.

Figure 4.7   The App Store helps you improve your sales by showing links to similar apps that customers also bought.

The "heavy users" of your app can be thought of as a market "niche" that you should attempt to dominate. Targeted marketing means targeting, communicating with, selling to, and obtaining feedback from the heaviest users of your business's iPhone/iPad application. For example, if your market is a specific set of gamers who only like a particular type of game, you've got to make sure that your app and marketing message is spot on with that group.

If you have developed a health-related iPhone/iPad app, ask yourself who will be the most likely buyer: the patient or the caregiver? If the app is a reference to various health symptoms, it's probably targeted to someone who needs to know more about the health issue. If the app is geared to giving treatment options, it may be targeted to a health care worker. Savvy iPhone/iPad marketers will recognize the best market for their app and provide appropriate messaging to their particular audience, or in other words the "heavy users" of the apps.

The other important point here is that once you have identified your target market, you can keep them coming back for additional applications. Every customer win should be cared for so that you can sell them additional apps or other products from your own website. Smart developers plan to sell not only one app but also a series of apps to the same customer. In an effort to build their brand, some developers are also selling other items on their product websites, including hats, T-shirts, and so on. This is not to build another income stream but to help establish a brand and keep their customers coming back to their site. Don't be a one-hit wonder. Think longer term and get to know your market segment well. In turn, they will treat you well.

 Note

A number of developers are developing their game apps in such a way that they are constantly updating them to generate customer interest. Their strategy has been to first attract a following to their app and then constantly release updates to keep the customer coming back. This accomplishes several things. First, it keeps the customer engaged in using the app because a lot of app buyers tend to get bored rather quickly. It also gives the app developer another opportunity to go out with a press release announcing the new version that helps drive sales on a continuous basis.

Another technique that app developers are using is known as the in-app purchase. This can either be used from a free app to drive sales to a selling version of the app, or developers can create add-on options into their paid apps to help drive app sales. Coin Dozer, one of the App Store's highly downloaded game apps, uses this technique to sell users additional coins for its arcade game. A brilliant way to keep customers engaged with your app and spending more money on it, too! The topic of in-app purchases is discussed in greater detail in subsequent chapters. Notice in Figure 4.8 that in-app purchases are listed on the app's store front page. This is true for any app that utilizes in-app purchases.

Figure 4.8 All in-app purchase options are listed on the bottom left of the storefront for each app.

Summary

Market segmentation is a necessity when selling an iPhone/iPad app. Segmentation starts when you post your app on the App Store through the categorization required by the store. Some developers are not sure what category their app should be placed in and should seek the opinions of others for help. Game developers can use one or two subcategories to help them segment their game within a very large market.

Beyond the App Store segmentation, as a developer you must also look at and understand the market from a demographic perspective. This will help you craft the right message, one that allows your audience to understand what your app does. What gender mostly uses your app? If it's a motocross app, your most likely buyer is a male teenager, although female teenagers might buy it, too. If you've developed a lifestyle app, your buyer might be a hobbyist or a professional player of some sort.

Knowing your market is important. You don't want to waste time and money trying to advertise and market to an audience that doesn't care about your app.

5

Building Your App's Total Message

Some people think marketing your iPhone/iPad app consists of doing a little advertising and a press release. Actually, marketing your app, especially if you want to see steady and consistent sales from the App Store, requires that you do a number of things very well and over a period of time. I call this group of marketing activities creating your app's "total message," and it includes every aspect of your marketing effort, from how you name your app and the icons and graphics you display, to your product website and App Store wording. Table 5.1 lists the components of the "Total" app message. Check each category and give yourself a grade that reflects your progress in each area.

All the activities listed in Table 5.1 are a means of communication and can help you convey the value of your app and its unique qualities to your buyer. You may not fail to sell your app by not doing them, but your odds of success are much higher than if you sit back and do nothing.

Table 5.1   How Well Are You Doing Creating Your App's "Total Message?"

Marketing Component	My Grade (haven't started, not bad, pretty good, very good)
Descriptive App Name	
Polished App icon	
Descriptive App Store written content	
Clean and simple product website	

The more complete your total message, the more likely someone will like what he or she sees on your product website and the App Store and then buy your app. When people visit the App Store online or from their phones, they are either simply browsing for something fun to download or they are searching for a specific type of app.

The "browser" type of visitor is usually looking for an app to just pass the time. He may be looking for an action game or a puzzle or some other app for short term entertainment. Perhaps he is looking for an app to keep one of his kids occupied, but he's not sure which to go with. Most buyers start a search by looking at the "What's Hot" or in the "New" categories, or they will look at the Top 25 lists for purchase ideas. The Top 25 is further broken out by Top Paid, Top Free, and Top Grossing categories. The other type of buyer comes to the store looking for a specific solution to a problem. It could be a student looking for help with homework for a particular class, or maybe she's preparing for the SAT exam. It could be a businessman looking for an app to help him in his sales activities or to better manage his finances or track customers. Or it could be a mom looking to get more organized with her daily activities such as shopping and budgeting.

Regardless of the apps they seek, buyers will be presented with pages upon pages of apps that are in that category. So even when they have found the category they want, they still may have to wade through hundreds of apps. If you can make your app stand out, it's more likely that visitors will stop and take a look at your app. That's the first step in getting them to buy! If you can't get someone to stop and look at your app, your sales will be disappointing. Take a look at the apps shown in a PC view of the App Store in Figure 5.1. Note the apps that catch your attention and ask yourself why these particular apps make you stop and look.

Figure 5.1   Which apps attract your attention and why? Understanding buyers' thought processes will help you devise ways to attract them.

Most people visiting the App Store are first attracted to the colorful icons. It's simply easier to scan the page looking at the graphics to see if one of them is of interest rather than reading every description. Buyers can sort the list of available apps by "[app] Name," "Most Recent," and "Release Date," but most buyers will scan the screens (or their iPhone screens) looking for an icon that grabs their attention. If an icon looks interesting, most people will read the name of the app and its category and then decide whether to click it. Some apps do a better job conveying their value than others. Can you find the apps shown in Figure 5.2 that do the best job conveying what they do?

If visitors to the App Store like an icon and the name of the app, they will then click on the app for a closer look and more information. When delivered to your App Store product page, they will again be drawn to the graphics that you have on your storefront. They will click through the graphics on your product page to get a quick idea of what your app does. And finally, if they like what they see, they will read the text description on the right side of the page. If your app is a game, they are going to look at the description to figure out a few details of how the game is played.

If the premise of the game is simple and the buyer likes the graphics, they will be more influenced to buy/download your app. They will make a buying decision. If the app is free (or a lite version), they will decide if they want to download it and try it out. If the app costs money, they will decide if they want to spend the money to download it. An example of the app buyer's decision progression is shown in Figure 5.3.

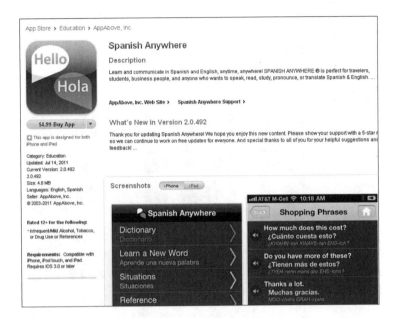

Figure 5.2   Some apps do a better job than others in instantaneously conveying what they are about.

 Note

Your goal as a marketer is to visually and textually anticipate and answer the buyers' questions and concerns, helping them to make informed decisions and convince them that your app is the right one for them. By addressing all the points covered in this chapter, you are making it easier for potential buyers to make a decision about buying your app. You are connecting the dots in the buyers' mind about how your app can meet their particular needs. Not doing some of these steps does not mean sales failure of your app, but why not cover all your bases and improve your chances of sales success?

Choose an Effective App Name

An effective iPhone/iPad app name can help increase your sales because the buyer does not have to invest as much effort to understand what your app does. The more you make buyers work to understand what you are selling, the more likely they will go somewhere to find an app that does what they're looking for. This is not to say that all apps will fail if they don't have a descriptive name. However, if your app is a

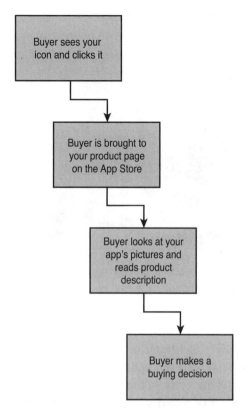

Figure 5.3   The decision process of a visitor on the App Store starts visually and then moves to the app's written description.

nongame app such as a utility, financial calculator, weight loss tool, and so on, you can improve your results by describing what the app does in the name.

You can use several words in your app name to be creative and also describe what the app does. For example, if you have written a calorie counting app, you could call it something like "Melt Away Pounds (Calorie Counter)." From the name you immediately understand what the app does. Figure 5.4 shows an example of an app that combines a straightforward name with a description of what the app does. Notice that the icon along with the title gives you an immediate impression of the app's purpose. I know instantly that the app is educational and directed to a young audience. This type of naming works very well on the App Store for educational and utility-focused apps.

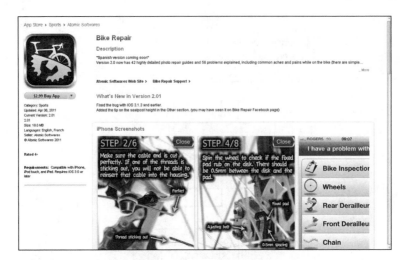

Figure 5.4   An example of a straightforward naming approach with the product name first, followed by a brief description.

Game apps have much more latitude in their naming options. You are only limited by your imagination and what you think will resonate with your target market. Remember your target market from Chapter 3, "Identifying Your App's Unique Value?" If you can focus on a catchy or memorable name that will resonate with your target audience, you can establish a stronger following for your app. There are many categories of games, and this can help you determine the best type of name for your app. If your game is educational, you'll probably want to name your app more descriptively, such as "High School Math Blitz I: Algebra I and II Refresher" or "High School Math Blitz II: Geometry and Trig Refresher." Figure 5.5 shows a game app in the Action category that is cleverly and memorably named. Figure 5.6 shows a game app in the Racing category that also has a name that resonates instantly with the viewer.

Other games are more seasonal and are named for a particular holiday. So usually the holiday is the first part of the name followed by the type of game. Again, the reader can get an instant picture of what the game is about. The holiday games are impulse buys attracting a buyer's attention for only a short time. Many developers have a collection of games for different holidays to keep their sales rotating around each month of the year. A seasonal example is shown in Figure 5.7.

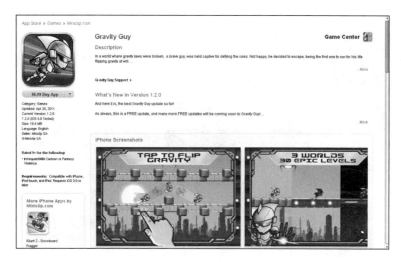

Figure 5.5   This game app has a catchy name that is clever and memorable (at least in the author's opinion)

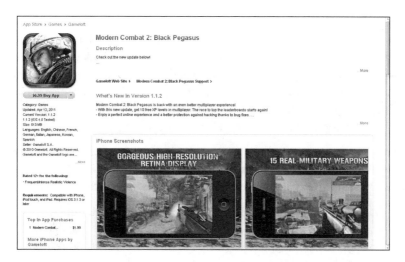

Figure 5.6   App names for games can be geared to your audience age and gender for maximum sales impact.

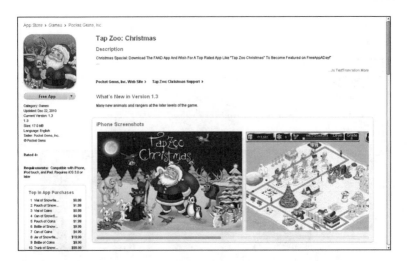

Figure 5.7   Seasonal games are named for the holiday and the type of game.

Basic App Naming

You should consider a number of ways to approach naming your app. First, if you plan to develop a series of apps under a brand name, then think of app names that are flexible and will support your overall brand. If you are developing a series of science apps for high schools students, your brand may be called "Science Guy," and your apps will start with your brand connected with a dash. For example, "Science Guy—Chemistry" or "Science Guy—Physics," and so on.

You can use roman numerals for some apps names such as "Crazy Flips I" and "Crazy Flips II," or you can choose names such as "MyStory—The Prequel" or "MyStory—The Sequel." Other general naming rules include the following:

1. Make sure your app name is easy to pronounce and spell. You want your app to be easy to remember from a word-of-mouth standpoint. You also want your app to be easily searchable in the App Store. Apps with difficult spellings may be hard to locate in the store.

2. Beware of app names that might mean something else in a foreign language. Nova comes to mind....

3. If possible, keep the app name short. You have limited space under the app's icon to display the name. If the name is too long, it will be truncated under the icon, or you'll have to use an acronym to spell it, which makes it lose some its value from a simplicity standpoint.

4. Be sure to check on trademarks and other reserved names. For example, Freeverse, Inc., has the rights to use the name Skee-Ball for its skee-ball app. So although there are other skee-ball apps for sale on the App Store, they cannot use skee-ball in their actual name.

5. Stick to names that don't offend any group of people. Offensive app names may appeal to some buyers, but you'll narrow your audience considerably with that approach.

6. Check for domain availability for your app name. With so many domains registered, this may be difficult, but it helps to have the same domain name as your app. If you are building a brand and developing a number of apps, then register the domain name for your brand first.

 Note

While researching your name, you can go to many different domain registration sites to check availability for your domain/app name. Sites such as GoDaddy.com and Register.com are just two of hundreds of sites that can help you.

Get Creative

If you're having trouble coming up with a good app name, you can follow some simple strategies to help you move the process along. Write down answers to the following questions and list as many ideas as come to mind. Then focus on the question where the best answers come to mind. This is most likely where you're going to find the best name for your app.

- What does your app do? (It calculates net worth, organizes coupons, tabulates investments, and so on.)

- What is your app's benefit to the consumer? (It makes a busy working mom's life easier, helps students get better grades, teach teens how to drive safely, and so on.)

- What will happen for my buyers? (They will feel better, look better, run faster, become smarter, and so on.)

- What are the key features of your app? (There are 10 levels of play, zoom, and pan function, 150 inputs, 3D graphics, enhanced sound, and so on.)

- How are you different from competing apps? (This is the only app to have such and such, multiplay features, and so on.)

- What makes your app unique? (Voted #1 by *MyApp Magazine*, and so on.)

- Can your app play off a mainstream word or phrase already in use? (If it's a photo utility, use the word "photo" in the app name, for example. A good example of playing off of other products for a product name is shown in Figure 5.8.)

Figure 5.8   This app name is playing off the ubiquitous Photoshop name.

Search for Synonyms

If you've found a few words that might work for your app name, you can also check for synonyms to see if there are any similar words that might work even better for your app name. You can use the thesaurus in Microsoft Word to get started with similar words, or you can go to one of many thesaurus websites, such as www.thesaurus.com. This site provides a multitude of synonyms for almost any known word and also provides a handy synonym map showing similar words branching off the root word you have entered.

Use Google or Yahoo to Help

If your app is a game, you can get lots of ideas by simply searching a particular topic in Google or Yahoo for ideas. For example, if your app is a road-racing game, you can get lots of ideas by going to Google or Yahoo and typing in "Road Racing." You will find an unlimited list of ideas. Some other topics that might help you in your search are listed here. Simply go to Google or Yahoo and type them in:

- Stars and planets (games, science, astrology apps)

- Finance and money (financial, education, utilities apps)

- Sports players and teams (sports, health and fitness, education apps)

- Cartoon characters (games, other apps)

- Presidents of countries (education, books, other apps)

- Travel (navigation, education, books, and other apps)

- Shows and entertainment (entertainment, other apps)

- Fitness training (health, fitness, education, other apps)

- Children's books (books, games, education, other apps)

- Electronics and computers (games, sports, education, other apps)

- Music and musical instruments (games, music, books, other apps)

Select and Test Your App Names

After you have selected the three names you like the best, run them by family and friends to see which name gets the highest vote. You have to ask more than one or two people, though. Try to ask at least ten people which name they like the best and why. It's important to understand which name triggered the best response, so you can continue to develop your marketing approach knowing what resonates with your buyer.

App Store Text: Lighten It Up

In this mobile economy, people are reading less when it comes to their communications. Attention spans are short and, with the crush of information thrown at us each day, there is limited time to listen to each seller's message and review buying options. Hence, the reason for the 15-second TV commercial and the massive popularity of Twitter. When buyers read the text for your app on the App Store, they are interested in downloading it.

Most people will not make the investment in time to read your words unless they have more than a casual interest in your app. So you've gotten them this far in the process, and you need to make the most of your words. Figure 5.9 illustrates good balance of text and white space, helping the reader to understand quickly the benefits of your app. There is no exact science to perfect content. However, the rule of "less is more" works best. Here are ten suggestions for your App Store text to help you captivate your reader's attention:

1. List any promotions, discounts, or sales events at the top of the text to meet the demands of any of your impulse buyers. Use asterisks to call out a sale or noteworthy review or event.

2. Post solid magazine, newspaper, or other leading reviews of your app next to the top of the text to reinforce the value of your app from the start. Testimonials, especially from well-known publications, can influence your sales.

3. Describe what your app does in a few quick sentences. The reader wants to know right away!

4. Talk about the benefits of your app toward the top of the page (feel better today, hours of fun, lose weight fast, learn this skill now, improve your health, and so on).

5. Use short paragraphs to describe your app. Two to three sentences work well. Avoid big blocks of paragraphs. Most app buyers will skim through it and won't read it completely.

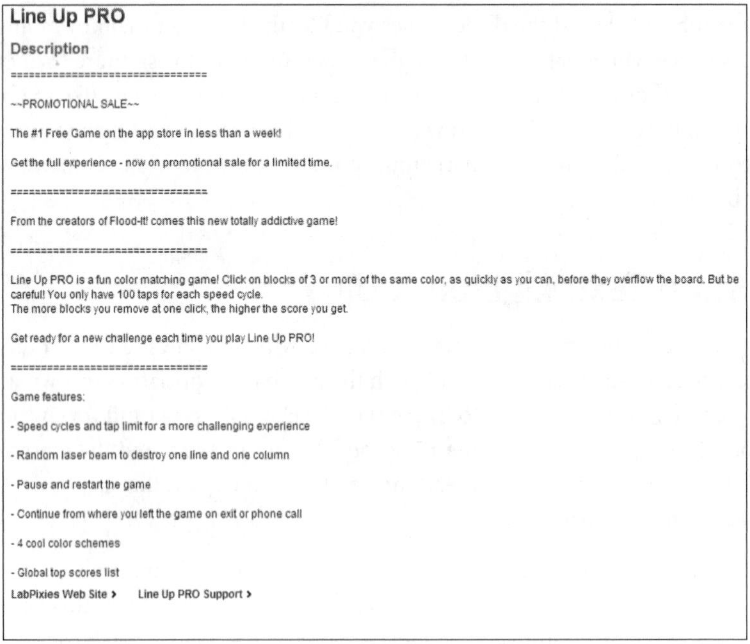

Line Up PRO

Description

================================

~~PROMOTIONAL SALE~~

The #1 Free Game on the app store in less than a week!

Get the full experience - now on promotional sale for a limited time.

================================

From the creators of Flood-It! comes this new totally addictive game!

================================

Line Up PRO is a fun color matching game! Click on blocks of 3 or more of the same color, as quickly as you can, before they overflow the board. But be careful! You only have 100 taps for each speed cycle.
The more blocks you remove at one click, the higher the score you get.

Get ready for a new challenge each time you play Line Up PRO!

================================

Game features:

- Speed cycles and tap limit for a more challenging experience

- Random laser beam to destroy one line and one column

- Pause and restart the game

- Continue from where you left the game on exit or phone call

- 4 cool color schemes

- Global top scores list

LabPixies Web Site ›   Line Up PRO Support ›

Figure 5.9   iPhone app example with good balance of text.

6. Use bullets to describe your features. Bullets help lead the reader through the key points of your app, and we are accustomed to go through bulleted lists.

7. Include a note to have the buyer look at your other apps, too, if you have them up on the App Store.

8. Include a "What's New" section describing the latest updates (if it is an updated app, of course).

9. List any updates that are coming up in a "What's Coming" section.

10. Review your text periodically to make sure it's still reading the way you like. Sometimes, rereading text after a few days or weeks helps us to see things in a different light. Have someone else take a look at the text to make sure it's on message.

 Note

There is an exception to the short text rule, and that's in the book category. Sometimes it helps to include a compelling paragraph from the book. Where the reader might be interested in seeing an excerpt, go ahead and include it. The App Store does provide an ample allowance.

Make Graphics Your Focal Point

The phrase "A picture is worth a thousand words" is well suited to the App Store and to selling your iPhone/iPad app. Good graphics help sell your product. Spend time to ensure that your graphics showcase your app in the best possible way. It is possible, for example, to turn your graphics horizontally for a different look rather than showing the pictures of your app vertically. You can showcase your app with a mix of vertical and horizontal photos. The examples shown in Figures 5.10 and 5.11 demonstrate good use of photos and graphics for several apps.

 Note

Some apps only have one or two photos posted on the App Store. This is a big mistake. The App Store allows you to post up to five photos of your app, and you should use every last one of them. To not use all five photos is like being given 30 seconds to do a TV commercial and using only 20 seconds. Use every last tool at your disposal to display your app in its best light.

Figure 5.10   This example shows two of five slides. Notice how the graphics can help explain the usage of the app.

Figure 5.11   This app makes use of vertical and horizontal positioning of its graphics.

Make Your App's Icon Jump

Another very important aspect of building a solid marketing message is to select an icon that helps convey the meaning of your app. The easier it is to see visually what your apps are about, the easier someone can make a decision to take a closer look at them. For example, if your app is utility-related, select a graphic that conveys the type of utility this app provides. Figure 5.12 shows a good example of an icon that clearly conveys what the app can do for the buyer. Adding a few descriptive words to the icon can also strengthen the visual message.

Figure 5.12   The most effective app icons clearly show a connection with the app's function.

 Note

> If you've had your app posted for a few months and you're not seeing as many sales as you like, change out your app for a new one. People get accustomed to seeing the same icon over and over again and may pass right over it. If you post a new icon, you'll attract new buyers.

Another great use of the icon is to post a promotion using part of the app. Let's say you've decided to have a 50%-off sale for a holiday weekend. You can modify the bottom of your icon or top-right/left corner announcing your sale. Figure 5.13 gives you an example of using the icon to convey your message. This is a wise thing to do, and app sellers know that a buyer is skimming the App Store. If they see 50% off or a 24-hour sale, they will hopefully be inclined to click the icon to find out more.

Figure 5.13   You can use your app icon to announce that your app is on sale.

Build a Simple, Clean Product Website

Your product website should be similar in look and feel to your App Store product page. A carryover between the two sites will help build buyer confidence in your app and that you are serious about your business. A sloppy website with broken links does not inspire confidence when a buyer is seeking more information about your apps. This does not mean that you have to spend a fortune on your site, but it must look clean and simple. This means that your home page should have graphics and showcase your app just like the App Store. For more suggestions on creating and promoting your website see Chapter 6, "Electronic Word of Mouth." For now, let's focus on the website message.

You may be building your own website, or perhaps you've hired someone to help you out. Either way, chances are you will be the one coming up with the messaging for your site. It is imperative that you learn to write well and convey the app or app's value to your reader. Obviously, web copy will vary in style, readability level, and length depending on the type of apps you are selling. The sole purpose of your site is to make sales, and your web copy should reflect that. Persuasion, clear product descriptions, rationale for buying, and so on will all be important. On the other hand, an app site for games may well have short copy that needs to be extremely well written to keep your viewers interested and willing to click around.

 Note

iPhone/iPad apps can only be purchased from the iTunes App Store. So the job of your app product website is not only to instruct and inform potential buyers, but to persuade them to click over to the App Store and buy your app.

Developing Great Web Copy

Outstanding web copy helps your website get visitors. To create great copy, you need to understand what your audience wants to read. For more information on this, see Chapter 4, "Identifying Your Target Audience."

There are lots of different rules and recommendations about how to write good web copy, but the bottom line is that you want to write copy in such a way that it pulls in your visitors. You want to create a statement at the top of your site that clearly identifies what your apps do. Don't make the visitor to your site hunt around trying to figure it out. People will click away in seconds if they don't find a clear explanation of your app. When you write your content for your website, your goal is to get visitors to learn about your app and want to click the Buy Now button that takes them over to the App Store.

Make your visitors feel good about your app—this is the key to drawing them back on a regular basis. Your website can include tips and tricks, frequently asked questions (FAQs), and occasional promotions to keep them interested in returning.

The best advice is to make your writing interesting. Look at some other sites that sell apps similar to yours and get some ideas. There's nothing wrong with seeing how others are building their websites, especially if they are on the top sellers lists on the App Store. It almost goes without saying, but I'll mention it anyway: You must make sure your content is spell-checked and grammatically correct. Failure to do even the simple things will make you come off as amateur.

If people think your website looks sloppy, they naturally think your app will be equally poor. Nothing says careless quicker than a spelling error. Use active voice style and keep your tone friendly, informative, and snappy. Keep their interest! Make your copy compelling if you want them to keep coming back. An example of a well-written home page for an app is shown in Figure 5.14. Here are some other important tips:

- Your content should quickly describe your app at the top of the page.

- Your web content should be as entertaining as possible. Be sure to have a gallery of pictures showcasing your app.

- The website should inform your visitor as to what your app can do.

- You must educate your visitor with FAQs and videos. Always have a YouTube video demonstrating your app.

- Your website must convince your visitor to buy. Always have a prominent Buy Now button configured to take your buyer directly to your app on the App Store.

Figure 5.14 Compelling web copy will keep your visitors' interest and help lead them to the App Store to purchase your app.

Make Your Content Usable

According to web design experts, most web viewers scan web pages rather than read them word for word. If you adhere to certain web content principles, you're more likely to have success in keeping your visitors and convincing them to click over to the App Store:

- Use highlighted keywords. (Hypertext links serve as one form of highlighting; typeface variations and color are others.)

- Create meaningful subheadings (not "clever" ones).

- Use bulleted lists just like on the App Store (such as this one, but not too long).

- Write short paragraphs. (Your readers will skip over any additional ideas if they are not caught by the first few words in the paragraph.)

- Use the inverted pyramid style, starting with the conclusion first.

Mastering your web content will help you achieve greater sales of your app. Remember to update your site whenever you update your app. You want to list new features you have added and anything else that might be of interest to your reader. See Figure 5.15 for an example of how you can showcase your app's updates on your website. This site is light and easy to read. Notice that the description and the Get Balloons and Get Balloons Lite buttons are placed prominently at the top of the web page.

Figure 5.15   Keep your website updated frequently with the latest features, tips, and promotions. Always have your Buy Now or Download App Now button prominently displayed on your home page, as the Get Balloons and Get Balloons Lite buttons are here.

Strive for Immediate Positive Reviews

There is nothing like getting a good reference. Whether you realize it or not, we all tend to listen to what other people say about things, and in part we base our buying decisions on what others have said. How many times have you ask friends if they liked certain movies? If they told you the movie was terrible, chances are you went go to another movie. But if you read reviews online or in the paper from the so-called movie experts, you might still be inclined to go anyway, regardless of your friend's experience. You may take more stock in what you read than what you heard from a friend because you judge the movie critic to possibly be a better source of information. But what if in another situation the movie critic gave another movie the thumbs down, but ten of your friends raved about it and said you must go see it? The chances are pretty good that you would go see the movie, despite what the critics said. In the latter case, you were probably swayed by what the majority said about the movie.

What about the last time you went out to dinner and asked for someone's advice on finding a good restaurant? Again, if they raved about a certain place, you would most likely go and give it a try. Other people's opinions about a product or service make a difference for many app buyers. We want to trust what we hear and read about products. It makes us feel safer if we see that others have made a similar purchase and have good things to say about it.

You may be wondering if reviews really matter for a $0.99 app—or a $2.99 app for that matter. If you are a game developer and trying to hit the Big Win (see Chapter 1, "Your iPhone and iPad App Marketing Strategy: Grand Slam or Base Hits?"), then reviews aren't going to matter too much. Most impulse buys are done straight from the iPhone/iPad, and buyers aren't going to the App Store to read what people are saying. However, if your app is in the Steady Wins category (again, see Chapter 1), then reviews do matter. The buyer has more time to look at your app, read a few reviews, and get a general idea of what the majority of the people think about it. A preponderance of good reviews makes potential buyers feel good about their purchase. A preponderance of bad reviews is a cause for concern in buyers' minds, and some will be inclined to look elsewhere for a similar app without the poor reviews.

But can you trust the customer reviews that are posted for each app? Well, yes and no. Apple changed the App Store not too long ago, requiring any reviews to be written by actual buyers of the app. In the early days of the App Store, any 10-year-old could post a review without buying the app, and the results could be very damaging to your sales. The App Store has definitely made the review process more democratic. However, many app developers would like the ability to respond to the review postings; something that Apple has yet to allow on the App Store.

Note

> If an app does not show any reviews, it means one of two things: Either the
> app has just been posted (or an update has just been released) and it's too
> early for any reviews to be posted, or the app has languished with no buyers
> and has not received any reviews. An app that is selling extremely well will
> generally have many reviews (in the hundreds or sometimes thousands).

If you don't have any reviews yet, you can use some of your free App Store promotion codes to give to friends to download your app and post a review for you. Ask them to give an honest assessment of the app and post some credible comments. If you've written a great app, you will get some great comments. Glowing reviews that go over the top to point out how good the app is are suspect. A lot of readers can tell if they are authentic. Obviously, having some customer reviews is better than none. But sometimes you have to get things moving along, and having a few family members and friends comment on your app can be helpful as long as they have used the app and are completely honest in their comments.

Summary

Marketing your iPhone/iPad app requires much more than just a press release and a few emails to family and friends. For best results, you need to build a total app message. Your message starts with giving your app an accurate and powerful name that will stick in the minds of your buyers, making it easy for them to pass along the app name to others. Next, you must have an app icon that helps your marketing efforts by its descriptiveness graphically or by including the name of your app in the icon. Your icon, combined with the app name, helps a buyer instantly understand what you app does and its value. Having a nondescriptive icon means your buyer has to dig a little deeper to understand your app. The more you can help a buyer "connect the dots," the more likely you'll get a sale.

Another part of your total app message is your App Store and product website text. Light and airy is the best approach because most buyers are not going to invest a lot of time reading text. Remember to post prominent reviews in your text and state a few key benefits of your app, along with some bullet points to describe key features on the App Store. You can always go into more detail about your app on your product website in an FAQ section or through a user guide. You want to strike a balance between conveying the strengths of the app without overwhelming readers with content.

II

Delivering Your Message

6 Electronic Word of Mouth 89

7 Using Social Media in Your App Marketing 111

8 Timing Your Marketing Activities 125

9 Getting the Word Out About Your App 135

6

Electronic Word of Mouth

One of the biggest challenges for any developer is figuring out the best marketing strategy, tools, and techniques to successfully sell their iPhone/iPad apps on the App Store. Your app, for example, may already be posted on the App Store and you are experiencing moderate sales success. Now you're looking for what else you can do from a marketing standpoint to influence even more downloads. Or you may be getting ready to launch your app and want to learn what you can do to get people excited about your app and start sales off strong.

As mentioned many times in this book, getting your app approved for sale on the App Store is only the first step (and probably the easiest) in the selling process. It takes a special mix of marketing activities to get your app noticed and to produce consistent sales success. Each marketing activity discussed in this chapter, when well executed, will contribute to more downloads of your app.

Simply rewording your app's top description on the App Store, for example, may result in an increase of 10–25 downloads per day if your original wording did not get right to the point about what your app does. An example of a crisp introductory sentence is shown in Figure 6.1.

Figure 6.1   Having a crisp, to-the-point, introductory description is vital to your selling success.

Adding a more descriptive app icon that speaks better to what your app does may result in 25–35 more downloads per day. An example of a great App icon is shown in Figure 6.2.

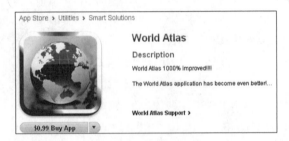

Figure 6.2   Having a recognizable and understandable app icon is critical to getting customers to click your app for more details.

Improving the app graphics that are displayed on the App Store helps you increase your downloads by some percentage as well. An example of crisp and clear graphics is shown in Figure 6.3. Each one of these seemingly small marketing activities also helps you build positive word of mouth.

Word of mouth (or word of mouse as they say in the Internet world) is one of the most powerful methods of getting your message out about your app. Word of mouth is all about building momentum for your app and getting everyone, espe-cially key influencers, to talk about your app to help generate buzz. Some app sales start off slowly and then gain momentum over time as the apps get noticed through various marketing activities. With consistent marketing you can increase the momentum of sales and even help your app become a best seller. Other apps take off almost immediately because of a good review or other good press.

Figure 6.3 Clear and easy-to-understand graphics can help instantly convey the purpose and value of your app to App Store visitors who quickly scan the store for interesting apps.

 Note

For an iPhone/iPad app to become a best-seller it has to have certain characteristics; it should be well written, have broad applicability and market reach, stay under 20MB in size, and be appropriately priced. Not all apps will fit all these criteria. In fact, only a small percentage of apps on the App Store meet such high criteria. Some iPhone/iPad apps will be good sellers, but not best sellers because their market may be limited or their applicability is focused on a narrow solution. This is partly why game apps are so popular. They have broad appeal, and the audience tends to be quite large. This is also why there are so many game apps for sale on the App Store. You can make a lot of money selling games if you hit on the right app, but your competition is extremely tough.

Word of mouth is a reputation-based form of marketing. If used properly, this form of marketing can be an extremely powerful way to get your app noticed and increase sales. It can take some time to get the ball rolling, so don't be discouraged if your app hasn't achieved momentum in the first few weeks of sales. Word of mouth marketing is probably the most powerful marketing tool you have if used the right way and you give it enough time. Granted, you will see and hear about apps that take off all by themselves without much effort on the part of the developer. These are the "black swan" apps that are in the right place at the right time with the right audience, and there's no easy explanation for their success.

Good, useful, or cool iPhone/iPad apps will prompt your buyers to recommend the app to others through email, blogs, or personal conversations. Earning a good reputation for your app is hard work. Your good reputation, however, can be extremely effective in helping you sell more apps and when you release follow-on apps to your user community.

In contrast, a bad reputation can be damaging to your overall app sales, and a bad customer experience can result in additional loss of sales opportunities if word gets too far around. Negative experiences prompt people to tell others about their poor experience using your app, and sometimes they write about their disappointment on the App Store app reviews.

 Note

> You will always have a few people who write negative responses to your app. There's no getting around it. Sometimes people purchase an app thinking it does one thing and then they discover it doesn't do what they thought. They become upset and write a negative review. People even write negative reviews for free apps! However, as long as your ratio of positive reviews is much greater than your negative reviews (10 to 1 or so), your sales will not be impacted too much. People will also write negative reviews if they can't install your app on their particular devices. Sometimes, an app built for a newer version of iOS won't install on an older iPod, for example.

Positive External Reviews

Sometimes a developer is lucky in that his or her app gets a positive review by an iPhone/iPad app review site. That review gets picked up by a blogger or other news agency, and it can be off to the races in app sales. If you're not fortunate enough to get such a review, you have to "prime the pump" to help increase the likelihood that your app will have the same sales outcome over time. This means that you can't rely on getting a lucky break by a reviewer just stumbling upon your app. Instead you have to employ other techniques to get the word out about your app and get reviewers to notice you. Don't ever give up on getting reviews from as many sources as possible. Try to obtain write-ups in several magazines and websites that would be interested in showcasing your particular app because it's topical to them.

For example, the app shown in Figure 6.4 was launched to help people locate health-related apps on the App Store. The developers of this app sought out publications that focused on health related devices and solutions for the elderly rather than only going after an iPhone/iPad app reviewer. The elderly are part of this app's market, and it was a good fit for this publication to do an article. This site (www. eldergadget.com) was interested in doing a write-up about this app because the senior crowd is very interested in iPhones/iPads and iPhone/iPad apps. The article gave the developer good press and helped strengthen the launch of his app.

Figure 6.4   AppsForAll launched their Healthful Apps application by doing a press release and mentioning an article written about their app in www.eldergadget.com (http://www.eldergadget.com/health/10404).

 Note

Your strategy for obtaining reviews for your app should be to contact as many iPhone/iPad app review sites as possible that are likely to review your app. Do not submit a nongame app to a game review site because it will simply get ignored. Seek out sites that give you the best chance for a review for your type of app. Utilize any and every contact you may have at these review sites to get your app noticed and reviewed.

Seek out other venues to get reviews of your app. For example, if you have an app that helps people learn how to garden, look for web and print publications that are focused on gardening and make a few inquiries to see if they would be interested in reviewing your app for an article. You'll be surprised how many publications will be interested in doing such a story. The reason is simple. Publications are always looking for topics that would be of interest to their readers. The iPhone still carries the "cool factor," and for those readers outside of the traditional tech world, the iPhone/iPad and apps that are germane to their interests carry strong interest. You will probably have to arrange a call to demo the app for the editor or writer of the publication if he doesn't have an iPhone, but it is well worth the effort, and you circumvent the long lines at the traditional review sites.

A truly successful marketing campaign requires that you have a coordinated presentation of your message and offer for your buying audience. You will want to engage in multiple marketing "touch points" to get the word out such as blogs, product reviews, and other social media tools. All of these delivery options presented to your prospects in a coordinated (or at least steady) fashion will lead them to purchase your app. In short, you have to develop a following for your app. As mentioned before, sometimes the pickup for an app is fast (usually implies a bit of luck), and other times the sales momentum takes more effort on your part. If you have a truly well-written app and it's not getting the downloads you deserve, then it's time to roll out a marketing plan and use the ideas presented in this book to make more sales happen.

Coordinated Marketing Effort

The first step is to make sure that all your marketing content uses your newly created unique message, as discussed in Chapter 1, "Your iPhone and iPad App Marketing Strategy: Grand Slam or Base Hits?" By marketing content I mean every written word and every graphic you use to convey the value of your app. This includes content for your product website, videos on YouTube, product descriptions, blog entries, and so on.

If, for example, you have decided to focus your message on the fact that your new game app offers the fastest action play around, then all your new app's marketing materials will have the same messaging to emphasize fast action play. You will want to make sure the following items are updated to carry your new app's message:

- **Icon**—Carefully evaluate your app's icon to ensure that the graphic describes your app and conveys the value of your app. This is easier than it sounds and requires you to spend some serious time on the creation of this key graphic. If you are concerned that your logo may not convey what your app does, you may want to consider developing another graphic or adding text to the graphic that gives the app's name.

- **Website**—All content on your website should express, convey, and highlight your unique message (e.g., fast action play), leaving no doubt in the minds of your customers as to the key values of your app. If you are selling a game app, then focus on the levels of play or other benefits of your game as you have identified from Chapter 1.

- **App Store app page**—All your content and graphics displayed on the App Store will help direct the reader to your app's key values and encourage them to make a buying decision of your app. The first few sentences on your App Store page that describe your app are crucial. Make sure you get right to the heart of what your app does and the value it provides in the first two sentences. If someone is interested in knowing more, he will click the "More" link to open up the description for more details.

- **Email templates**—If you send out emails, make sure your template (the header, footer, and text) are updated with your unique message (text, graphics, design, and so on).

- **Email signature**—Be sure that your email signature (personal email, product website email) includes your app's name and website. Each time you send out an email, they will see this small advertisement in the email.

- **Other delivery methods**—Videos, Twitter Profiles, and so on should all contribute to driving your app's marketing message as discussed in more detail later in this chapter.

Generating Demand

Demand generation is the process of delivering your app's marketing message to the most receptive audience and getting them to respond, either to review and/or purchase your app. Somehow, somewhere your app has to get in front of the people most likely to buy it. You can sit back and hope they find it, or you can take some steps to help the buyer "connect the dots," as they say. There are many options to choose from when it comes to creating demand for your iPhone/iPad app. The challenge is that every program you implement costs something: time and/or money.

Not every program is always worth the investment for every type of app. For example, does it make sense to rent an email list to promote your app if you don't already have a list? I believe it's generally not a good use of your marketing funds to rent an email list to generate demand for several reasons. First, it's difficult to target your specific buyer with a list, and second, the expense will eat considerably into your profits especially if it's a lower priced game app.

Now, does it make sense to build your own email list from your product website? Absolutely! Your product website should have a box on your home page for people to opt-in and subscribe to receive product updates, newsletters, new app announce-ments, and so on from you. You can even add an option into your app to gather email addresses. Your own email list will become very targeted and specific to your type of app buyer, much more so than trying to buy a list from a broker. Over time you will have a very valuable email list that is highly relevant to your marketing efforts.

Reaching Interested Buyers

There are many possible avenues to obtain buyers for your iPhone/iPad app. Utilizing the different sources outlined here will assist you in creating a large and targeted approach to leverage when rolling out your new iPhone/iPad app. Here are a couple of other time tested realities as you deploy your demand generation plan:

- All app buyers are not created equal. Eighty percent of repeat business for your apps will come from 20% of your customer base. Take special care of this 20%! You do this by knowing who they are and keeping them updated on every aspect of your apps and your future plans.

- The most important download you ever get from a customer is the sec-ond download. Why? Because a second-time buyer is at least twice as likely to buy again as a first-time buyer.

- Maximizing direct mail and email success depends first on the lists you use, second on the offers you write.

- Time limit offers, particularly those that give a specific date, outperform offers with no time limit practically every time.

- Free gift offers, particularly where the gift appeals to self-interest, out-perform discount offers consistently.

- Sweepstakes offers, particularly in conjunction with impulse purchases, can increase order volumes by up to 55% or more.

- People buy benefits, not features. But in the case of an iPhone/iPad app, features matter.

- The longer you can keep someone reading your website or App Store description, the better your chances of success and getting a sale.

Choosing the Right Delivery Methods

It may seem like there are limitless possibilities to reach your audience; therefore, choosing the right delivery methods can maximize your marketing dollars and allow you to grow your sales faster and hopefully beyond your expectations. To begin determining which delivery methods would be best for your app, consider the following questions:

1. Where does your target audience go to obtain information (examples: online, websites, blogs, and so on)?

2. How does your target audience make purchase decisions for your type of app?

3. Is interest in your type of app driven by certain websites?

Three Key Areas

In today's very competitive app marketplace, a marketing strategy that ensures a consistent approach to offering your iPhone/iPad app in a way that will outsell the competition and keep your costs down is critical. However, in concert with defining a marketing strategy, you must also have a well-defined methodology, a week-to-week plan for implementing your strategy. After you've completed the necessary steps to define your app's unique selling points and have created a solid marketing message, it is time to deliver that message to your targeted audience. There are three distinct methods (and many derivative methods) that you can use to deliver your app marketing message to your audience. We will take a look at examples and ideas in each of these areas:

1. Direct marketing for your app

2. Promoting your app

3. Establishing a community

Direct Marketing for Your App

Direct marketing can be done through direct mail marketing or email marketing. Here we look at the pros and cons of both methods.

Direct Mail

Although certainly not a new marketing concept, there are some areas where direct mail marketing may be of benefit to you. Direct mail includes postcards, flyers, or letters mailed directly to a potential buyer, reviewer, or trade show group. Direct mail has pros and cons just like any marketing medium and must be evaluated in the context of your particular app. First are the pros of using direct mail.

Pros

- Direct mail can be persistent, meaning that if you send someone a post-card, he might put it on his desk and read it several times before deciding what to do with it. So you may get multiple opportunities for people to pick up a postcard and act on it.

- Getting a reader to look at your ad more than once is obviously a very positive thing and can be cost effective if it leads to the desired behavior.

Cons

- Direct mail is expensive and difficult to track response rates. Postcards are generally the least expensive route within this category of advertising, with letters being the most expensive. A postcard printed in four colors front and back will cost you around 50–65 cents (including postage) for an average mailing of 1,000. An envelope, letter, and postage could easily cost you $1.00 per recipient to send out.

- This means your app will have to be priced much higher to absorb the cost of sending out a mailing. I don't recommend doing a letter mailing for your app under any circumstance. It's just too costly, and you won't see the return on your investment in terms of app sales.

Now, before you dismiss postcards completely there are a few possibilities that you should consider in your marketing plan. First, if you plan to attend trade shows where you have the opportunity to showcase your app, you can print off 50–100 postcards inexpensively by using sites like www.vistaprint.com. It's always a good idea to have something printed to hand out to remind people how and where to get your app. Second, as you solicit reviewers for your app you can send the reviewer (or reviewing company) a postcard showcasing your app. This just might nudge them to take a look at your app in the sea of apps they are solicited to review. Sending the reviewer a postcard will help you to stand out in the crowded field. It's worth a shot in my opinion.

 Note

Getting a reviewer or industry expert to review your app is much like getting a company to notice your résumé. Most employers want you to submit your résumé electronically for tracking and filtering purposes. However, it doesn't hurt in some cases to also send them a printed résumé to increase the likelihood that you'll get noticed by the hiring manager. Similarly, your app is vying for attention in a very crowded field, and you want to stand out. Sending a postcard to a reviewer gives your app that little edge that might make the difference between getting noticed or ignored.

Email

Email is generally the most inexpensive form of mass marketing to reach large audiences—and with somewhat predictable results. Industry averages say that emails have an open rate of 20–40 percent (depending on the industry) and then 10–20 percent click through to your website. Like regular snail mail, email also has it pros and cons.

Pros

- Email is great for building relationships and keeping your app buyers up-to-date with offers, information, and newsletters.

- Some email campaigns can generate up to a 5–10% response rate, with additional tracking options to fine tune your messaging—such as tracking click-through rates on links embedded within the email.

- You can quickly adjust and tweak your message or call to action quickly based on response rates.

- Email also allows the audience to respond to the offer immediately by directing responses to your specific landing page on your website or to the App Store.

- Email can be used to easily send promotional codes or invite users to join a registration-based community.

Cons

- In recent surveys, email is declining in terms of use by younger users who prefer other means of communication through newer social media tools.

- Email is easily deletable, and with so much spam many email users may ignore or not even receive your message.

- Email is ineffective in attracting the attention of an app buyer if he doesn't check email often. You need to go where the user is, which is on his iPhone or iPad. The next section on advertising goes into detail on how to capitalize on this emerging trend.

 Note

Email can be used to reach out to your contacts on a consistent basis, but it's important to send relevant and timely information to avoid boring and annoying your readers. Direct marketing success is dependent on a well-maintained database of current buyers with valid email addresses.

A promotion for your new app via a monthly newsletter or a targeted piece designed specifically for a campaign can be effective use of direct mail. If you can locate a newsletter that might be willing to carry the announcement of your app, this is the best approach. I would be willing to bet that very few iPhone/iPad developers have tried this approach...yet. It is crucial to always create a compelling call to action and a strong offer whenever you use this type of approach. You must give your audience a reason to respond. Direct mail generally nets a 1–3% response rate.

 Note

The best list you can ever have is the one you build organically over time with customers and contacts who want to be contacted with information about your iPhone/iPad app. Start now with this goal but remember it takes time and patience.

Promoting Your App

Advertising your app is another way to increase sales and get the word out about your app. Advertising can also be effective to build your overall brand image if you are a larger development company and have the budget, time, and money. For most independent developers, effective advertising requires you to think more creatively and constructively about how to get the word out about your app. Think in terms of getting free advertising where your app has some appeal and a reporter or writer is interested in giving your app some press.

Your App in Traditional Media (Newspapers, Radio, TV)

You might think it's crazy to pursue these options, but let's look at a few ways you can get free press on TV or in your newspaper. You have to approach this from the standpoint that newspapers and local television stations are always looking for stories that will be of strong interest to their reading or viewing audience. If your application is newsworthy or could fit into one of their columns or news segments, then you've got a shot at getting some free publicity for your app. Naturally, if you have a very narrow type of application, you'll have to look harder for a way to pitch your app to the press.

Newspapers

The good, old-fashioned printed newspaper is still alive (for now), and it's actually a great medium to help you gain exposure for your app. Keep in mind that if your story runs in newsprint, it will also run in the online edition of the paper in most cases. There are so many opportunities to reach out to editors and writers to pitch your story, and reaching them has never been easier given they all post their email addresses at the end of their columns.

The best approach is to take a look at your local paper and see which categories would fit for your particular app. Most papers have a technology section, so you at least have one category to focus on. Larger papers also have other sections that will fit more closely to your particular type of app. You can approach all reporters/editors in any category that you think might be a fit. Don't worry if you contact the wrong person. They will usually forward your message to the right person, or they will respond with a contact for the right person. Table6.1 shows you certain app categories and how they correspond to sections of your local paper.

Table 6.1 Various App Categories and How They Align with Sections of Your Local Newspaper

iPhone/iPad App Types	Section of Local Newspaper
Games	Sports, Technology, Entertainment
Lifestyle	Lifestyle, Technology, Entertainment
Health	Health & Fitness, Technology
Plants & Gardening	Home & Garden, Technology
Navigation	Travel, Technology
Education	Education, Technology
Finance	Financial, Technology

These steps will help get the media to review your app:

1. Match your type of app with the right section of your local newspaper.

2. Take note of all the articles written and find the email addresses of the section's editor and some of the writers.

3. Draft an email with a catchy headline about the value of your app. For example, if you have a gardening and houseplant app, you could contact the home and garden editor of your local paper and say something like this in your email:

    Subject Line: New iPhone/iPad App Helps Owners Keep Their Gardens Alive!

    Dear Editor (find and use the person's real name),

    We have recently completed this exciting new iPhone/iPad app that allows an iPhone/iPad user to take care of their gardens with clear pictures, descriptions, and tips for many garden varieties across the United States and Canada. Because of your coverage of home and garden topics, we feel this app would be of great interest to you and your readers. We would be happy to provide you with a free copy of this app and give you a demonstration of its benefits. I look forward to hearing your response!

Kind Regards,

Your Name

Your Phone Number

You will find articles written for your local paper on iPhone/iPad apps for most major cities. Simply go to your newspaper's website and type **iphone apps** into the search box. Typing **iphone apps** into the search of the *Arizona Republic*'s website (www.azcentral.com) for example, revealed many articles, such as the one shown in Figure 6.5. The creators of this app received free press, and this article was syndicated in other papers across the country as well.

Golf pro, duffer launch iPhone app

by Jane Larson - Jan. 7, 2010 12:00 AM
The Arizona Republic

Larry Slivka's very expensive golf lesson is paying off.

The Scottsdale retiree and his neighbor, professional golfer Kevin Streelman, weren't sure what would happen when they developed a software application for iPhones that coaches amateur golfers as they encounter tough shots on the course.

But in the two months since the pair released Golf Like a Tour Pro, they have sold more than 7,000 copies at $4.99 each. Golfers throughout the United States and in 63 countries from Denmark to Sri Lanka have downloaded their iPhone app.

Figure 6.5 An example of a local app getting coverage in the Arizona Republic.

After an article is published by one newspaper, it may be picked up by other papers across the country depending on the interest or importance of the app. Sometimes even a very large paper like *USA Today* will pick up a story from another paper. Getting newspaper coverage for your app can help you create the momentum that your app needs to build strong sales.

Radio and TV Advertising

Radio and TV advertising might also be effective in some circumstances. Many entrepreneurs believe that radio and TV advertising are beyond their means. Although this may be true for national TV slots, and national advertising is usually out of the entrepreneur's price range, appearing on local stations or on smaller cable television stations can sometimes be free. For example, if a local station does a technology show once a week, you might be able to get on it to demo or discuss your app. There are also a number of local (city-owned) stations that may want to do a story on iPhone/iPad apps targeting a broad base of users or more specifically focusing on a smaller market for the busy sales rep, the stressed commuter, or perhaps a health segment. Again you can reach out to your local station and pitch them on the idea that they do a story around a topic that just happens to match the very app you've written.

The best way to reach a reporter is to go to the station's local website. On most sites you will find a link to the reporters, and they are usually listed by categories such as News, Weather, Sports, Entertainment, and so on. When you click their biographies, there are usually email addresses where you can contact them. Use the same email approach discussed previously in the newspaper description to reach out to these reporters.

Radio is the last area that you may want to explore. Radio is more difficult because you have to explain your app rather than show it. Radio is also very broad in its reach, and so part of your listening audience may not own an iPhone or an iPad. Some radio shows have technology segments once a week usually on slower days/times like Saturday mornings. You can do a little digging on a radio station's website to look at their programming schedule to see if there might be an opportunity for you.

 Note

The ease with which you're able to get a story written about your app often depends on your app and current events. Don't give up easily. It takes persistence. It's free advertising, and it can mean the difference between your app selling okay and selling extremely well.

Advertising Your Apps

First, there is a difference between marketing and advertising, and it's important to understand the distinction. The premise of this book is about how to market your iPhone/iPad apps, which is a process and includes multiple steps. Part of the marketing process includes a single component known as advertising. Advertising, in the iPhone/iPad sense, is concerned with the placement of ads on the iPhone or iPad itself to either help sell your app or to generate revenue selling other apps or products. A developer can make money selling an app to interested buyers or by selling space on the app to host other ads.

Typically, developers who want to make money selling ad space on their apps will provide a free app to encourage thousands of downloads. They will carry ads on their apps with the hope that the iPhone/iPad user will click on one of their hosted ads. Each click pays the owner of the free app a percentage of the revenue generated for each ad. Therefore, developers of free apps are incented to develop the very best apps possible to achieve huge volumes of downloads, thus increasing the potential that someone will click through on one of their hosted ads.

There are at least six major vendors vying for ad revenue in the iPhone/iPad ad market. Two such companies have taken center stage in early 2010, Admob and Mobclix, who are considered dominant players in this space. There's no doubt that mobile advertising is big business and getting bigger every month. Analysts peg the market to grow to $1.3 billion by 2013 up from $68 million in 2010. Just like any type of advertising, it's important to determine how effective it might be for your particular needs in selling your app. In most cases the shotgun advertising approach does not work, and you end up spending a lot of money and don't reach your target audience. Mobile advertising is certainly more targeted (to mobile users), but the challenge is reaching your type of app buyer. Just because someone has an iPhone or iPad does not mean they are your target audience. So you have to understand whether the service you intend to use can target very specific users interested in your app. In the next sections we take a look at a few of the major players in the mobile ad provider market.

The other large consideration is whether to give your app away for free and try to make money by generating ad revenue. A full discussion of this option can be found in Chapter 10, "Pricing Your App."

 Note

If you choose to use a company to advertise your app, always start off with a small test before going too far and spending too much money. Just like with Google Adwords, you can set your budget low to test things out and evaluate your success.

AdMob

AdMob (now owned by Google) offers pay-per-click (CPC) advertising on thousands of mobile websites and iPhone/iPad apps for iPhone/iPad developers. You decide how much to pay per click through their auction-based pricing system. The minimum amount to start an ad campaign is $50.

AdMob allows you to target your ads to iPhone/iPad and iPod touch users only, so that you pay for clicks from users who can download your app. Your ads will appear on mobile websites and inside other iPhone/iPad apps. You can also target your ads to specific geographical locations. However, as mentioned earlier be careful and do a small test. Just because someone has an iPhone or iPad does not mean he or she will be interested in your type of app.

AdMob's free Download Tracking tool tells you how many downloads of your app were driven by each of your ads, helping you to optimize your ad spending.

You can also choose to serve AdMob ads inside your app. You can use AdMob's Download Exchange—a free way to drive downloads of your app. When you show ads for other apps inside your app, free ads for your app are shown inside other apps.

If you have more than one app, you can use AdMob House Ads to show ads for your app inside your other apps—another free way to cross-promote your apps.

AdMob provides free, real-time reporting to help you monitor your campaigns, optimize performance, and manage costs.

Mobclix

Mobclix is another ad platform that provides analytics and monetization through advertising and distribution for application developers. The company also provides a mobile ad exchange as well. App developers can use the Mobclix platform to choose from 20 ad networks including Google AdSense for iPhone, Yahoo Mobile Publishers, and many others. App developers sign up with their ad inventory, and ad networks bid for the spots on their apps.

Pay Per Install

Another option for gaining additional downloads is to look at pay per install programs such as those offered by Flurry and Tapjoy. At the time of this writing, Apple was coming down hard on pay per install programs by rejecting apps that include this option in their apps. The programs are designed to display your app in other apps allowing the user to gain "points" or "credits" if they install your app. If your app is installed you are charged a fee for someone downloading your app.

For example, let's say you have a game app that you are giving away for free. You have in app purchase capability built into the app and if someone wants to unlock additional levels of the game, they can pay for them through an in app purchase. When you sign up for a pay per install program such as Tapjoy, you agree to pay them a per install charge each time your app is downloaded. This charge could be $.25–$.50 per install for example. Through the program, your app is displayed in other apps on their "app wall". A user is incented to download your app (or other apps on the wall) to receive extra game credits, talk time, coins, or other virtual currency. When your app is installed, you are charged by Tapjoy for that install. Companies have spent tens of thousands of dollars to have their apps downloaded.

Paid Search

Google, Yahoo, and other search engines provide the capability to perform a paid search to locate your app's product website. Be very careful when employing any type of paid search because it will dramatically eat into your profits. You are basically paying for potential customers to click over to your site when they do a Google (or Yahoo) search for your products or services. When they perform a search, your website will appear in the "paid" listings section of these search engines. When a user clicks over to your website, you are charged a fee for each click through.

There are pros and cons to using paid placement programs. The benefit is that you can get immediate exposure to your product website. The downside is that anyone can click through to your site "kicking tires" and can cost you a lot of money every month with perhaps few new sales. You can place caps on how much you want to spend each month for clicks on your website. This all depends on your budget.

If your app is priced between $0.99 and $1.99, paid search is probably not worth the bother because your cost for click throughs will be very high when compared to the price of your app. The challenge with paid search is that it's going to direct traffic to your product website. You then have to get the visitor to click over to the App Store to purchase your app. The odds of this happening drop dramatically for this two-step process. Again, you will be disappointed when your credit card is charged a bundle for click-throughs and your sales have not grown much. An example of a developer using paid search is shown in Figure 6.6.

Sponsored Links

Mind Games - iphone games
The **iPhone** Brain Game Collection
20 Unique Brain Teasers - $2.99
www.chemicalx.co.uk

See your ad here »

Figure 6.6 Paid search can be very expensive for low cost apps. The app shown in this example is selling for $2.99 on the App Store.

There is some value to using paid search initially when you are building your overall brand as an iPhone/iPad app developer. So from the standpoint of driving awareness about your products and services, paid search can help you initially to gain traffic to your website and showcase products/services in front of potential customers. Having this mindset is better than hoping to achieve sales from paid search. But be sure to experiment slowly and optimize keywords at the lowest possible cost per click.

I recommend that you view Adwords (and similar programs) as a way to drive immediate attention to your website because you have not established the site with organic traffic. As you optimize your site over time to appear higher in the search rankings, you should depend less and less on paid search for web placement. See Chapter 7, "Using Social Media in Your App Marketing," to learn how to increase your web traffic.

 Note

> An online presence for your business is an absolute must! Some app devel-opers think they can get by without a website. You can't! Your customers can only go to two places to find your app: the App Store or the Internet. If they go first to the Internet to look up whatever they are looking for, you want to be included in the search results to answer their need. But do this as cost effectively as you can. There are many books and articles on how to increase your search engine optimization (SEO). This topic goes well beyond the scope of this book.

Online Advertising

With the prevalence of Internet users today, online advertising has become increas-ingly effective because that's where the buyers are. Online advertising includes plac-ing company information, products, and a description of your app on online listings and iPhone/iPad app directories, and so on. These listings can be free, but you can often upgrade your presence if you determine the site drives traffic to your business. Banner ads, skyscrapers, or other graphic advertisement can be a great way to drive traffic to your product website.

The goal behind online campaigns is to drive traffic to your website or a specific landing page of your website. Look to place banner ads and paid listings on web-sites that searchers who might be looking for your app would likely visit. Remember that you are paying for the exposure and click-through rates to your website. You must have a compelling offer to entice the click through to convert to a lead.

 Note

> Advertising in online communities allows you to get your app some expo-sure very quickly, but a better way to get online exposure is by getting someone to write a review of your app and post it to his or her site. Seek out local newspapers as well to write you a review especially if your paper has a technology section.

Advertising on online review sites is also possible but will cost you more money. Many of the big name brands will use ad space on popular iPhone/iPad app review sites.

Building a Community

Your customers should be your biggest fans—and you should treat them well to keep them coming back and recommending and using your apps. Maintaining an accurate user list or having a way to reach out to your customers is imperative to a successful customer retention program. Selling to an existing customer is far easier and less expensive than obtaining a new one.

Create targeted email campaigns, leveraging your list to do the following:

- App promotions that you may offer
- Software updates
- Cross-sell opportunities with other apps that you may implement
- Answers to common app questions
- Tips and secret features with your app
- Leader boards showing the high score leaders if you are selling a game

Treating your customers as if they're valued will guarantee a loyal customer base for years to come. Establishing registration-based communities allows you to maintain contact with your database on a frequent basis. Having customers register for a blog (RSS feed) is another great way to build your list.

Another way to build a sense of community is to tie your app from the user to the developer. Some apps lend themselves well to developing this type of community. Look carefully at your app and consider ways you can create a strong sense of community. The more you can interact with your buyers, the more likely they will be to come back and buy more of your upgrades or more apps from you. For example, for certain game apps, you can create a leader board. The top three or five leaders can submit their scores from your app to your website, drawing people over to your site and creating a sense of community.

Another company has developed an app that helps diagnose problems and recommend the best houseplants for your particular environment. As part of a strong tie-in and sense of community, the creators of this app have provided functionality called "Ask Judy" as an extra feature of the app. This service allows anyone to send in a photo of their plant with an email to ask questions and get advice about his plant. This helps establish a strong community or link back to the user's website and gives the user a sense that a real person is answering questions and giving personal advice. An example of this clever idea is shown in Figure 6.7.

Figure 6.7   You can build a strong sense of community when you provide a link between the user of an app and the developer.

Summary

The Internet and its myriad tools have made it possible for independent developers to gain significant exposure for their apps while managing their unique budgets. Using the right marketing techniques, the independent developer can build his brand and gain exposure for his app in ways unheard of just a few years ago. The challenge for an independent developer is to determine which tools will have the most impact for his particular app.

Generating positive press and positive word of mouth takes hard work. For the developer who is aggressive, there are many opportunities to get the word about his app. There are still many opportunities to garner free press through newspapers, TV, and radio if you are willing to contact editors and reporters and pitch your app's concept. Be willing to give them a free copy and be willing to demo the app, answer questions, and even help write the article if necessary. Free press in a newspaper means that the article will be posted online. When online, the news of your app can be syndicated across many media outlets. The bottom line is you must achieve momentum to get your app sales moving.

7

Using Social Media in Your App Marketing

When you hear the term "social media," what comes to mind? You're probably thinking of Facebook, Twitter, Digg, YouTube, and many other social websites that allow you to interact within a community of common users. But social media is really much more. It also includes blogs, RSS feeds, LinkedIn, del.icio.us, StumbleUpon, and many other social marketing activities, which I discuss in this chapter. Make no mistake, social media marketing takes work!

One of the biggest mistakes developers make is thinking that using social media will generate leads and sales of their apps. In reality, social media is more about creating relationships with a community of users and developing potential buyers. Eventually, the community will become buyers and ongoing users if you've gone about your relationship building in the right way and if you've given it enough time.

To be successful with social media you must establish yourself as a respected participant in your area of interest and earn the respect of that community. This takes time and steady work.

Harnessing the power of social media does afford app marketers the ability to reach large groups that share common interests. The great benefit of social media is that it is typically free for you to sign up. Within minutes you can register an account and be logged on to a social media site. There are thousands of sites that you could join, but remember that social media is like being at a party. You can only be a part of a few conversations to really be effective. Jumping from conversation to conversation at a party is not effective, and the same holds true for social media sites. You simply won't have the time to devote to more than a few of them on any consistent basis.

> ✉ **Note**
>
> Choose your userid for social media sites with some care. If you are required to use your name, then use your real name or a subset of your real name. If you are asked to create a fictitious userid that will show up when you post comments, blogs posts, reviews, and so on, then choose a userid that will help your brand and your app. If your company is Apps R Us then try to use appsrus for your userid. Always be thinking of how to extend your brand or your app's name wherever you can.

Registering for social media sites may be free, but that's where free ends. There is a cost as far as your time. It takes time to develop a following in social media, and it takes time to establish a presence. So even though you may get online and registered quickly, the real work comes when you want to get established in your community. You have to earn the respect of others by visiting and commenting on different posts, adding value to conversations, and answering questions where you can provide insight.

The activities of social media will open up opportunities for you to talk about your apps after you build a relationship with your readers. If you barge into an online community with the expectation that you can tout your app, you may be in for a surprise. Other members of the community will recognize your intent and will either call you out on your posts or ignore them. You must "earn" the right to be a part of the community without outward attempts to cash in. Longer term, your results will be positive as you make new connections, establish yourself on the Web, and reap new sales of your app.

Here are some ideas to help you get started using social media to establish a presence in your community and become a positive influence:

- **Start sooner than later to establish a presence**—You cannot launch an app and hope to be known in your community on Facebook or other sites a day or week later if you have never visited them or made a single posting. Building up contacts and friends takes time in the real world, and it's the same online. If you have not done so already, sign up for a few sites such as Facebook, Twitter, and iPhone/iPad app blog sites that pertain to your type of app. Create a Facebook Fan Page to begin showcasing your app and generating interest. If your app is highly unique, be careful about disclosing too many details on your fan page. You can still generate buzz and interest about your app without giving away all the details. Do this before you even start coding your app if possible, and you'll be ahead of the game. You can hire companies to help you generate thousands of fans on Facebook. This can help you tremendously when you go to launch your app as you can post your press release, videos and other topics of interest on your fan page. Go to Facebook and search on "Shine Inside" (http://www.facebook.com/home.php#!/ShineInside). This company was able to gain over 10,000 fans through the help of another firm prior to launching their "Happy Rabbit" dating app.

- **Actively participate**—To be seen you have to post comments on a regular basis. Join groups and discussions that are focused on your type of app. Be helpful in your posts with information that others will find valuable. After you have become established, you can begin to talk about your app if you have posted it to the App Store. If you haven't posted your app, you'll want to be careful about how much information you disclose so your idea doesn't get copied in full. Chances are very good that someone is developing a similar app anyway but not exactly like yours.

- **Pitch bloggers and influencers**—Over time you will have a greater degree of comfort asking bloggers to discuss your app in one of their blog posts. This is one of the fruits of having a relationship with people on the Web. An influential blogger can help your sales tremendously if his blog is widely read or the post is picked up by other bloggers. If your blog post is mentioned by Digg, for example, you could see sales of your app skyrocket.

- **Write an article or two about your area of expertise**—If your area of expertise is jewelry making, then write an article offering tips and advice about jewelry making. If your expertise is finance, then give people some good financial advice with no strings attached. People love articles framed around "10 tips" or "Five Reasons Why..." These types of titles peak our curiosity, and we want to read more about it. At the bottom of your article you can post your contact information and your product website and maybe the link to your app if you're lucky. Always ask the editor of the publication what they will allow you to post at the end of your article.

- **Offer to write a guest blog**—After you get to know a few bloggers and have established a rapport with them, you can approach them to write guest posts for their blogs. Many bloggers will agree to let you do this. Why? Because often they are looking for ideas and ways to beef up their blog posts. Having a guest blogger gives a blog a shot in the arm and creates additional interest from its readers.

Selecting Your Social Media Tools

The first step to selecting the right social media tools is to understand where your audience is and how they communicate online. In other words, don't just sign up for a bunch of social media sites thinking you'll do a little marketing of your app without first understanding where your buyers are and how they exchange information. If you have developed a really cool app for bowlers, you can do a search on different social media sites to see how many bowling fans there are in any given community. A search for bowling fans on Facebook, for example, reveals multiple fan groups. One fan group is shown in Figure 7.1.

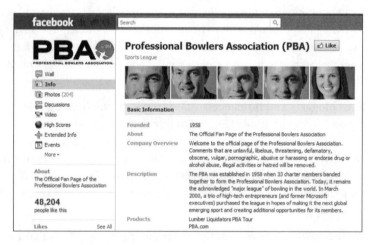

Figure 7.1 A search for bowling fans on Facebook reveals multiple groups, one of them quite large.

You can review groups for any topic of app you are trying to market. However, there are many groups listed on Facebook that are very small, sometimes 10–100, and that usually means there's not a large enough community on that particular site to really do any effective marketing. You want to locate audiences that are several thousand in order to be effective. This means that you have a strong community of similar users on the same site, and this can work well for your marketing efforts.

 Note

Locating and joining a group that corresponds to your app does not mean you start spamming the group about your app! Join the groups so you can see what people are talking about and how you might join and provide value to the conversation.

Using Facebook

Facebook has become an extremely powerful tool for creating a community and attracting users from a social perspective. In fact, Facebook has some 650 million registered users and is still growing. It has such a large collection of users that it simply can't be ignored. You won't reach all of them, but your goal is to do the best you can to reach your market of interested users and buyers. Need more encouragement? Here are some more reasons why you can't ignore Facebook as part of your marketing plan:

- Of the 750 million users, roughly 140 million are from the United States.
- Half of the registered users login daily to Facebook.
- Your app buying audience is on Facebook.
- There are over 75 million users who access Facebook from their mobile devices.
- Ten million members become fans of fan pages each day.

Your Facebook Marketing Objectives

Using Facebook, you want to accomplish several things. First, you want to be found by people who are interested in buying your iPhone/iPad app. Second, you want to connect with these potential customers and establish a relationship with them. You can use Facebook to create a business page for your app within a few minutes. You can start to build your page by going to www.facebook.com/pages/create.php and filling in the details, as shown in Figure 7.2.

facebook

Create a Facebook Account

○ I already have a Facebook account
○ I do not have a Facebook account

Email:

New Password:

Date of Birth: Month: ▼ Day: ▼ Year: ▼
Please enter your own date of birth. (Why is this required?)

Security Check:

e∐G

Can't read the text above?
Try another text or an audio captcha

Text in the box: What's this?

☐ I have read and agree to the Terms of Use and
Privacy Policy.

Sign Up Now!

Problems signing up? Check out our help pages

Figure 7.2 Facebook's main screen to create a business page for your iPhone/iPad app.

After you have given your fan page a name, you can fill in a description of your app and add videos and photos of your app. Of course, one of the links you want to add to your site is a link to the app on the App Store. This is critical! You can get the URL to your app on the App Store by going directly to your app, highlighting your icon, and right-clicking with your mouse. You will see two options: Copy Link and Open Link. You can copy the link and then paste it into your fan page. An example of accessing your direct URL link is shown in Figure 7.3.

Figure 7.3 Obtaining the direct web link for your app's URL on the App Store is done by going to your app on the store, clicking on the link, and then right-clicking with your mouse.

When you have completed all the details for your page, you can then invite your friends to become fans of your business (app) page. This will help you to initiate the viral marketing process for your app. When people join your Fan page, it's published in their news feeds for all their friends to read, further helping the word to get out about your app. An example of the ever popular Pocket God app with its Facebook fan page is shown in Figure 7.4.

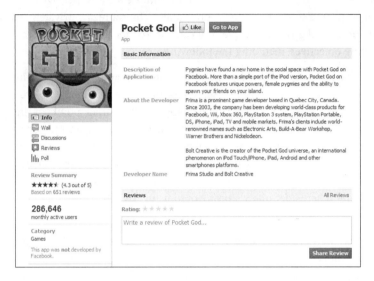

Figure 7.4   The Pocket God iPhone App has many thousands of fans who read up on the latest buzz around this extremely successful app.

Facebook also offers advertising based on click-through activity. You can create an ad for your app's page and target the ad to a very specific subset of people generating huge amounts of traffic to your page. Be careful though. Just like Google Adwords, you can set your own budget and spend lots of money on people clicking through. So go slowly and see if the results generate sales of your app. It's one thing to get traffic to your site, but you need to convert surfers into buying customers too.

 Note

> Obviously there are entire books written on the subject of Facebook and how to utilize the power of this enormous social site. The important point to remember here is that you should consider using Facebook to help you market your iPhone/iPad apps because it's inexpensive and easy to get started. Just like your own product website, Facebook is another extension of the App Store for driving interest and buyers to your app. The more accessible your app is to your buying audience, the more apps you will sell.

Tweeting

Twitter has burst on to the media scene in just the past several years and should also be considered a valuable tool in marketing iPhone/iPad apps. Because Twitter only allows you to send 140 character messages, you must be very concise in your posts. Twitter is meant to allow you to communicate a short message to whole groups of people at the same time. You can also communicate privately to a single person or a small group of people. You can use Twitter to accomplish a number of marketing objectives, including the following:

- **Create a following for a soon-to-be-launched app**—Use your name to sign up for Twitter and then search for other Twitter users who are or might be interested in your type of app. At appropriate points in the conversation, insert your own comments (tweets) and start to contribute to the conversation. You'll be surprised how quickly others will start to follow you. At some point you can mention the app you are working on. Remember, contribute first and then talk about what you're doing. There's definitely a protocol to using Twitter successfully, just like any social media.

- **Help maintain a sense of community**—If you have already launched your app, you can put the Twitter logo on your personal website and invite others to follow you on Twitter. This allows you to keep in touch with users of your app and keeps interest alive. You can also add the Twitter logo to other social media sites you join.

- **Forward other relevant posts to your followers**—When you do a press release be sure to Tweet out to your followers with a link to your announcement. Ask your followers to do you a favor and retweet the post to their followers. This will help you spread the word about your app, and this helps you establish a sense of community with like-minded users of your app.

- **Drive traffic to your site**—When you have a large enough following, you can use Twitter to drive people to your product website and directly to the App Store to review your latest app or app updates with your improved graphics, sounds, and so on.

- **Post comments or questions about your app**—One of the best ways to communicate to your followers that you are working on a fix or an enhancement to your app is to tweet about it. This will help get conversations going about your app.

Twitter allows you to create a personal account or a business account with less delineation. If you already have a personal account on Twitter, keep that account for personal communications. You can set up a separate account for your brand or your app. It doesn't hurt, though, to tweet about your app to family and friends. If you plan to build multiple iPhone/iPad apps, then you should create a Twitter ID that is inclusive of your brand, such as iPhoneAppsGuy or some name that will describe your company rather than a single app. An example of the Twitter account creation page is shown in Figure 7.5.

Figure 7.5   Creating a Twitter account for your iPhone/iPad brand/app can be done in minutes.

Just like any social network site, setting up your account is the easy part. Building your contacts happens over time. You can do a search for different people with the same interests as your app and begin to follow them. To follow someone, you simply click on his or her Twitter icon and then click Follow. In many cases when you follow someone, he or she will also follow you back.

One of the fastest ways to utilize Twitter is to find someone else who has thousands of followers to tweet about your app. So if you've written a great sports app, see if you can locate a sports star that either you may know or a friend knows. See if you can get an introduction with that person to see if he or she would be willing to Tweet about your app. Obviously, this may be a long shot but worth pursuing if you have some acquaintance with a sports or TV legend. The benefit to you could be huge.

 Note

There are whole books dedicated to making the best use of Twitter. However, the important thing to remember from an app marketing perspective is that this tool is at your disposal to assist you in marketing your apps. Twitter is helpful when you want to communicate short messages to your audience either to ask a question or to direct them to take a look at your app.

Using Blogs

Blogging has been around for some time now and is still an incredibly popular and powerful communication tool. Blogging can help you market your iPhone/iPad app in several ways. The first and easiest way to utilize blogging is to get to know some bloggers that write about iPhone/iPad apps. These people having already established a following with their blogs can give you a hand in getting a review of your app or at least giving your app a mention. There are many blogs that do iPhone/iPad app reviews to which you can submit your app. It's always best if you have established some type of relationship with the blogger before reaching out for a review. Obviously if he know you he will be more inclined to look at your app ahead of someone else's. An example of an app review site that is a blog is shown in Figure 7.6.

Figure 7.6 A blog that functions as an app review site.

Be sure to search on blog sites that discuss the topic of your particular app even if they don't typically review iPhone/iPad apps. They might just be interested in discussing your app as an interesting blog post. Remember that most bloggers are usually looking for good topics to blog about. Sometimes even the best bloggers run out of ideas, and you may come along at just the right time with a very interesting app for them to discuss.

 Note

All bloggers that do app reviews will ask you for a promo code for a free download of your app. Don't request all 50 promo codes from Apple at once. These promo codes have a four-week shelf life, and then they expire. Only request promo codes from Apple as you need them. If you update your app, you will receive another batch of 50 promo codes.

The second way to utilize blogs is to create your own. If you don't have a product website for your app, you can use a blog page to set up a site quickly. It is easy to set up a blog to discuss and showcase your apps. You can post videos and graphics to your blogs. Starting up a blog is free and easy; you can go to WordPress (www.wordpress.com), Typepad (www.typepad.com), MovableType (www.movabletype.com), and Blogger (www.blogger.com) along with hundreds of other blog sites.

After you have your blog set up, you can promote your app(s) on your blog. Post the press release about your app on your blog and integrate your blog into other social media sites such as Facebook and LinkedIn so more people will visit your blog and comment on your posts.

 Note

Having your own blog is a time commitment. You have to enter posts at least a couple of times each week or you won't build up a following for your brand or your apps. Once again, building a following is hard work and takes persistence. If you stop blogging for weeks and months at a time, you won't attract much of a following. It's interesting, but in this time-crunched society, we always look at the posting dates of articles and especially blogs. If we see January 6, 2009, as the last post, we tend to click away, looking for newer content.

Using RSS

RSS or Real Simple Syndication can be considered a subset to blogging. RSS feeds help you spread your blogs and help people keep in touch with you whenever you have a new blog post. Using RSS, your readers can filter and aggregate similar content so that they are receiving the content they desire. You will want to provide RSS capability on your blog and your product website so that people can sign up for your blog posts and receive information that is important to them. There are a number of RSS tools a reader can use to aggregate content such as Google Reader, GoogleNew, YahooNews, Feedburner, and so on.

Using LinkedIn

LinkedIn started out as a site for business professionals to stay connected, and although it has morphed into much more, its primary purpose remains the same. Just like many social media sites, LinkedIn has added lots of additional features such as complex search capabilities, advertising, job postings, and groups. Its power for you as an app marketer lies in the fact that there are literally thousands of groups that you can review and join to take part in discussions and promote your apps. For example, a recent search of LinkedIn for "iPhone apps" revealed 51 such groups. An example of such a search is shown in Figure 7.7. They are sorted by group size by default, with the largest groups at the top of the list. A search of "iPhone developers" reveals 129 groups, some with more than 10,000 members!

Figure 7.7 A search of groups on "iPhone apps" results in 51 groups.

If you haven't signed up for LinkedIn, you should. This is an opportunity for you to showcase your developer skills or marketing skills and to showcase your apps with a professional community. It will take you about half an hour to do a really nice job of listing all your skills and attributes for this site. After you have registered, you can locate and join iPhone app groups that allow you to contribute your expertise and inform people of your apps and their availability.

LinkedIn's advanced search functionality also lets you locate people, groups, or companies that you may have an interest in contacting. For example, you can search on "iPhone app developers," and LinkedIn will respond with a list of more than 3,000 developers! Perhaps are looking for another developer to team up on a project; this is a great site for doing that.

Don't forget to post your app announcement on your Linkedin page as well. I currently have approximately 400 friends on Linkedin, and when I post they all see it, and may forward it to other people. The power of social media is incredible.

 Note

It will take some time for you to build up your connections to other people. Many on LinkedIn have earned a badge of respect with more than 500 connections. That's a nice network to have when you are looking for development opportunities or any type of work. It's also a great network to post a comment to the "What are you working on?" link when your app is ready for sale.

Using YouTube

One of the most powerful ways to get your message across about your app is through a YouTube video. There are now more than 1 billion YouTube downloads of videos each day. This is because most people would rather watch something about your app than read about it. So a video is a must when you are trying to market your iPhone/iPad apps. Your video should be posted on your product website and blog. It should also be used when contacting reviewers to attract their attention. Reviewers are so stretched for time that they would rather watch something than read about it. You can post a link to your app's video wherever you have an online presence.

Creating and posting your own YouTube video has never been easier. With a video camera or app recording software and your app, you can create a compelling video that will eventually be viewed thousands of times, perhaps millions of times if it catches on or "goes viral." We all probably know about the famous "Will it Blend?" videos posted on YouTube a few years ago. In one video segment the founder of Blendtec grinds up an iPhone (http://www.youtube.com/watch?v=qg1ckCkm8YI) in his blender! The video has had more than 8 million views and has created remarkable sales for this company. The video was catchy and provocative, something you need to think through carefully when you create yours. A screen capture of an iPhone app product video is shown in Figure 7.8.

Figure 7.8 YouTube videos can be incredibly powerful to help sell virtually any product, including your iPhone/ iPad apps.

Video Basics

Here are a few basic ideas to help you develop your iPhone/iPad app video:

- Keep the video short! No more than two minutes in length.

- Make your video engaging. Humor, where appropriate, doesn't hurt.

- Write out a script to cover what you will say in the video. Shooting the video without a script will look like, well, you shot the video without a script!

- You can create a video with tools such as the iPhone simulator provided by Apple to all developers. This tool will allow you to run and demonstrate your app click-by-click on your Mac. You can use recording tools like Snapz Pro X ($69) to record your app while in the simulator. No need to purchase expensive tools, but if you want to get fancier, you can look at Adobe After Effects ($179) for amazing video editing capabilities. Apple also provides Final Cut Pro for video editing.

- Present the video in a "problem, solution, demo" format. State the problem your buyer is having. Then state the solution your app provides. Demonstrate the app in a brief demo.

- In your video, ask the buyer to go to your product web page or blog and the App Store to learn more.

Summary

In this chapter I have discussed the value of using social media to help you market your iPhone/iPad apps and build your overall brand. Social media marketing is more about having conversations with your community of buyers rather than developing outright leads. When you have invested time into developing your social media strategy, you can look for opportunities to discuss and showcase your app.

There are many ways to utilize social media to help you market your iPhone/iPad apps. Developing a successful social media strategy takes some time. You can shrink the time required by partnering with bloggers, Twitter users, and LinkedIn (or other) groups who have already established a presence in your market area.

8

Timing Your Marketing Activities

For most developers, getting an app's message out will take some time and consistent marketing efforts to make buyers aware of the app. The good news is that so few apps have any marketing at all that your marketing efforts will likely pay off. Even if you apply only some of the marketing methods recommended in this book, you're bound to see improvement in your sales. If one marketing activity doesn't work, you can try something else until you get some positive results. I have to reiterate that you must have a well-written app. You can't market your way around a bad app.

Some marketing activities should be timed for maximum impact. Other marketing activities are equally effective at any time as long as they are part of a consistent marketing plan. For example, a press release announcing the launch of your app or relaunch of your updated app should be timed as close as possible to when your app is posted for sale on the app store. I tell you how you can line up your posting date with your press release date later in this chapter.

Other activities such as getting articles or blog posts out about your app, getting reviews, seeking partnerships to comarket your app, and so on can and should be done before and after the launch of your app. These activities must be done as part of your marketing plan. It's ideal to have them coincide with your press releases, but it's usually quite difficult to make all of this happen at once. If you can get a press release, app review, and a blogger all talking about your app at the same, you will generate the best outcome.

 Note

> Be sure to allow adequate time to get someone to blog about your app. If you want a blogger to write about your app as your app launches, you will need to allow at least a month prior to the launch and press release to get someone lined up. People generally don't return phone calls and emails too quickly, and these things take time to get in place.

As I discussed in Chapter 1, "Your iPhone and iPad App Marketing Strategy: Grand Slam or Base Hits?" successful marketing is delivering the right message at the right time to the right audience. If you have effectively segmented your market and you have a clear message to deliver, then you want to look at the timing of your marketing campaigns and activities. Each app will vary as to how important the timing of your marketing needs to be. For example, if you are selling a holiday app, then it obviously will have a certain shelf life, and you'll need to time your announcement and marketing very carefully.

App Buying Cycles

App buying cycles vary with each customer. Some people buy apps daily for a few days or weeks, and then they get busy with other things and don't buy again for a few weeks. Other buyers will make an app purchase (or free download) a couple of times a week. Some people only buy an app monthly. And other app buyers show no pattern at all, only buying and browsing the App Store every once in awhile. App activity for new buyers of the iPhone, iPod Touch, and iPad is strongest when they first purchase the device. Over time, their buying activity tends to taper off.

Note

In Q1 2011 (reported in late April 2011) Apple sold over 16 million iPhones and over 8 million iPads worldwide. Apple also reported that it sold 300,000 iPhones in China, which is only a year or so into using the phone. So there are millions of new customers all looking for apps to download, so you have a vast market waiting to buy your apps. At the same time, the app store has swelled to over 375,000 apps.

The problem with many apps is that they are downloaded and used only once or twice and then they are not looked at again. Buyers have limited dollars and limited space to store apps. So they are choosy about the apps they download, even the free ones. After buyers reach a saturation point of apps, they generally tend to use only a few apps on a regular basis that help them with their daily activities.

So even though someone may have downloaded 148 apps, she tends to use 10 or fewer on a daily basis. The rest of the apps just sit there and aren't used much at all. Occasionally, a buyer will do an inventory of his apps and delete ones that are no longer appealing. Apps that are useful and frequently updated will remain on most people's iPhones/iPads.

Is Your App Seasonal?

Some app sales are definitely influenced by seasonal activities such as the weather, sports, holidays, current trends, and so on. As a marketer, you want to make sure that you understand the external influences that may impact sales of your app during the year. Timing the delivery of your app becomes more important if your app is seasonal. If you release a Super Bowl app in July, you may not see as many sales as you would if you released it in December or January.

Many iPhone/iPad games are somewhat immune from this issue because they can be played year round and aren't tied to any particular season. Holiday-themed games will definitely see more sales around the particular holiday on which the app is based. Racing games and other mind challenging apps are not tied to any holiday and can be sold all year.

 Note

If you are developing a very seasonal type of app, think about building multiple seasonal apps to cover the entire year. If you build multiple apps, you'll have a steadier stream of income selling your apps. If one app is selling slowly, another app may pick up the slack.

Other utility type apps will be influenced by the time of year that the app is most likely to be used. Tax-related apps, for example, will have a stronger showing early in the year due to the April 15 tax deadline in the United States. Other countries will have similar deadlines, so if your app is focused on another country, you'll experience the same thing. Financial apps such as banking, personal finance, and so on will do well during the entire year due to their daily use.

Health and Lifestyle apps will also do fairly well during the entire year unless the apps recommend activities outdoors that are not suited to the current season. A learn-to-ski app is going to do best in the winter months when people are thinking about skiing. A camping app is probably going to do better in the spring and summer than in the winter.

Table 8.1 shows a number of different topics and events during the year and how app sales may be impacted. Although not an exhaustive list, it does give you an idea of how some iPhone/iPad apps can be subject to sales fluctuations during the year. This does not mean you should not consider writing such an app. It simply means that you should be aware of seasonality for apps and understand beforehand whether your app might be impacted by these factors.

Table 8.1   The Time of Year or Specific Events Can Impact Sales for Certain Apps

App Category	Indoors/Outdoors	Subject to Seasonal Influence
Sports Apps	Either	Sometimes
Financial Apps	Indoors	Taxes yes; others no
Food/Cooking/Holiday	December	Yes
Food/Cooking/General	Either	No
Health and Fitness	Either	Sometimes
Lifestyle	Either	Sometimes
Games	Indoors	Rarely
Social Networking	Indoors	Never
News	Indoors	Never
Navigation	Either	Never
Education	Either	Rarely
Music	Indoors	Sometimes
Photography	Either	Never
Utilities	Either	Never
Business	Indoors	Never
Weather	Either	Never
Travel	Outdoors	Sometimes
Entertainment	Indoors	Sometimes

Winning Marketing Activities

In Chapter 1, I talked about hitting the grand slam with your app. Your strategy should be to try to hit the grand slam but also make base hits. Sometimes the grand slam happens all by itself with some positive reviews but in most cases you have to work it. This way you hedge your bets. You may or may not hit the grand slam with your app, but with consistent marketing activities, you're going to have some base hits in terms of consistent sales. Here are some ideas that can help you launch a winning app where timing is everything:

1. Identify an app that has never been developed before. This is more difficult than it sounds. With tens of thousands of apps on the App Store, the chance of you coming up with an app that has never been done is challenging but not impossible. Sometimes you have to look for an app idea to solve a problem.

2. Develop apps that recommend other apps. For example, there are apps that help you address the sheer volume of apps available on the app store by scouring the App Store and recommending the best apps in that category. These "Recommender Apps" as I like to call them are making headway in 2011 and 2012.

    Some apps are geared to recommending apps for a specific category or to several categories that might contain the same app. These Recommender Apps help you save time by giving you a list of apps that have been reviewed by the app developer or by peer review.

3. Sign an exclusive sponsorship deal. If you have a well written app that is seeing steady sales, you can search for corporations that are looking for apps that fit their marketing models. Most corporations either build apps themselves or look to partner with a popular apps that will give them a marketing presence on the app store. If your app is extremely well written and has broad appeal, you may be a candidate for such a partnership. Start by evaluating your app to see if it would be a fit for any company that might be interested in building a brand. The Gas Cubby app is a great example of such a partnership.

    Gas Cubby has been selling well for the past year and half and has a strong following of users. With a partnership with Honeywell (FRAM), they are now offering a free Gas Cubby app for FRAM advertising on it. The developer of this app will receive ad revenue through an arrangement made with Honeywell. An example of this app is shown in Figure 8.1.

Figure 8.1   Signing an exclusive sponsorship deal could be a way for you to realize huge downloads of your app and strong advertising revenue.

4. Gain national and prestigious recognition for your app. This method can work for almost any app, but actually the apps with a fairly narrow buying audience may have an edge. This is because the editors of publications that would cover your app are probably easier to contact and may be more responsive to doing a story about your app.

    You can contact editors that would be interested in reviewing and writing about your app by going to their websites and looking up their contact information. Landing a review from MacWorld would create tremendous buzz for your app. An example of such a review is show in Figure 8.2.

Timing the Launch of Your App

There are a few things you want to do before choosing a date to announce the availability of your app. First, review the upcoming date as best you can to see what other big announcements might be occurring on that particular date. You can Google or Yahoo! dates and check the News sections of these sites to uncover big news events that might be coming up.

 Note

If Apple is making a big announcement on the same day, you may want to look at doing your announcement the day before or the day after. At least make your press release go live at 8 a.m. London time in an effort to get your news out early.

Figure 8.2   A positive review in a major publication can generate strong traffic for your app.

Now you might think that it doesn't matter because your press release is small by comparison to that of a big company, but keep in mind that you are trying to get other news agencies to pick up your announcement and do a write-up on it. If there are too many announcements competing for their time, your announcement may get overlooked. It's best to find a time on the calendar that doesn't have so many big press releases going out.

Submitting Your App for Review

When you submit your app for review by Apple, you can specify a day you would like your app to go live on the App Store. Reviews (at the time of this writing) generally took one to two weeks to receive approvals if there were no problems with the app. If you select a release date for three weeks from the date of your submittal, Apple will honor that date and post your app on the day you have selected.

If you select a release date before they actually complete the review of your app, they will release your app to the App Store as soon as it's approved. Therefore, if you want to time the release of your app with a press release announcement, you should select a date beyond two weeks to make sure that you have some control over the posting of your app. An example of setting the date for your app's submittal is shown in Figure 8.3.

App Store	US*	Mexico	Canada	UK	European Union*	Norway	Sweden	Denmark	Switzerland	Australia	New Zealand	Japan
Customer Price	US$1.99	$20.00	CA$1.99	£1.19	1,59 €	11.00Kr (NO)	15.00Kr (SE)	12.00Kr (DK)	2.20Fr	AU$2.49	NZ$2.59	¥230
Your Proceeds	US$1.40		CA$1.40	£0.72			0,97 €			AU$1.58		¥161

Figure 8.3   You can select the date you want your app made available on the App Store. If your app is not approved by the date you have selected, your app will be made available immediately upon approval.

 Note

The Apple Developers Guide has the following verbiage about setting the date for your app: "Availability Date—the date when your application will be available for purchase on the App Store. If your application has not been approved by Apple prior to this date, your application will go live as soon as it has been approved. This is a global date, and applies to all territories selected. If you change this date, it will apply to all versions of your application, not just the version where you are making the change."

Summary

In this chapter, I have covered the importance of proper timing of your marketing activities. Buyers of apps are influenced by a number of factors, including how recently they have purchased their iPhones/iPads, how many apps they have already downloaded onto their devices, and how much money they feel they can afford to spend on apps.

Your app could be subject to seasonal influences if it is based on a holiday or particular event during the year. You may see 65–80% of your sales during a few months out of the year if your app is designed to help someone with a certain challenge such as taxes.

Use a press release to announce the availability of your app and try to time your press release to within a few days of the launch of your app. This will help drive momentum for your app and build sales. The press release is only one aspect of your marketing plan. You also need to include marketing campaigns targeted to your specific audience. These campaigns will help drive awareness and sales when executed properly and consistently.

9

Getting the Word Out About Your App

A press release is one of the most powerful ways to get the word out about your app. A lot of independent developers may not understand that a press release can serve as a launching platform to begin to get the word out about an app. In fact, you shouldn't just consider one press release but many well-timed press releases to help you build momentum.

There are some key points to creating a successful press release. First, the press release must be well written to attract a following and "pick up," which means getting news agencies, bloggers, and other online outlets to write about and carry the story in their publications.

Writing quality press releases is not for the faint of heart. It takes an experienced writer to capture and convey the key value of your app and interest your busy readers. Certain style elements must be followed in the press release so that it reads like a press release and not like an advertisement. Additionally, the press release must be positioned so that it gets into the right hands and is reposted by other news outlets. Developers may think that if they have a hastily written press release in hand, they can simply email it around to a few people, and like magic the word will get out.

There are, however, a number of online outlets that will help you get the press release pushed into the path of prospective readers and news agencies. Some of these press agencies have broad reach into major news organizations, newspapers, and other publications. These PR companies can be highly effective in helping you get your press release out to the masses via the Internet, giving you the muscle you need to get the word out and perhaps start that snowball of downloads that you seek. There are some PR firms that charge for their services and some that are free. As is usually the case, you get what you pay for. Free press releases will not get the coverage you want in the timeframe you want.

In this chapter, I first discuss how to write a press release for maximum impact. Next I talk about how to deliver your press release to the right outlets to get the coverage you need. I also cover some of the most well-known PR firms that can help you electronically distribute your press releases around the world.

When to Write a Press Release

The first question often asked is when to write a press release. The following situations warrant issuing a press release for your app:

- **Newly shipping app**—If you have just placed your app for sale on the App Store, this a perfect time to issue a press release. You want to get the word out, and this is a very good way to alert the public and your buying audience that you just posted your app for sale on the App Store.

- **Updated app**—If you have just updated your app with new features, fixes or other enhancements, you want to let your audience know about it. A press release is a great way to announce that your app has been updated.

- **Free app issued**—If you have just issued a free app to complement your paid app. This is an excellent time to issue a press release announcing your free app. It will drive instant downloads and absolutely help you spur sales of your paid app.

- **In app purchases added**—If you have added in app purchase capability to your app, a press release is the perfect way to get the word out. You can let everyone know that the app is still free to download and if they want additional features, functionality, etc. they can purchase additional level(s) within the app. You can describe these levels and the benefits from not only downloading your app but also buying additional functionality.

- **Second app in a series**—Perhaps you have written a second app in a group of similar apps. A press release shows a steady drumbeat of activity for your apps and your brand. One developer built eight apps, and so each week for eight weeks he did a press release for each one. This kept his apps in the news and helped him build his audience base.

- **Download milestone reached**—If you have achieved a significant number of downloads and you want to let the world know that your app is doing well. Depending on your type of app, you can issue a press release when you achieve several thousand downloads or more.

- **Placement of your app into an App Store category**—If you are fortunate enough to have your app placed into the "New and Noteworthy," "What's Hot," or "Staff Favorites" categories, you will definitely want to issue a press release announcing the good news.

- **New developer added to your team**—If you are building a small company and a brand, you can issue a press release announcing the addition of a new team member to your company. At the same time, you can mention in the press release that you are the developers of such and such apps to remind them about your apps.

In short, you can do a press release for many reasons, and you should always be thinking about when you are going to issue your next one. Marketing is all about keeping your message in front of your audience. If you see your sales slowing for your app, a good way to energize them is to do a press release. If you go to any medium to large company's website (Apple, Intel, IBM, Google, Adobe, Mobclix, Admob, and so on), you'll notice they have frequent press releases, and they post them in the media centers of their sites.

Apple, shown in Figure 9.1, has frequent announcements, many in the form of official press releases. If you Google "iPhone or iPad apps" in the news section, you'll see all kinds of hits for the latest news for iPhone and iPad apps, as shown in Figure 9.2. Each time you do a press release you should post the press release to your own product website. You can easily create a "News" or "Media" tab for your site. Newer press releases can be placed on your home page for a month or two following the issuance of your press release.

Figure 9.1   Apple's website has frequent press releases, which are displayed on its website. You should always post your press releases and news items to your own product website as well.

Figure 9.2   A Google News search for "iPhone and iPad apps" reveals the latest news stories for this selected topic. You can sort by date or relevance.

Do You Have What It Takes?

The first step to writing your press release is to figure out who will write it. Do you have the writing skills necessary to produce persuasive and crisp copy that will move your audience into action? Do you want to learn how to do it? Or should you hire someone to handle this aspect of your marketing plan? Either approach is fine. The important thing is to make sure you end up with a quality press release.

If writing is not your forte, then it's best to find someone who can write it for you. Perhaps you know someone who is a good writer and can help you out. There are lots of writers in every city around the world. Preferably you want to locate someone who focuses on writing press releases. They will be able to produce the writing fairly quickly and in the format that is required for publication and distribution.

Note

How much will you pay to have someone write a press release for you? Plan to spend somewhere around $250–$400 to have a professionally written press release. Be sure to ask the person you are considering hiring for some samples of their work and some references. Ask them if they've written iPhone or iPad app press releases before. Experienced writers will gladly send you some samples.

If you have decided to take on writing the press release yourself, then read the next sections of this chapter to learn the nuts and bolts of writing a press release. You will want several people to review and proofread your press release before you send it in to any online firm for distribution. Online press release sites also have editorial reviews before they allow your press release to be launched. They review it for relevance, appropriateness, formatting, and other criteria. It's a good thing that they review your press release before it goes out. They can often pinpoint errors and offer suggestions to make your press release a better read. They also have certain standards about how and where in the release you can use your website address and other contact information.

You only have a few seconds to attract your reader's attention. You need to figure out what's top in the minds of your readers and message to that immediately in your headline so you can attract the attention of the media, bloggers, and others. You must then point out in the first paragraph what your news is and how it will benefit the reader. The rest of your copy is in support of your headline and first paragraph. Boiling out the key elements of your app and why it's so important to your reader will try your writing skills like never before!

Writing Your Press Release

The first step to writing your press release is to define your objectives for writing it. Understanding your goals and audience will help you position your press release for maximum results. Are you trying to get your app noticed by various reviewers or bloggers? Are you trying to build your brand and drive traffic to your website? Perhaps you are trying to generate revenue for your app and you want to create news that will cause readers to go to your product website or purchase your app.

You'll want to write your press release in such a way that you are attracting your target audience. If you haven't read Chapter 4, "Identifying Your Target Audience," you'll want to go back and read that first. This chapter will help you to message your audience in the best way possible.

The beauty of an electronic press release is that you can include web links, video, and graphics in compelling ways to capture your reader's attention. The online press release can come to life in ways that a printed press release cannot. Depending on the type of app you have written, you will want to consider different options for your announcement. If you are launching a new game app, a video is a great way to get your reader to take a look at how your game is played. At a minimum you'll always want to include your product web page and a link to the App Store so people reading your news release will click over immediately to your app on the App Store and buy it right away. An example of using a video clip (along with web links) in an iPhone app press release is shown in Figure 9.3.

Figure 9.3 This iPhone app press release has an embedded video clip hosted on YouTube showcasing the app.

The Anatomy of a Press Release

All press releases have some common components: the headline, the body, company information, and contact information. For an iPhone and iPad app press release, you will want to have a headline, body, company website, and a link to your app. An example of an iPhone app press release is shown in Figure 9.4 and includes all of the previously mentioned components.

Houseplant 411 iPhone App Announces New Update

Scottsdale, AZ   Jan 12, 2010 in iPhone

[prMac.com] Camp Verde, AZ - JAMF Enterprises, LLC today announced that an upgrade to its best-selling indoor houseplant consultant application, Houseplant 411 (TM) v1.1, for the iPhone and iPod Touch, is now available for download on Apple's App Store. In its newest version of this best-selling app, Houseplant 411 has added 20 new houseplants to its database bringing the total to 70. Search terms have also been expanded to include the degree of difficulty of plant care, making the tool more versatile for any experience level. An entirely new section on plant propagation has been added and is appropriately linked to individual plant screens.

Houseplant 411 creator and indoor plant expert Judy Feldstein commented, "We've broadened the scope of our coverage for indoor plants in this release, enabling literally millions of homeowners and businesses to obtain accurate advice for the care of many of the most popular indoor plants. Houseplant 411 is a timesaving and money saving app allowing you to quickly diagnose existing indoor plant care concerns and to select the best plants prior to purchase for your particular indoor environment based on temperature and lighting recommendations."

iPhone and iPod Touch users have a simple yet powerful tool at their disposal to help diagnose plant problems and restore the health of their indoor plants. As in the original version, this app goes well beyond just providing indoor plant recommendations. Don't see a particular plant in the app or still have questions? Houseplant 411 includes the incredibly popular "Ask Judy" feature allowing you to send an email to HouseplantConsult with a photo of your plant and your question. The experts at Houseplant Consult will promptly get back to you with the answer to your individual plant problem.

Houseplant 411 features include:
* Browse 70 houseplants in alphabetical order
* Search for recommended houseplants based on lighting requirements, ease of care, plant usage, suitability for offices, flowering, and those that clean the air.
* Create unique lists of your favorite indoor plants for future reference
* Get help for any plant question with the "Ask Judy" feature
* Find numerous links and articles, tips and tricks for plant care with the push of a few buttons

Device Requirements:
* iPhone or iPod Touch 3.0 or later

Pricing and Availability:
Houseplant 411 is $4.99 (USD) and available worldwide exclusively through the App Store in the Lifestyle category.

Houseplant 411 (v1.1)
Purchase and Download

HouseplantConsult is your personal online plant advisor. Founded by a professional plantscaper and interior plant designer with 35 years experience, HouseplantConsult provides advice to thousands of indoor plant owners in homes and offices around the world through its popular iPhone App: Houseplant 411 and its "Ask Judy" electronic request line. Copyright (C) 2010 JAMF Enterprises, LLC. All Rights Reserved. Apple, the Apple logo, iPhone and iPod are registered trademarks of Apple Inc. in the U.S. and/or other countries.

###

Figure 9.4   An example of an iPhone app press release.

 Note

When using one of the online organizations to launch and distribute your press release, you can write up the press release using Word and then you simply copy and paste into their online forms. I discuss several of the more popular online PR firms at the end of this chapter.

The format for an iPhone and iPad app press release is fairly standard. After you have created one press release, you can use the same layout for other press releases you may create in the future. The biggest challenge of the press release is not the layout but writing the creative copy to convey your message. This is where the key values that you identified in Chapter 2, "What Makes a Winning iPhone/iPad App?" will come in handy. You will want to use those key value statements in either the headline or the body of your press release. Table 9.1 shows the elements of an iPhone app press release along with each section's characteristics.

Table 9.1   iPhone and iPad App Press Release Components and Characteristics

Components	Characteristics
Headline	Eye Catching, 20 words or less
Summary	Builds off headline, two sentences
Body	Supporting content, two to three paragraphs
Contact Info	Your website, link to iTunes App Store

Writing Your Headline

Your headline is the first component of your press release and will be displayed at the top of your press releases' webpage. The headline is where you attract readers' attention and entice them to read on. This sentence or two must be crisp and provocative. This is your hook to get the reader pulled in. If you fail to capture the reader in the headline, the chances of her reading on are slim.

You also want to make sure you are using keywords or phrases in your headline that will be picked up by search engines. These keywords will help your press release to be pushed along when prospects perform a search. For example, the phrase "new iPhone/iPad game" or "new iPhone/iPad app" works well to help your headline to be picked up by Google, Yahoo!, and others. Here are a couple of examples of good and not so good headlines:

Not so good headline:

"iPhone Developer Announces New iPhone Game"

Good headline:

"New, Highly Interactive iPhone Game RasterBlaster HS Math Hits iTunes App Store This Week"

Not so good headline:

"Scientific iPhone/iPad App Ready to Sell on App Store This Week"

Good headline:

"Science4School Group Releases New Chemtastic iPhone/iPad App for High School Students on App Store"

Not so good headline:

"New iPhone/iPad App Helps People with Their Bills"

Good headline:

"New MoreMoney iPhone/iPad App Helps People Manage Their Finances and Save Money Instantly"

Hopefully you see the differences between headlines in the three examples. You have to approach writing the headline from the standpoint that your reader knows absolutely nothing about your app. Often when writing, we take leaps in our explanations because our minds tend to fill in the blanks. You must assume your reader will not fill in any blanks about your app. You must clearly state what you're announcing.

Use the name of your app in your product announcement. If someone does a search for educational games, for example, your app's press release and product website are more likely to show up because you have seeded the search results.

Notice that your headline should not be lengthy. Most headlines are 20 words or fewer. Again, this will challenge your writing skills to see how crisp you can be in creating a headline that is eye-catching and includes your app's name, your brand's name (if you have one), and some keywords to help those search engines find you.

Your headline must also be a lead-in to your summary, which is discussed in the next section. The headline is the setup for the entire press release. Your reader must be able to grasp immediately the essence of your announcement so they want to know more about it and will read on, at least to the summary section. If you can get a reader to read the headline and the summary, he is most likely to read the body of the press release as well.

Summary Copy

The next step in writing a successful iPhone and iPad app press release is to create a powerful summary statement. The summary builds off the headline and is two to three sentences that succinctly cover what your press release is all about. With your headline and summary statement, your reader must be able to grasp all the key information about your app and why this is a newsworthy announcement. If you can get your audience to read these two pieces of information, you are well on your way to having a successful press release.

The summary does not need to repeat the heading, but you can add some additional flavor about your app and why it's game-changing for your reader. For example, you can include the name of your company or brand if you didn't already do it in the headline. You can expand on the headline by adding more detail about the app and its importance to your reader. You want to highlight unique characteristics of your app or explain a new angle on an old problem. In the headline, you are announcing to the world that you have a better mousetrap. In the summary, you're basically explaining why you have the better mousetrap.

Keep in mind that you also want to include keywords and phrases in the summary statement that you believe will be popular with search engines. Again, write your press release with an eye toward how someone might search for your app and make sure those keywords are being used in your headline and summary. These keywords include iPhone, iPad, iPhone and iPad apps, game apps, educational apps, lifestyle apps, (any App Store category that fits your app), App Store, iTunes, Apple, smartphones, mobile phones, and so on.

Using several examples from the previous section, I now add summary statements to them:

Headline:

"New, Highly Interactive iPhone Game RasterBlaster HS Math Hits iTunes App Store This Week"

Summary:

"RasterCorp expands its lineup of iPhone game apps by adding a new interactive math game geared to high school students. RasterBlaster offers four levels of play incorporated into learning modules for algebra, geometry, and trigonometry."

Headline:

"New MoreMoney iPhone/iPad App Helps People Manage Their Finances and Save Money Instantly"

Summary:

"MoreMoney takes the hard work out of shopping and budgeting by helping you build your own shopping list with prices automatically imported through bar code scanning. Take the MoreMoney app with you to the grocery store, scan items you typically purchase and see your total before you get to the checkout line!"

The summary should also serve as a transition to the body of your press release. Again, the headline should link to the summary, which should link to the body of your press release. Remember to give the reader more information than you gave her in the headline. A press release is designed to lead the reader down a path of wanting to know more and more information about your app.

Developing the Body Copy

The next component of your press release is the body. This is where you can expand on the comments you made in the headline and the summary as well as provide supporting quotes, sample graphics, web links, and so on to substantiate your claims. You want to still write this section with the idea that your reader knows nothing about your app. But you've piqued their curiosity with the headline and summary, and now they are interested to know more. Keep your writing focused on your primary and secondary messages and don't try to say too much.

 Note

> The body of the press release can be 300–800 words in length or typically three to five paragraphs. It is, however, better to create a shorter press release than a longer one, especially in the iPhone/iPad app world where brevity is expected. You want to adequately convey your message but not make it so lengthy that the reader gives up on it.

One of the most powerful ways to strengthen and give credibility to a press release is by providing quotes from experts who can vouch for your app. If you are selling a game app and you can get a quote from an expert in your game area, that will help strengthen your press release. If you are selling a financial app, then try to get a quote from a financial expert. If you have a sports app, then get a sports star if you can. You get the idea.

 Note

> If you have trouble getting a quote from an expert in your app's area, then get a quote from the founder of your app company or the lead developer. If that's you then you can include your own quote in the press release and relate your number of years of experience doing development work.

Keywords are also very important for the body of your press release. You have the space to include keywords in multiple sentences and paragraphs and the body of the press release. You want to reinforce your message in the body of the press release without going overboard.

After you have provided quotes and supporting information for your press release, you'll want to give your reader a call to action. What is it that you want your reader to do? If you want him to learn more about your app, then be sure to give him your product website address and ask him to visit. You should always include the download link to take the reader directly to the App Store to purchase your app.

Embedded Links

Embedding links in your press release is a very powerful way to drive traffic to your product website and drive sales of your app. You want to position your web links at the right spots in your press release. Keep in mind that many online press release services will designate where you can embed links and limit the number of links that you can embed into the copy. So you need to choose carefully how you'll use your links. If you have a product web page, be sure to provide a link directly to your app's web page. In other words, if your app is not on your home page, be sure to provide the whole link directly to your app. Don't make people search for it on your site.

Also be sure to include a link in your press release to your app's page on the App Store so people can go directly to it, read about it, and make a purchase. You want to make it as easy as possible for your reader to grab a copy of your app. Some online press releases will allow you to embed a graphic with an embedded URL. If so, you can use the common App Store logo shown in Figure 9.5

Figure 9.5　Use the App Store logo in a press release that allows graphics to lead the reader directly to your app.

Some online PR services provide additional areas where you can add links to your product website or to the App Store. Don't overdo your embedded links as your press release may get flagged as spam and ignored by a lot of publications and readers. Some online PR services will also check your press release for too many links prior to allowing it to be launched. They may reject your press release and ask you to remove the links from the body of the announcement.

Attaching Multimedia to Your Press Release

The great thing about doing an electronic press release is that you can use images, video content, pdf files, and web links. These elements help you bring your press release to life, gain the attention of many readers, and increase your search rankings. If allowed by the online PR service, always include a graphic of your app's main screen or the app's icon in your press release. You can graphically convey what your app does in a split second with a graphic. Don't waste this opportunity to reach your readers.

 Note

Most online PR services allow you to attach an image to your press release. Some may charge you more for this option as they know it's definitely a value add. Using a graphic in your press release will display in Google

News and Yahoo! News, so it's definitely worth the extra cost. Use .jpg format for images and keep the image to less than 1MB in size. Your online service will restrict uploads that are much larger than this.

Don't forget the keywords in graphics, too. Be sure to think of appropriate keywords or phrases that you can use to describe your graphic. Always give your graphics a name that includes a keyword such as "Main screen for the new Mega iPhone/iPad App." If your online PR service allows you to write a longer description of the image, be sure to use this space (with keywords) to describe it.

You should also look to add PDF documents where appropriate. For example, you could attach a little document in PDF format that gives further details about your app and shows more screen shots of how your app can be used. Anything that you can add to your press release that will create additional value will increase your readership and make your press release even more visible.

Press Release Signature

One of the last steps is to provide your digital signature. Your reader will want to know who composed the release and how they can contact you with additional questions about your app. If you have hired PR firm or individual to write your release, you will want to direct your readers to them. Online PR services will ask you for the appropriate contact information. It's usually called a profile or corporate contact page, and you simply fill in the contact information.

As part of the profile, you will also fill out information about your company. If you are an independent developer, then you'll want to create a short page about the types of apps you create, how many years of experience you have, and so on. You want your reader to be comfortable contacting you or your contact person. For example, you could say the following:

"RasterBlaster is the creator of innovative educational games for the high school market. With its launch of RasterBlaster HS Math, the company now has five iPhone/iPad apps to help high school students improve their grades and test scores. Founded in 2009, RasterBlaster has achieved outstanding success with two of its apps making it onto the App Store's "New and Noteworthy" category. RasterBlaster can be reach at www.rasterblaster.com."

If you should be contacted about your press release, this is a good thing. Most iPhone/iPad app press releases don't attract a lot of questions, but if yours does, that's a good thing! If your press release is timely and relevant to world events, then you are much more likely to receive requests for more information from the media. Answer the questions of those that make a query, and they will help you spread the word about your app. Be ready to send your interested media screen shots, photos, and even promo codes of your app.

Be sure to include a web link as shown in the previous example so your readers can reach you. Some online PR services allow you to put your email address in the signature area as well. Always include an email address and phone number so you can be reached easily.

Don't forget to have your online PR service push your press release into areas of bloggers and other forums that might not see the release in Google or Yahoo! news. RSS, or Really Simple Syndication, will help you get your press release to bloggers and other news sites around the world. Most online PR services will allow you to set up your press release for RSS feeds. Don't ignore this simple option to get more mileage out of your press release.

Publishing and Distributing Your Press Release

There are a number of online outlets for publishing and distributing your press release. Two of the more popular sites for iPhone apps are PRMac and PRWeb. Both sites offer excellent service with very good results, although they vary in price and capabilities.

PRMac (www.prmac.com) offers good capability and distribution at a very affordable price, less than $20 per press release at the time of this writing. They also offer free immediate distribution. If you want to specify a time and date, then there is a charge. They are focused on all news that is Mac-related. You can select iPhone as a distribution category when you launch your press release. An example of PRMac's home page is shown in Figure 9.6.

PRWeb (www.prweb.com) offers solid online PR services with lots of flexibility. At the time of this writing their prices ranged from $80 to $360 depending on how much coverage and how many options you wished to add. Most iPhone/iPad app press releases will need at least the $200 option to get the best coverage. If you wish to add embedded video to your press release, then you will need to add $160 to the cost, bringing your total to $360.

PRWeb has the potential to reach millions of readers and tens of thousands of news sites and bloggers. It is an excellent service with great coverage and depth. An example of the PRWeb home page is shown in Figure 9.7.

A number of developers are using PRWeb for their first press releases announcing the availability of their apps on the App Store. They follow this up with additional press releases about their apps using PRMac which is less expensive. Doing multiple press releases every month or so helps keep your app in front of your buyers and helps you to build your brand.

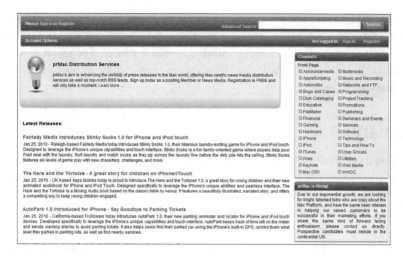

Figure 9.6   PRMac is focused on news releases for Mac-related products including iPhone and iPad apps.

Figure 9.7   PRWeb offers a powerful online PR solution and is geared to a broader audience for distribution.

When to Launch Your Press Release

There are certain times and days of the week that seem to work best for launching press releases. Monday, Tuesday, and Wednesday are good days to launch a press release for your app. This is because most people are looking for news after the weekend and will be interested to read about your announcement. As you move later in the week, people tend to be less interested in reading announcements as they are preoccupied with work and other issues. Fridays are generally not as good to issue an announcement as earlier days in the week.

You should aim for your press release to hit at midnight the day before you want to issue your announcement. This will allow those in Europe to pick up the announcement first thing in the morning and start to spread the word. Then your announcement will be available in the United States when people come into work or log on to their computers.

Summary

Writing a press release is an important tool to announce the availability of your iPhone/iPad app. You can use the press release as the starting point of your marketing efforts. Press releases should be issued whenever you post a new app for sale on the App Store and whenever you have updates to your apps. If you do not feel you have the experience or skills to write a press release, you should look to hire someone who does. A press release must be written in the right way to attract the attention of journalists and have it picked up by other news outlets.

Should you consider tackling the process yourself, this chapter discussed the nuts and bolts of writing a press release. All press releases have common elements including the headline, the summary, the body, and the contact section. Understanding the format of a press release is not difficult. Your challenge will be to pull the key elements of your app's value to the surface and message to those key points. A successful press release will draw your reader in and get him to take action by either forwarding the information on to someone else or buying your app himself.

III

Pricing Your
iPhone/iPad App

10 Pricing Your App 153

11 Conducting an App Pricing Analysis 167

12 Selling Value over Price 179

13 Breaking into the App Store Top 100 189

14 Level the Playing Field with a Free App 201

15 The App Pricing Roller Coaster 215

16 App Promotions and Cross-Selling 223

17 Using iPhone/iPad Analytics 235

Pricing Your App

It has been said that the exercise of pricing an app is as much an art as it is a science. There is no doubt that pricing is a challenge, especially with iPhone/iPad applications because the App Store is so large with many different price points, mostly at one dollar. The state of the economy over the past several years has not helped the situation for developers given people are evaluating their purchases more closely. Even a $0.99 app is scrutinized as the customer decides whether to spend their dollar on your app or someone else's. It's also very possible that the low price apps have been highly influenced by the fact that the iTunes store started out selling songs for $0.99, which I believe set the stage for the App Store pricing to some degree.

Many developers, however, are simply following the herd, pricing their apps low with the hope of gaining acceptance and market share. However, the goal of this chapter is to get developers to focus on delivering value instead of just a low price. Many developers are finding that they can't make enough money at $0.99 to break even let alone realize a profit.

Understanding your audience and delivering value can help you price your app appropriately in this cutthroat market.

Regardless of the current economy, iPhone/iPad app developers would do well to carefully examine all aspects of pricing as it pertains to their product, make careful pricing decisions, monitor and measure sales, and make adjustments as needed to maximize their revenue. Keep in mind the purpose of this book is to help you maximize sales for your app through better marketing. And marketing includes the challenging area of pricing.

 Note

> The right price for your iPhone/iPad app is where your profits are maximized. Thus, the highest price you can charge without reducing your pool of customers is your goal. Knowing the exact price to charge is difficult, but you can get fairly close to the right price based on how steady your sales are and customer feedback via the reviews and comments they make.

You need to consider a number of factors when pricing your iPhone/iPad app. For starters, look at competing apps in your category and then ask yourself the following questions:

- **How much do your competitors charge for a similar app?** Take a look at the App Store and review how many apps are similar to yours. Have you produced a Battleship game that is similar to other Battleship apps? For example, a recent search for Battleship games on the App store revealed at least 15 similar apps.

- **What are the differences between your app and someone else's?** Do you have more features? Do you have more levels of play if it's a game? If you are offering a new financial calculator app, does it offer something more than the other calculator apps on the store?

- **How does your app rate against the competition?** Do you feel that your app has better graphics? Better sound? Are there more exciting types of play? Have you confirmed this with your reviewers, friends, followers, customers?

- **How do you define your app and its market?** If you are selling an app for sales reps only, have you attempted to define approximately how many sales reps are in North America or any other country? How many of these sales reps might own iPhones/iPads? Having this knowledge will help you make a better decision in the pricing process.

- **How does your app compare to free apps?** If there are many similar free iPhone/ iPad apps, you will need to strongly communicate and market the value of your app. Overcoming objections to free is a high hurdle but can be done with the right marketing. See Chapter 14, "Level the Playing Field with a Free App," to learn about the pros and cons to creating a free version of your app.

 Note

Remember, the old adage "You get what you pay for" applies to anything, including iPhone/iPad apps. Many free apps are downloaded and never used.

Additionally, ask yourself the following questions from a cost perspective. These questions will help you get some context on how much you need to recoup:

- **What were the actual development costs or time involved for your iPhone/iPad app?** Knowing your development cost is important in helping you determine the price of your app as I discuss later in this chapter.

- **How much would the app cost to be developed by another company?** Larger development firms can often create an app less expensively than a small developer because they already have developers and graphic designers on staff and can redirect their efforts to that iPhone/iPad app. If you know someone who works for a development firm, ask her how much her company typically spends to develop an app. Sometimes independent developers have to outsource some of the development for graphics or other complex requirements to outside agencies or other developers.

Competing Against Free Apps

One of the more challenging aspects that iPhone/iPad app developers are coming up against from a pricing perspective is competing against free. Many developers get discouraged thinking that their apps might not fare so well against competing free apps. However, if your app truly has functionality that goes beyond what a free app can do, then you should not worry...as much. In fact, some free apps (whether it is your own free app or another) can help drive sales of your app because users find that free will only take them so far and then they have to pay to gain additional functionality. If you think creating a free app is for you, then read Chapter 14 on how to develop a free version of your app. Consumers want a deal, and the word "free" is programmed into everyone's brains at birth! Nevertheless, we also know that in many cases we get what we pay for.

 Note

Don't be intimidated by free. If you have developed a unique app, use your app's unique features as your marketing angle.

Consumers have also learned that free apps could mean risky software with a clumsy interface that does not really solve their problems. They also know that free may mean lots of advertisements that sometimes get in the way of a useful app. So how can you effectively position your paid app to compete against free apps? Following are a few ideas that will help you out.

Make Your App Better

It should go without saying, but your app must provide greater functionality, better graphics, and more features than a free app. Many free products are often stripped-down versions and offer minimal functionality. Make sure that your iPhone/iPad app is more robust and feature-rich without compromising the ease of use or functionality. Include features and functions that are not available in the freeware competitors and then use these features to promote your product.

Make Your App More Intuitive

Your iPhone/iPad app design and program operation should be intuitive and should not require advanced instruction for the primary functions. Your buyer should be able to operate the basic features of the program immediately after installing it and without needing to refer to any documentation to figure out how to get started. Consider developing a video on your website to guide the user through the primary features, as well as the more complex ones.

Provide Better Graphics

Initial impressions matter. Use professionally designed graphics, attractive color combinations, and a modern User Interface (UI) to distinguish your application from any freeware alternatives. Yes, you are going to spend some money here, but it is worth the expense if you want a successful app. If you are writing a game app, it is a necessity to have catchy graphics.

Note

Getting your app to stand out is always possible against free apps. Carefully look at the free apps and design your app to take advantage of the free app's weaknesses.

Create Documentation

The one thing that is so often lacking with free applications is any documentation or tutorials. Instructions (beyond the app's in-product instructions) seldom exist at all. Create short documentation and tutorials to assist your users in how to use your iPhone and iPad app. You can post this documentation (a PDF file) on your product website designed to help market this app, or you can imbed this in your app. This documentation does not need to be lengthy at all. Just having it provides a value add.

Offer Some Technical Support

No, I don't mean offering 24x7 coverage or an 800 number! But do offer a way for your customers to reach you if they have a question about your app. Your product website should have an email form they can fill out or a contact email address. Do not rely solely on product reviews from the App Store. Someone may never make a comment on the App Store but might send you an email instead.

Developers of "free" iPhone/iPad apps may have little incentive to invest their time providing ongoing technical support for an application that generates no income or revenue. This depends on the developer's objective, of course. Some developers are trying to build a brand with free apps, and so updating their apps is very important, and they want to get feedback from those who download their apps. But other free apps won't offer much in the way of support. Distinguish your apps and your brand by providing fast responses to any customer complaints or bugs that your user community has identified.

Develop a Reputation for Customer Service

Do not discount the value some customers place on customer service even with a simple app purchase. Invest some energy into providing superior customer service for any technical issues brought to your attention. It's unfortunate that the App Store does not allow developers to respond to reviews posted about their apps. Perhaps in time they will offer this capability.

If you see a negative comment on the App Store or someone sends you an email, be sure to respond immediately so the individual knows that you're acknowledging and addressing the problem. People who take the time to write to you will also take the time to write a positive or negative review.

Go Viral

Recruit and encourage "fans" of your iPhone/iPad app to promote your products for you. Reward customers who faithfully endorse your application by providing free upgrades or other perks such as giving them an advanced copy of a soon-to-be-released update to your app or a $10 iTunes gift card. Some developers offer prizes for the most referrals received from a particular buyer of your app. This requires some registration capabilities on your site. For example, you can have a button that says, "Refer a Friend," allowing a user of your iPhone/iPad app to send a message to a friend. You can track the referrals and give away a prize at the end of the month.

Some Pricing Misconceptions

So you have just completed your app and you are trying to figure out the best price to charge. Often, developers think that in order to compete on the App Store they must price their apps very low, like $0.99. Your thinking may have been influenced by one of the following:

- You see a lot of downward pricing pressure on the App Store from what you've read and think you had better not price your app too high.

- You think customers will expect you to charge only $0.99 for your app, given you believe everyone else is. You succumb to the pricing pressure.

- You think that pricing your app at $0.99 will help your app to make it into the top 100 sales results. You rationalize that your low price will make up for it in volume sales.

- You see dollar signs looming and think your low price will attract tens of thousands of buyers even if they have no use for your app.

Caution is recommended *against* adopting any of these mindsets and dropping your price right away. Any one of these thoughts can quickly result in low revenues, no immediate paychecks from Apple, and discourage you from creating more apps for the App Store in the future. Let's review each of the previous thoughts in a little more detail.

You see downward pricing pressure and think you should follow suit. Yes, it was true that overall average prices were falling on the App Store. But more recently, prices seem to have stabilized, and some categories have actually seen slightly higher prices, even with games. Because the App Store was a relatively new store-front, developers and buyers were trying to find that sweet spot where buyers would buy and developers would receive fair compensation for their work. What I am learning over time is that while prices have stabilized for iPhone/iPad apps, many are being sold at two to four times the $0.99 price, and they're seeing steady sales. Base your initial app price on a rational determination of how much time and money you have put into the project, the size of your buying market, and other fac-tors I discuss later.

You think customers will expect you to charge only $0.99 for your app. Not so fast. If you truly offer unique functionality for your product, you can certainly charge more for your app as a starting point. Pricing your app at $0.99 is like putting your newly published book in the $5 bargain bin at your local bookstore! Is that where you want your work of art to go first? How will you discount from there? How will you do any promotions or entice users to buy additional apps if you are already at the lowest price point possible?

Next, you think that by entering the market at $0.99 you will easily enter the top 100 in sales and make up for the low price in volume. As more apps are being added everyday to the App Store, your chances of making it in this exclusive club become narrower. You've got to use other means to help buyers find your app on the App Store.

 Note

Let's face facts! The chances of entering the top 100 in sales on the App Store by only pricing your app at $0.99 is getting slimmer by the day as more and more apps are added to the store. Pricing alone is not going to get you into the top ranks of app sales. You have to have an incredible app.

Last, you want to see dollar signs as soon as you launch your app on the App Store. This is a mistake. We all want to make money, but you need to adopt a longer-term vision if you want to be successful selling on the App Store. Unless you have very deep pockets like a large game developer, you most likely have little to no brand awareness. Building a brand takes time and big bucks unless you happen to be one of the lucky few to have a bestselling game or other app. This is getting harder and harder, and the reality is that most developers won't make it into that cherished cir-cle through luck alone.

So what's your best option? You have to level the playing field as best you can, and that's by offering your users a free version of your app. Let your users "try before they buy." You want to establish a following for your app, and one of the best ways to do that is to offer them an iPhone/iPad "Light" app that allows them to preview the app, test drive it and get a feel for it, before committing monetarily. This is a long-term strategy, and I've emphasized throughout the course it takes some time.

Offer a Free Version of Your App

I touch on building a free app briefly in this section but please refer to Chapter 14 for more in-depth information on developing a free app. You can use a free app as a way to build a strong following for your paid app or to utilize in app purchase capabilities. As an independent iPhone/iPad app developer you can offer a free application in order to compete with the big players on the App Store. Offering a free app helps your customers gain confidence in your product and allows them to use it without risk. Various studies from analytics companies such as Pinch Media and Flurry.com indicate that a free-app strategy is a must going forward. You can see their blog at http://www.pinchmedia.com/blog, which includes strong research evidence that this strategy works. In one blog post, they stated the following:

"...even if you're the proud steward of such an uber-brand, remember that free trials drive discovery of your title, helping increase the adoption of your paid version and ranking in the Paid App category. And don't forget that all the previously disadvantaged Indies now have a shot to take away your consumer with their free trial."

In this blog, Flurry sums up this recommendation by saying that everyone, regardless of their success on the App Store, should have a free app. The decision rests with you of course and is dependent on how much time you have to create a free app. You can always go back after you've launched your paid app and develop a free app. Or you can offer an app for free to see what type of response you get from it. Both strategies can work to eventually help you achieve sales of your paid apps.

Setting Your App's Price

Now that I've got a few misconceptions out of the way, the question then remains, "How do I price my app?" You've come this far to develop a great app, so don't pass up this crucial exercise to make your app as successful as possible in the market. Everyone defines success in his or her own way. Perhaps you want to generate $20,000 a year in additional income from an app that cost you $5,000 to create. You might not be able to live on that income entirely, but it sure doesn't hurt if it's additional income to your regular job.

Or perhaps you have grander ambitions and want to generate $100,000 in app sales for a product that cost you $20,000 to create. If you start at a $0.99 selling price in either example, you would have to generate 28,572 downloads to achieve $20,000 or 142,858 downloads to achieve $100,000 in sales! These are huge numbers of downloads regardless of how successful the app is. Again, starting at a $0.99 sales price, it is going to take forever for you to achieve either breakeven or any profits!

In both examples, the breakeven is not factored into the equation. I'm assuming you want to make some money selling your iPhone/iPad app. But for the record, you would need 7,143 downloads at the $0.99 selling price to break even in the first example if the app cost $5,000 to produce. The second app example would require you to realize 28,572 downloads just to break even!

 Note

> You must conduct a breakeven analysis to determine how different price points will affect your breakeven timing. See Chapter 11, "Conducting an App Pricing Analysis," to learn more about how to conduct a pricing analysis for your app.

For the previous examples, you may have spent less developing your app, and so your breakeven might be lower. But regardless of the cost, you need to calculate your breakeven so you at least cover the costs of development and marketing. Let's look at a few strategies that are often used by developers for pricing their apps:

- Price high initially and measure the results. Pricing high does not mean you pick a random high price. It means that you choose a price that falls in the high end of the range for your app's category. For example, if you are pricing a game, the range is generally priced between $0.99 on the low end and $1.99 on the high end. So a high price initially would be $1.99. However, pricing higher in your category means you've got the features to back up your price. You can't just start out with a high price because you want to make more money! An example in the App Store of different game apps and their respective prices is shown in Figure 10.1.

- Price mid-range and measure the results. Pricing in the mid-range means you've looked at your category, measured the lowest price and the highest price, and then selected a price somewhere in the middle for your app. For example, you are selling an app that helps someone improve their fitness. This type of app has all kinds of competitors and prices. The price range for this type of app is free to $6.99. So after some research you feel your app is worth more than free but less than $6.99. So you start at a price of $2.99. An example of these types of apps is shown in Figure 10.2.

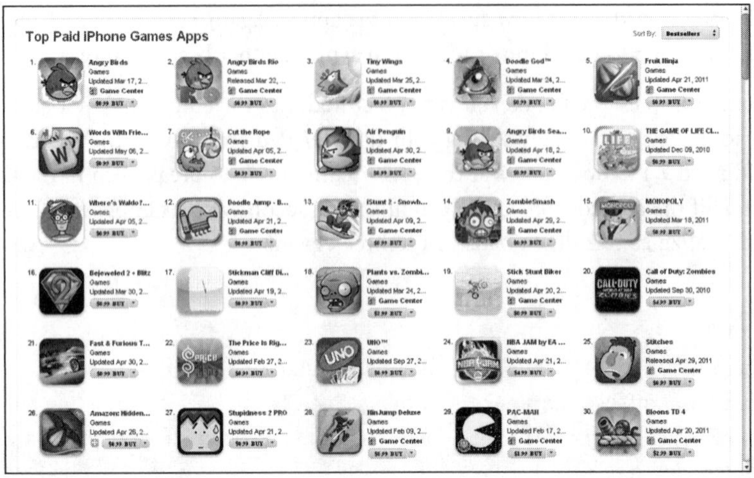

Figure 10.1   Researching Games apps on the App Store reveals most prices fall between $0.99 and $1.99.

Figure 10.2   Pricing in the mid-range means you search for the highest and lowest priced apps and set your price in the middle.

- Price low and make it up on volume. Most developers do very little in the way of pricing analysis for their apps. They simply take the low price at $0.99 and wait to see what happens. For many apps, especially games, this may be the right price. But, again, some research should be done to determine if that's where the starting price should be set.

Regardless of which strategy you end up adopting, you want to perform a breakeven analysis to know how many apps you will need to sell at different price points to break even. The following pricing discussion makes a few assumptions as outlined here for simplicity:

- Nearly all apps on the App Store fall between $0.99 and $9.99. As you calculate your price, you are most likely going to look at price points in this range to set prices.

- I make the assumption that your app will not make it into the top 100 most downloaded apps. This is not being pessimistic just realistic given you're an independent developer and most likely don't have a huge following for your app yet. If you are not selling a game app, you may never get into the top 100, sorry.

- Because you are probably not in the top 100, you will most likely sell at most 100 downloads of your app per day. For the following examples I assume 100 sales per day.

My first example assumes no marketing costs to launch the app.

Let's assume you have spent $5,000 to develop your business application. You believe you can sell 100 apps per day. But let's be more realistic and say you can sell 100 apps per day to start out. Your sales numbers based on different price points would resemble the following.

The results of my breakeven analysis is shown in Table 10.1. They indicate that it will take at least 70 days to break even for an app that cost $5,000 to develop, and I charge $0.99 per download. Doubling the price cuts the breakeven time in half to 35 days as shown in the second row that is shaded. Obviously, as the price goes up for my app, the time needed to break even goes down as shown in the prices from $2.99 to $5.99. But, it's not that simple to simply kick the price up a couple of bucks to lower your time to break even. This is where you have to review other similar apps to see what you can realistically charge for your app. If your app is clearly out of the pricing range for similar apps, your app will not sell.

Table 10.1   A Basic Breakeven Analysis at Different Price Points for an App That Costs $5,000 to Develop

App Price @100 Sales/Day	Gross Sales	After Apple Commission	Breakeven Reduction (1st Sale)	Days Left to Breakeven ~
$.99	$100	$70	($4930)	70
$1.99	$200	$140	($4860)	35

Table 10.1   A Basic Breakeven Analysis at Different Price Points for an App That Costs $5,000 to Develop

App Price @100 Sales/Day	Gross Sales	After Apple Commission	Breakeven Reduction (1st Sale)	Days Left to Breakeven ~
$2.99	$300	$210	($4790)	23
$3.99	$400	$280	($4720)	17
$4.99	$500	$350	($4650)	14
$5.99	$600	$420	($4580)	11
$9.99	$1000	$700	($4300)	7

 Note

If you have only incurred your time in app development, you should still calculate the cost of developing your app based on estimated hours spent on the project times an hourly rate.

As you can see by looking at the table, pricing your app at $0.99, it will take you over two months to break even assuming you spent $5,000 to develop your app. Again, as an independent developer your development costs will vary. But if you haven't spent real dollars, you most certainly have spent long nights writing code! So you should calculate your hours spent in development and estimate some sort of development cost.

Based on Table 10.1, I am of the opinion that it's better to price your app higher first and carefully monitor the results. By this I mean in the $2.99 to $5.99 range (*for nongame apps!*) so that you've got room to adjust your pricing if needed. If you have developed a game app, the pricing sensitivity is much greater, and you will need to price in the $0.99 to $1.99 range as a starting point.

If you have done what I call "pre-launch" marketing activities, you will have established a following of early adopters who will gladly pay your entry price. In the last section of this course I discuss how to develop a marketing plan for your app. The marketing plan is ideally implemented at the start of your development project, not at the end, so you can begin to establish a following for your app prior to its launch.

Table 10.2   Pricing Analysis Showing a 20% Marketing Expense with a Resulting Increase in Sales

App Price @150 sales/day	Gross Sales	After Apple Commission	20% marketing expense for app	Take home net ~
$.99	$150	$105	$30	$75
$1.99	$300	$210	$60	$150

Table 10.2 Pricing Analysis Showing a 20% Marketing Expense with a Resulting Increase in Sales

App Price @150 sales/day	Gross Sales	After Apple Commission	20% marketing expense for app	Take home net ~
$2.99	$450	$315	$90	$225
$3.99	$600	$420	$120	$300
$4.99	$750	$525	$150	$375
$5.99	$900	$630	$180	$450
$9.99	$1500	$1050	$300	$750

After breakeven, you can begin to enjoy the fruits of your labors. Table 10.2 shows how much you could make on a daily basis assuming a 20% marketing expense that may bring you 50% more in increased sales.

The issue with any pricing assumption is trying to figure out how elastic the pricing model is for iPhone/iPad apps. Over time, elasticity will become more predictable. Some bloggers have said that lowering their prices has had some effect on sales but for a limited time. Others have said that lowering the price has had no effect on their sales. Who do you believe? Well, they are both right. It depends on the type of app and variances in mileage. So the best approach is to experiment at a price point that makes sense for your app based on your research, breakeven analysis, and type of application.

If you are confident that your app is unique and has qualities and features that no similar app provides, price it higher and measure the results. If over a few weeks your sales start to drop off, you can carefully begin to reduce the price and measure the results. If you are doing solid marketing, driving visitors to your site, and have created a following through the marketing methods discussed in earlier sections, then there is no reason why your app (nongame) cannot continue to sell at sustainable levels for many months or possibly years to come.

Some app sellers have also found some success in offering limited time offers where they drop the price for a few days only to spur sales. If you have a certain promotion you want to do around an event, you can often spur sales by offering a temporary price cut. Let's say you offer a financial calculator that includes special tax features. You may want to reduce your price for a few days around tax time to spur sales and let your app take advantage of this particular time of year.

 Note

Do not undersell yourself by pricing your app too low to begin. You can always lower your price, but it's harder to raise it.

Summary

There is more to pricing your app than just setting the price at $0.99 and hoping for the best. Developers would do well to carefully review pricing of similar apps before setting their own prices. As part of your pricing analysis, try to determine the range of prices for your particular category of iPhone/iPad app. You do this by checking the App Store and taking note of the range of prices found. When you have a price in mind, compare your features with the features of similar apps in your price range. This will help you feel more confident about your price.

Pricing your iPhone/iPad app at the higher end of the range for your category will give you the pricing flexibility to lower your price when needed or when you want to do a sales promotion and temporarily drop the price of your app. Do not immediately set your price at $0.99 unless you are confident that all competing apps are priced in the same range.

11

Conducting an App Pricing Analysis

Although you may think it's a little over the top to do a pricing analysis for an iPhone/iPad app, these skills will come in handy as you build your brand and start to build multiple apps. A pricing analysis (or cost/benefit analysis) is also an exercise you should do prior to developing your app. So many developers (or entrepreneurs) think of an idea for an app and set out to develop it or contract with someone to develop it without thinking through entirely what it might cost them. It's easy to get caught up in your life-changing, world-domination idea for an app, but prudence should take the upper hand.

A cost/benefit analysis will help you predict whether you are likely to break even on your app and start to make a profit on it. As an independent developer, a cost/benefit analysis is probably not an exercise you are used to, but it's pretty important to count the costs beforehand so you don't end up in financial trouble down the road.

The App Store is littered with half-baked apps that were very costly to produce and have left the developers with no hope of ever recouping their costs.

Think about it. On the low end you may spend $2,500.00 to develop your app. (And that's really on the low end!) If you price your app at $0.99, it will take more than 3,500 downloads just to break even on your costs after Apple takes its 30% cut. It's also not uncommon for a developer to spend upward of $30,000.00 to develop and market an iPhone/iPad app. It will take tens of thousands of downloads to break even when this much money is spent to develop an app.

So it's critical to do a little math before you get started down the development path to make sure your finances can handle the costs you are going to incur. Who knows? You may decide after doing a little analysis that building a particular app is not worth the price and scrap the project until you can find an idea that will work.

 Note

Game apps, as I've mentioned before, tend to fall into a tight range of $0.99 to $1.99, sometimes $2.99 and a very few over $4.99. As you define the market for your type of app, you may find that the number of potential buyers is quite limited. To make money from your app, you must identify a price point where you can make some money and the buyer will still be inclined to buy.

The challenge for many developers of nongame apps that usually don't fall into the $0.99 pricing category is deciding what they should reasonably charge. So it helps to have some background on how to go about performing a cost/benefit analysis for the more expensive types of apps. Setting an accurate price is crucial to determining a breakeven point and attempting to do some amount of forecasting.

Cost/Benefit Analysis

A cost/benefit analysis is a process to help you understand the total anticipated costs of your app development project as compared to the total expected financial benefits. This analysis will help you determine if this project is worthwhile for you as an independent developer or your development team. If the results of your analysis show that your financial benefits outweigh the costs, you can proceed with the development of your app with greater confidence.

For simplicity sake, the iPhone/iPad app cost/benefit analysis consists of three components:

- Quantifying the app development costs

- Quantifying the benefits of developing the app

- Performing a cost/benefit comparison to make an informed development decision

Quantifying App Development Costs

The first part of the app cost/benefit process is to identify and quantify the costs associated with your app development. Your costs will fall into two categories: fixed and variable. Fixed costs include any expenses that are the same every month. If you are an independent developer or a small LLC, you may be renting some office space. You will want to include the monthly rent as a fixed expense for the expected duration of app development. If you have just bought a new Mac for development, you have incurred a fixed expense with that hardware purchase.

Variable costs can include things such as expenses you might incur if you pay a developer by the hour to develop your app. This could range from $50 (low end) to $200/hour (high end). Your labor rates could vary depending on how complex your app project is. You may hire a developer and find, to your dismay, that the person does not have all the skills you need to develop your app. So you end up hiring another more costly developer.

Another scenario is that the developer has underestimated how much time it will take to complete your app. Instead of the project taking 200 hours to complete, it takes 250 hours. This happens more frequently than you think. In fact, you should add 20% to the total cost of whatever estimates you receive from developers. You won't be too far off the mark, and you'll save yourself the shock of having to come up with more money because you will have anticipated this already.

 Note

If you are hiring an outside developer to create your iPhone/iPad app, you can ask him to give you a fixed bid price. Some developers will work with you on a per-contract basis. Keep in mind that if you want to change/add features to your app down the road (and you certainly will), the contractor will most likely charge you a change fee or add on an additional project fee to accommodate your request.

The following steps will help you quantify the costs you will incur during the app development stage:

1. Make a list of all monetary costs you think you will incur during the development stage of your app. These expenses include buildings, developer's payroll, training, travel, hardware, and so on.

2. Next, make another column with a list of all intangible costs that you are likely to incur. This would include your own time if you are developing your app, risks if the app fails, lost time on other apps, and so on. Granted, it is quite difficult to quantify these areas, but some attempt is better than no attempt. Table 11.1 gives you an example of the monetary and intangible costs you'll want to include on your list of overall expenses. (This is not an exhaustive list, and you should modify this for your unique circumstances.)

When you have a list of your anticipated monetary and nonmonetary expenses, you can add numeric values where appropriate. Do your best to estimate nonmonetary costs. This part of the exercise gets a little bit fuzzy, but it's still important to have some numbers down in writing. At the bottom of the table, add up the totals for each column.

Table 11.1 App Development Expense Table to Help Estimate Monetary and Nonmonetary Costs

App Development Items	Monetary cost estimate	Intangible cost estimate
Hardware (Mac, PC, networking equipment)		
Software (development tools, compilers, testing tools, and so on)		
Apple Developer Registration Fees		
Self developed app, Contract development costs (by project or hourly)		
Development training courses		
Office rent		
Product website development/web copy costs		
Marketing/advertising costs		
Opportunity cost of doing this app versus another app		
Miscellaneous (printing, postage, domain registration, programming books, and so on)		
Totals		

Note

If you are new to developing iPhone/iPad apps, you'll most likely need to get some training unless you are the type that can read manuals and learn by doing. Many people are best served by getting some training from experts who can teach basic (and not so basic) coding skills in a few weeks or months.

Online training, such as that offered by XcelMe.com (www.xcelMe.com), can cost as little as $97/course or under $500.00 for a bundle of classes. Other companies such as BigNerdRanch (www.bignerdranch.com) can cost $3,500–$4,750 plus your travel and lodging expenses, but they offer face-to-face instruction.

A sample of the table with some financial values included is shown in Table 11.2. These numbers assume that this person is a fairly new developer in the iPhone/iPad app space but has a development background and needs some training in this unique space.

Table 11.2   Estimating Overall Project Costs

App Development Items	Monetary Cost Estimate	Intangible Cost Estimate
Hardware (Mac, PC, networking equipment)	$3,000.00 (Macbook Pro + accessories)	
Software (development tools, compilers, testing tools, and so on)		
Apple Developer Registration Fees	$99.00 (or $299.00)	
Self developed app, Contract development costs (by project or hourly)		Self-developed (250 hrs @ 50/hr*) $12,500.00
Development training courses.	$450/online with Xcelme or another vendor	8 weeks time (3 hours/week @ $50.00/hr*) $1200.00
Office rent	Home office	
Product website development/web copy costs	$2,000.00	
Marketing/advertising costs	$1,500.00	

Table 11.2 Estimating Overall Project Costs

App Development Items	Monetary Cost Estimate	Intangible Cost Estimate
Opportunity cost of doing this app versus another app		No other apps scheduled
Miscellaneous (printing, postage, domain registration, programming books, and so on)	$250.00	
Totals	$7299.00	$13,700.00

*I am assuming that this person has development skills that would be worth $50/hr. This is a cost for her time. Granted, this may be low, but it's impossible to peg this number with any exactness.

As you can see from this simple analysis, you might spend more than $7,000.00 in real dollars to develop your first app. You may have the hardware already, and so you could deduct $3,000.00 from the total. Regardless, you would still be at $4,000.00 or more to develop your first app. If you added in your own time (non-monetary costs), you can see that you might spend $17,000.00 to $20,000.00 in time and actual expenses to develop an iPhone/iPad app. The question for you to ask yourself is if you still feel that your app can make you enough money to justify your time and expense to get the app created, approved, posted, and marketed to the App Store.

 Note

I am well aware that you can pay a foreign developer to get an app created for $1,000.00 in just a few weeks. It is highly unlikely that you will see success from such an app. The time worn phrase, "You get what you pay for," applies. Most often these apps are quickly designed and buggy. You're better off going to Vegas over a long weekend with your $1,000.00 and rolling the dice!

Quantifying the Benefits

Your next step in the cost/benefit analysis is to determine the expected benefits from the creation of your app. This is a little trickier than estimating the costs to build your app, but this step is a crucial part of the cost/benefit equation. Keep in mind that most of you, as app developers, are looking for monetary benefits from your first app. You'll need to spend a little time estimating potential sales of your app. Be sure to refer to other chapters in this book to understand market sizing and appropriate pricing for your app.

Some developers are offering a free app as a forerunner to another paid app or to demonstrate their skills and solutions in an effort to obtain consulting opportunities. In this case, they won't list a profit benefit for their app. Follow these steps to help you quantify the anticipated monetary and nonmonetary benefits of your app:

1. Create another list, similar to that which I used for costs, of all the monetary and intangible benefits that will be realized with the creation of your app (see Table 11.3). First on the list is the overall direct profit you hope to achieve from the sale of your app. Next might be additional investment capital you hope to attract by building a fantastic app. Other benefits might be less tangible, such as decreased production costs, name recognition, or building a solid app development reputation.

Table 11.3   A List of All Monetary and Nonmonetary Benefits You Hope Your App Will Achieve When Completed

Completion of App	Monetary Benefits	Intangible Benefits
Profit from sale of app*		
Additional investment capital if app does well		
Decreased production expense due to standard, reusable app structure		
Name recognition		
Building a solid app development reputation		
Totals		

*The profit assumption must be made by doing an estimate of your target market size multiplied by your app's per unit price. For more information on sizing your target market refer to Chapter 4, "Identifying Your Target Audience."

Next, assign some monetary and nonmonetary values to your list. In my example, I am assuming that a developer has created a productivity app and that this app will be sold for $4.99 on the App Store. The app is expected to have 5,000 downloads over the next six months based on marketing efforts. After you have filled in all the monetary detail for which you have information, add and total them up at the bottom of the table. Table 11.4 shows the inputs for both monetary and nonmonetary benefits.

Table 11.4 A List of All Monetary and Nonmonetary Benefits with Numeric Values Assigned

Completion of App	Monetary Benefits	Intangible Benefits
Profit from sale of app*	$17,465.00 (after Apple's 30% share)	
Additional investment capital if app does well	None	
Decreased production expense due to standard, reusable app structure	$3500.00	
Name recognition	Yes	Yes, not quantifiable
Building a solid app development reputation	Yes, I anticipate this app will lead to other projects, consulting deals ($10,000)	Yes, I expect this to lead to a stronger reputation in the app development community
Totals	$30, 965.00	

*The profit assumption must be made by doing an estimate of your target market size multiplied by your app's per unit price. For more information on sizing your target market refer to Chapter 4.

Performing a Cost/Benefit Comparison

With your evaluation of costs and benefits completed, you can now do a cost/benefit comparison, which is fairly easy. You are at a point in your analysis where you can weigh your costs and benefits to determine if it makes sense to build your app. Your outputs are only as good as your inputs. Your investment in gathering data is commensurate with the quality of your results. You can follow these steps to help complete cost/benefit comparison:

1. Compare your two total values for the monetary benefits first. If the total costs are considerably higher than the expected benefits, then you can safely determine that the project should not be undertaken.

2. If the total costs and total benefits are pretty close, then you need to go back and re-evaluate your assumptions for both the costs and benefits. If, after review you find that your numbers are roughly the same, then you can conclude that the project is not worthwhile from a strictly monetary standpoint. If profit is not your primary concern, then it may make sense to do the project.

3. If the total monetary and intangible benefits are much greater than the total monetary and nonmonetary costs, then the development of the app is worthwhile and will be a good financial and time investment for you.

The results for my fictitious example are shown in Table 11.5. As you can tell by looking at the table, the benefits outweigh the costs for building this particular app. I should also do a breakeven analysis to determine more precisely how long I think it will take before my app is producing profits for us.

Table 11.5   The Results of My Cost/Benefit Analysis Showing That Building My App Will Most Likely Be a Good Investment of Time and Dollars

Monetary/Nonmonetary Benefits	Monetary/Intangible Costs	Results (Benefit − Cost)
$17,465.00 (actual profit)	$7299.00 (actual costs)	$10,166.00 (actual net)
$30, 965.00 (profit + potential benefits)	$13,700.00 (actual costs + intangible costs)	$17,265.00 (net plus potential benefits)
Benefits > Costs (for this example)		Decision: Favorable to build app

 Note

When factoring how much time it will take to produce a profitable app, be sure to include two to three months of extra time for Apple to pay. Some developers have complained that Apple is slow to pay royalties on apps.

Breakeven Analysis

Performing a true cost/benefit analysis requires you to develop a breakeven point for your app so that you will have an idea of how much time it will take you to recoup your investment. It's not much of an investment if it takes you two years to make your money back. Ideally, you want your app to breakeven within a month of releasing it to the App Store. If it takes much longer than that, then your app is probably not going to be too profitable for you because it will not return payment soon enough for you to sustain a living or complete other projects.

When you have determined a price (please see pricing chapters), it's quite easy to plug the numbers into the breakeven formula as shown in the following:

$$\text{Breakeven Point} = \frac{\text{Fixed Costs}}{\text{App Selling Price (Less Apple's Commission)}}$$

This calculation lets you know how many total apps you'll need to sell to break even. When you've reached that point, you've recovered all costs associated with producing your app (both variable and fixed).

Note

For simplicity's sake, I do not include variable costs as a separate item in this example. When an app is complete, the expenses are considered complete for that version of the app. Because the app can potentially sell unlimited copies, the cost to produce each app after breakeven is basically zero.

After reaching the breakeven point, every additional copy of your app sold will increase your profit by the amount of the app's contribution margin. The app's contribution margin helps reduce overall fixed costs and can be defined as

App Contribution Margin = App Selling Price (Less Apple's Commission)

Using an Excel spreadsheet can help you figure out these calculations quite easily and figure out your own breakeven and contribution margin. An example using the $4.99 productivity app is shown in Figure 11.1.

Our $4.99 iPhone /iPad App - Breakeven Analysis	
Fixed Development Costs	$7,299.00
Price of App on App Store	$4.99
Contribution Margin (Apple's Commission Deducted)	$3.49
Breakeven (required paid downloads)	2090
Estimated Time to Breakeven	
100 downloads per day (variable)	21
Monthly revenue after breakeven	$2,189.70

Figure 11.1 An Excel spreadsheet helps us easily calculate the breakeven and contribution margin for our $4.99 app.

Some Caveats

If you think selling that many apps is possible but at a lower price point, then redo your calculation at a lower price point to see what the results look like. You can also look at your application development costs to see if it makes sense to cut the cost of your development through cheaper labor or adding less features to start out.

Keep in mind that the biggest unknown is your level of demand. A breakeven analysis cannot predict what the demand for your app might be. It is simply a decision-making tool that will help you avoid making some costly mistakes prior to development of your app. The best predictor for your app is the research you do around your target audience and what data points you can glean from communities and blog posts that are discussing apps similar to yours.

Summary

Counting the cost of an app before you start is simply wise. Going through the effort of performing a cost/benefit analysis will help you make a more sound decision about spending your hard-earned money developing and marketing an app that the buying community will want. The App Store is cluttered with apps that provide no real value to iPhone/iPad users, and the chances of many apps breaking even or turning a profit are slim.

A breakeven analysis will help you determine how many apps you need to sell to turn a profit and start seeing money come through the door. A breakeven analysis will not help you predict your app's sales; that information is gleaned from other research you do around your target audience and what buyers actually tell you they want. There is not an exact science to this complicated area of pricing and predicting sales of your iPhone/iPad app, but a little up-front cost/benefit analysis can go a long way.

12

Selling Value over Price

There is an ice cream sundae in New York City that sells for $1,000.00! It's hard to believe, but the restaurant Serendipity sells its Grand Opulence Sundae for $1,000.00, and they actually sell one or two of them a month. Who would be crazy enough to spend that kind of money on a sundae? There couldn't possibly be enough ice cream or toppings to make it that expensive. So, it would follow that people are drawn to this sundae for other reasons.

Obviously there are a few people who feel there is value in spending so much money on an ice cream sundae. But the value goes beyond just a bowl of ice cream. The person is also buying intangible benefits such as prestige, attention, adulation, appreciation, and so on. It's almost a guarantee that people who buy the Grand Opulence Sundae will not be sitting in a far away corner of the restaurant. They will want their friends and family and anyone else to watch the presentation and be impressed by it.

The desire to purchase this product starts with the restaurant's own description:

> "5 scoops of the richest Tahitian vanilla bean ice cream infused with
> Madagascar vanilla and covered in 23K edible gold leaf, the sundae is driz-
> zled with the world's most expensive chocolate, Amedei Porceleana, and cov-
> ered with chunks of rare Chuao chocolate, which is from cocoa beans
> harvested by the Caribbean Sea on Venezuela's coast. The masterpiece is suf-
> fused with exotic candied fruits from Paris, gold dragets, truffles and
> Marzipan Cherries. It is topped with a tiny glass bowl of Grand Passion
> Caviar, an exclusive dessert caviar, made of salt-free American Golden
> caviar, known for its sparkling golden color. It's sweetened and infused with
> fresh passion fruit, orange and Armagnac. The sundae is served in a bac-
> carat Harcourt crystal goblet with an 18K gold spoon to partake in the
> indulgence served with a petite mother of pearl spoon and topped with a
> gilded sugar flower by Ron Ben-Israel."

The restaurant has done an amazing job conveying the value of its product and
convincing a small number of people to purchase this sundae. It has sold the value
of its product by its description, coupled with the strength of its restaurant brand
and prestige. Through savvy marketing, it has convinced buyers to suspend their
focus on price and think about the excitement and quality of the product. Although
you may not have a $1,000 app (there is actually one app called iRa Pro that sells
for $899.99, shown in Figure 12.1), you're nonetheless going to have to sell the value
of your app, especially if it's above $4.99.

Figure 12.1   One of the App Store's most expensive apps at $899.99 is focused on a
very narrow market of mobile video surveillance.

Customers generally become price-sensitive in the App Store starting at about $4.99. If you are selling a game, price sensitivity starts at $2.99. There are a number of reasons why this is the case, including the following:

- **People have come to expect all things Internet to be free.** Because so much information is available at no charge, many buyers think everything should be free, including apps. It's only recently that online publications (for example, newspapers) are tiptoeing back into the paid subscription model. The iPad and subscription-based apps are helping to change the perception about paying for online content.

- **iTunes set a precedent with $0.99 music.** People who visit iTunes have become accustomed to all prices to be set at $0.99. This is not completely true, however; many albums for sale on iTunes are priced at $9.99 and up. But most people buy single songs.

- **People don't equate an iPhone/iPad app as having as much capability as a regular Mac or PC app.** Over time this perception will change, but some buyers think that a mobile phone means limited app capability, and so they instinctively believe that an iPhone/iPad app isn't as powerful as applications provided on other platforms.

- **People don't have unlimited funds.** If someone is looking at an app that is priced at $9.99, she has to forego buying several other apps at a lower price. The average App Store buyer spends $10–$20 a month, tops, on apps. If you factor in the cost of an iPhone or iPad plus the monthly subscription fees, it starts to add up for the average consumer. Therefore, consumers are sensitive about how much more money they will spend for iPhone/iPad app.

So if you have an app that is priced in the $9.99 range or higher, you need to spend some time focusing on selling value. An example of an app that sells in this price range is shown in Figure 12.2. This navigation app is geared to drivers, allowing them to view maps and listen to turn-by-turn navigation via their iPhones/iPads. The audience for this type of app is any driver who has an iPhone/iPad. The company that develops and maintains this app cannot make any money selling at $0.99 given the uniqueness of the app. However, their navigation solution is much less expensive than buying a navigation system for a car.

Figure 12.2   A higher priced app is generally focused on a more narrow audience such as automobile drivers who own iPhones/iPads.

Selling Value

Because you can't have a conversation with your buyer about the price of your app, you may be wondering how you convince someone that the value of your app is worth the asking price. This is really the crux of the issue. Buyers must think that they are getting what they pay for in terms of quality, usefulness, and return on their investment. If you can convince your buyer of at least one of these three points, you are more likely to achieve the sale. You have to let your app, App Store verbiage, product website, and reputation do the talking.

Selling Quality

One area of iPhone/iPad apps that has done a great job of selling quality is mobile navigation. Mobile GPS apps have really become popular over the past several years, and the quality has approached that of regular auto GPS systems. Still, buyers want to be sure they are buying quality when spending $20–$59 on an iPhone/iPad app. The graphics and accuracy of the GPS have to be of the highest quality. As you can see in Figure 12.3, pricing for navigation apps is between $20 and $59 from a number of competing companies. And, yes, there are a few free and $0.99 apps in this category but not of the caliber found in the higher price range.

You can also help buyers of this app understand that their iPhones/iPads can function as turn-by-turn navigation system when they need it without having to o buy a completely separate navigation system for their cars. Anytime your app allows the iPhone/iPad to function as another device, the customer is actually saving money by not having to buy a separate device. Be sure to point this out to your buyers, and immediately they will not be as hesitant about the price because you are extending the value of their mobile devices.

Figure 12.3 Mobile Navigation apps sell on quality and accuracy of their systems, keeping their prices far above the regular iPhone/iPad app price.

 Note

Many thought that after Google offered its free turn-by-turn navigation app that prices would continue to sink lower for navigation apps. And although it's true companies like Garmin (TomTom) have had to drop prices dramatically for their apps, the prices for high-end navigation apps have remained higher than the typical app (more navigation apps at $.99 have been introduced to the market, however).

Selling Usefulness

Anytime you can provide an app that saves people time in their business or dealing with their clients, you have an opportunity to sell your app a higher price. You can focus your app verbiage on how your app saves consumers time and makes them more efficient. The more efficient people are, the more clients they can see daily, and the more they can offer in terms of better service. Your app customer views this as a valuable tool if your app can provide this capability.

There are a number of productivity apps on the App Store, and some are geared to very specific audiences such as doctors, lawyers, financial advisors, dentists, and so on. Figure 12.4, for example, is an app geared to physicians that allows them to track their patients. Physicians can wirelessly write prescriptions and patient info to other databases at their office.

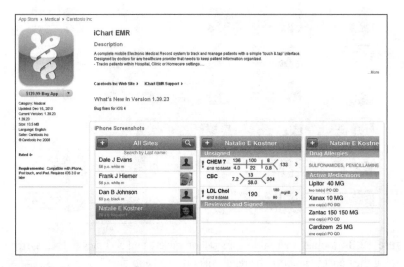

Figure 12.4 iChart EMR sells for $139.99 and allows physicians to track patients and health histories, write prescriptions, and transmit data to their main databases.

Other apps that fall into the usefulness category include calendaring and organization apps. To charge a higher price than free or $0.99, your app must provide connectivity to other systems or provide a level of functionality not typically found in the less expensive apps. Figure 12.5 shows an example of an app that uploads updates to iCal and Outlook.

Selling Return on Investment

The most expensive app on the App Store is called BarMax CA, which is currently listed for $999.99. Yes, a thousand dollars will get you all the materials you need to prepare for the California bar exam. The company justifies its price because it typically offers the same material in a classroom setting for $3,000–$4,000. The difference, of course, is that you don't get a live instructor on the iPhone/iPad. The app includes thousands of pages of prep materials and hours of audio lectures. The course takes about two months and consists of multiple choices, essays, and performance exams. And this can all be done from your iPhone/iPad. An example of this application is shown in Figure 12.6.

Figure 12.5   Productivity apps can justify a higher price when they connect to/update other common Mac and PC applications.

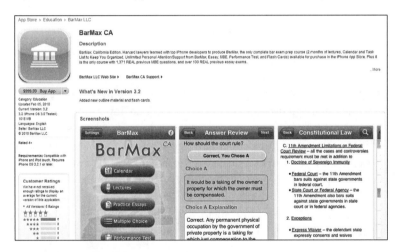

Figure 12.6   The App Store's most expensive (and legitimate) app is BarMax CA, which currently sells for $999.99.

If your app sells for more than $10, you should look for ways to communicate to your buyers that your app can save them money. One way to do this is through a case study on your product website or App Store verbiage where you explain an actual use case for your app, particularly how someone saved money by using your app. Through a case study, you should be able to demonstrate to your potential buyer how your app saved people money and how long it took them to save X dollars. When reading such an illustration, your buyers will take comfort in knowing that they will make up their investment in your app with just a few uses. This approach to selling takes away the risk for the buyer to some degree.

Additional Thoughts on Selling Value

Think about how many times you have had a particular problem; when you found the right solution, price was usually not an issue. You needed that solution, and you were willing to pay for it. The same holds true for the more expensive iPhone/iPad apps. Obviously the type of app I am talking about is one that is geared to a narrow audience with a specific need. Because you understand the buyers' problem and can provide them with a solution, they are willing to pay for that solution.

 Note

There are really two markets on the App Store: the Flea Market and Utility Market. We all love flea markets, and sometimes we are flea-market buyers. We browse and walk the aisles of the App Store looking for something fun and inexpensive. At other times we are utility buyers, looking for a particular app to solve a particular problem.

Here are some things to keep in mind:

- **Differentiate, differentiate, differentiate**—If there is nothing that makes you unique from your competition, you become common. Common means ordinary or not special, and the only way buyers select one common app over another app is price. Take inventory of your development skills, experience, and knowledge. If you have specialized skills in some area, think about developing an app for that skill set. Sure, you are going after a niche market, but it could be a very profitable niche market for you. If you are an expert in certain facets of your business, look to create an app to automate or improve your business. These and other differentiators can make you unique and valuable to the app buying audience.

- **Dropping your price too low can hurt you**—Depending on the type of app, you may be doing yourself a disservice by pricing the app too low. In some of the previous examples, your customers would question the value of your app if the price is set at practically zero. Most find the old adage holds: They get what they pay for in terms of quality and stability. A higher-priced app implies there must be something more to it. Again, this is generally not referring to game apps, which seem to all fall in the $0.99 to $2.99 range with few exceptions.

- **A competitive price adds perceived value**—This chapter is focused on higher-priced apps, and if you are selling a higher-priced app, do not drop the price so low that you are far and away the cheapest option in your category on the App Store. It's okay to be a little cheaper, 20% or so, but not 80%.

- **If there are few (or no) iPhone/iPad app competitors, price the app higher**—If you have created an app that could have a strong audience but lacks a strong competitive presence on the App Store, then look to Mac and PC solutions to see where they are priced. A good PC or Mac app (think antivirus software for the PC) sells for $24.99 to $39.99 all the time. Your app may be a utility or novel app that helps someone in a certain line of business and can be priced above $20.00, but keep in mind that you'll have to do a lot more marketing at this price.

The app shown in Figure 12.7 is an example of an HVAC app that helps people in the heating and air conditioning trades calculate duct sizes and pipe sizes. This app is currently priced at $23.99 and for an individual in this line of work; this is an acceptable price for this type of tool. I'm sure they've spent a lot more on other tools.

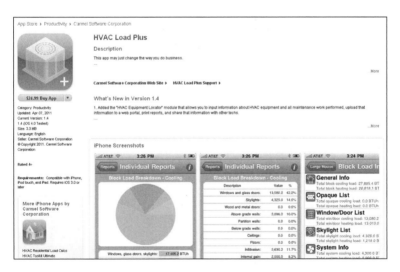

Figure 12.7   If there are very few (or no) apps that do the same thing your app does, you can charge a much higher (but fair) price to a limited audience.

- **Consumers want value and are willing to pay for it**—It may surprise you, but consumers are willing to spend a fair amount for an app that works well and solves their problems. They would rather buy an app that works and spend a little more than buy an app that is junk that doesn't work well or solve their problems.

Summary

If you have developed an app that does not fall in the game category and caters to a narrow audience, you should consider carefully the concept of selling value over price. Many apps will not become blockbuster hits on the App Store, but they serve a very specific audience. You want to maximize your revenue with this smaller audience by selling value over price.

Apps that improve productivity and help solve a problem or save money are candidates for value pricing instead low pricing. The key to selling value is that your web and App Store content must communicate one or all of the components: quality, usefulness, and return on investment. Buyers will almost always purchase your app if they believe they are getting more from your app than indicated by the price. The mentality for apps buyers depends on the type of app being sold.

People who are looking to play games or pass the time will be looking for low-priced and zero-priced apps. They tend to download an app and use it on average 10 times before they forget about it, become bored with it, or delete it off their iPhones/iPads. People who are looking to solve a specific problem in their profession, life, health, and so on will be willing to spend some money on an app. They also tend to use the app much more frequently, especially if it proves useful for one of the previous scenarios.

13

Breaking into the App Store Top 100

Perhaps the most popular question ever asked about marketing an iPhone/iPad app is "How do I get my app in the top 100 for my category?" Developers know that if they can get their apps into the top 100, they are certain to see massive numbers of downloads and huge sales volume. This accurate assumption was described as hitting the grand slam in Chapter 1, "Your iPhone and iPad App Marketing Strategy: Grand Slam or Base Hits?" Being in the top 100 in app sales is the Holy Grail for iPhone/iPad app developers.

The challenge, however, is unlocking the mystery of how to break into the top 100 in sales volume, which by the way, requires several thousand downloads per day. There have been rumors that some companies have bought their own apps for a few days to get onto the list, creating momentum. Although this is possible, it would be fairly expensive to achieve this feat and could only happen with a wealthy developer or large company with deep pockets.

Some developers are using pay-per-install programs such as those provided by Tapjoy and Flurry. These programs allow your app to be presented on what is called an "offerwall" where it is presented to other users to download as a way for them to earn virtual currency. If your app is downloaded and installed, you are charged a predetermined amount for the install. Companies with large marketing budgets can afford to spend large amounts of money to achieve more installs.

 Note

Apple has recently cracked down on pay-per-install programs by adding additional criteria to their download ranking calculation. This means that you must have positive ratings (and other positive factors) along with a high number of downloads to break into the top 100. Apple is attempting to level the playing field for apps and is trying to prevent companies from paying to push poorly written apps into high rankings on the App Store.

Otherwise, there is no one single formula for breaking into the top 100 (or top 50 or top 10, for that matter). This has been proven time and time again by developers who have told their stories of making it into the top 100 through articles and blog posts over the past two years. So although I can't pinpoint an exact formula for success, I can give you some common elements that are part of the most successful apps. These are things I know must happen to some degree to reach orbital velocity on the App Store.

Develop a Great App

Far and away the biggest reason an app makes it into the top 100 is because it's a great app. Hands down, this is the biggest reason, and yet so many developers seem to discount this first recommendation. They say to themselves, "Of course I have a great app. It's the best app to ever hit the App Store!" Then they don't give it too much more thought. But your rash decision to create the perfect app without really thinking it through could be your undoing. Ask yourself some of the following hard questions before you start development on your app:

- Are people really going to be interested in the app you are going to write?

- Will someone be willing to pay for the app you are going write?

- Are you so confident in your app that you will bet your whole reputation on releasing it?

- Are you prepared to work nights/weekends/holidays, whatever it takes to ensure the highest quality app gets produced?

- Are you prepared to take criticism and blunt appraisals about your app?

- Are you prepared to release updates frequently?

If you can honestly answer "yes" to all of these questions, then read on. As they say, you may have what it takes. In short, your app must be easy to use and difficult to master! Not an easy feat. But spend some time on the App Store familiarizing yourself with the best-selling free and paid apps. Spend a few bucks and download the most popular games in your category and study them to understand why they are so popular. You have to pick apart the app to understand how it ticks and why it's so appealing to so many people.

Figure 13.1 shows the most popular music app at the time of this writing, I Am T-Pain (grossing $3.5 million in sales and 1.5 million users). This app has a few key very successful ingredients. First, it has mass appeal because nearly everyone likes music. Second, it mimics the effects of auto-tuning, the extremely popular way to alter the pitch of someone's voice in a song. Third, the original software for this tool sells for several hundred dollars, and you can buy a similar likeness of that tool for less than $3. Fourth, the product is well written and has stickiness, meaning that users enjoy using the app over and over again.

Figure 13.1   A best-selling music app I Am T-Pain has many key ingredients required for a top-100-selling app.

Note

Build your app with an eye toward television. When you are designing and building your app, try to envision your app being selected for an Apple TV commercial. The quality of such an app would have to be of the highest caliber and the usability superb. Setting the bar this high helps position your app with the greatest possibility for success even if it's never shown on TV.

Beat Up Your App...Mercilessly

Nobody likes to be told that their baby is ugly, but in the case of iPhone and iPad apps, you must get second and third opinions on what people like and don't like about your app. If you have produced a game for teens, you need to get it into the hands of teens prior to launch. Send out an email or post an ad on your website that you're looking for early testers of your app. You can offer them a free version of the app when it ships or other things like T-shirts or other small gifts. If you provide them with a prerelease build, you'll have to obtain their UDIDs (unique device identifier). Apple allows developers to provide prerelease versions of their apps to up to 100 iPhone/iPad users. This allows you to conduct a fairly substantial beta test of your app prior to launching it on the App Store.

 Note

You need a way to solicit feedback about your app. Don't just have your testers give you random comments or tell you what they think. Create a structured survey form on your product website or through a service such as Survey Monkey (www.surveymonkey.com). Ask your beta testers to rank the level of play for your app, ease of use, graphics and sound, and so on. Ask them about 10 questions total so they can quickly give you their feedback. You can also leave a space for open comments on the survey to capture their suggestions.

Have Friends in High Places

It never hurts to have lots of friends and family who can help promote your app. You can offer them a free download through a gift card. Until recently, you could give anyone (up to 50) a free promo code to download your app and give it a try. You could then ask him to post a review on the App Store. In an effort to prevent falsified reviews, Apple has disallowed reviews to come from free promo codes. You can still give away free apps, but those who use the free promo codes will not be able to post a review of your app.

Now, what about the ethics of giving a free app through a gift card and asking for a review? I amwell aware of the reports about some companies creating fake reviews for their own or their clients' apps on the App Store. This is clearly not appropriate, and I am not suggesting that you ever take this approach. I am suggesting that you contact everyone you know, give them gift card apps, ask them to download the app, test it out, and write honest (and hopefully positive) reviews. This is no different than reaching out to a regular reviewer and asking him to give you an honest evaluation of your app. If you have created an outstanding app, you won't need to worry about getting a bunch of negative reviews. You will get a few, but that's just the nature of selling any product.

If you are fortunate to know reviewers at different companies, always solicit their help in providing reviews for your app. There are also a number of sites that have popped up recently that allow you to post your app for review by others. If someone likes your app, she can use one of your promo codes and download it. You can submit promo codes for all of your paid apps. These review sites definitely give your app more exposure if the right person downloads it and helps spread the word. An example of an app review site is shown in Figure 13.2.

Figure 13.2 The Daily App Show allows you to submit your paid app along with five or more promo codes.

 Note

It doesn't hurt to ask your users to write reviews for your app. If you offer an instruction page within your app, you can include a request at the bottom of your instructions saying, "We appreciate your feedback; don't forget to write a review on the App Store."

Cross-Promote

Cross-promoting your apps is a powerful way to increase sales and move you into the top 100. When you have one successful app, it's easier to build off that success with your next app. It's similar to an author who publishes a best-selling novel. The next book is much easier to get the same success because the author is a known quantity at that point. He has a following of readers, and they will most likely buy his next book.

You can cross-promote your app in numerous ways. If you have a PC or Mac app that you have already built, you can utilize that audience to promote your iPhone/iPad app. If you have developed a free version of your app, you can easily cross-promote the paid version in that app. For more information on developing a free app, refer to Chapter 14, "Level the Playing Field with a Free App."

Each time you introduce a new app to the App Store, be sure to issue a press release. In your press release, you should talk about your new app, but you should also mention the other apps you have available. For example, at the end of your press release, you can mention your company name and tell the reader you are also the developer of *XYZ* apps. The App Store also helps you cross-promote by showing other apps available from you, as shown in Figure 13.3.

Figure 13.3   The App Store helps you cross-promote your apps by displaying other apps available from the same company at the bottom of your app's product page.

Keep the Size Under 20MB

Many app purchases are impulse buys, especially games. People are browsing apps on their iPhones or iPads, and when they see an app they like, they download it from their devices. Because there is a 20MB limit, you should try to keep the size of your app below this limit. If you are building a game, this should be a high priority. If you look at the current, highest ranked, best selling apps, most of them are under 20MB.

Price It Right

As I've mentioned in many sections of this book, you have to do some homework on where to set your price. If you are hoping for a quick win, you've got to sell a game app, and your price must be between $0.99 and $1.99. Nearly all games are priced at $0.99. Some name-brand game apps are priced a little higher, but they have a large following and strong name recognition before launch. See the other chapters in this book that discuss how to price your app.

Integrate Your App with Other Apps

There are a number of very popular apps in the area of social media that you can build your app to work with or utilize. Search the App Store for popular apps around Facebook, Twitter, Living Social, YouTube, and many others. Look for ways to enhance or expand the use of these social networking sites with your iPhone or iPad.

When someone searches the App Store for a social networking app, your app will also appear in the search results. For example, when you search the App Store using the "Twitter" keyword, you bring up a number of apps that work with Twitter, such as the app shown in Figure 13.4.

Figure 13.4 Creating an app that works with extremely popular apps helps others find your app when they do a keyword search.

Optimize Your Web and App Store Copy

Carefully choose the name of your app and think about keywords you might be able to use in your app's name that will be common to users searching the App Store. Descriptive words such as *Easy*, *Fun*, *Fast*, and *Exciting* are all common terms used in searches. If your app has these types of words, your app is more likely to show up in the search results at the top of the list.

 Note

Apple keeps upping the quality of the App Store search engine. When the store was initially launched, the search capabilities were fairly primitive. But with each release of the iTunes client, the search capability seems to improve. They are becoming sophisticated in properly identifying the right apps for the search terms entered.

If your app is connecting to another popular app such as Twitter, Facebook, Myspace, and so on, be sure to mention these apps by name in the body of your copy. This can help your app to appear when someone does a search for these apps. You also want to add keywords to your web copy to assist people in locating your app. It is widely believed that the more keywords you use in your App Store copy, the higher you'll appear in the search rankings. Don't overdo it, but a generous use of keywords can't hurt.

Develop Your Brand and Promote It Like Crazy

If you plan to develop more than one app (and you should), then you want to think about building a brand instead of just an app. There are many young development companies vying for a piece of the spotlight in the app development world, and they are working diligently to build a brand. Some of the benefits of building a brand are the following:

- A brand allows you to build a bigger following as you reach a larger audience of iPhone and iPad app users across multiple apps.

- A brand helps your company attract venture capital if you achieve success with a best seller and desire to grow your business into a large-scale business.

- A brand allows you to cross promote your apps across your user base.

- A brand allows you to concentrate development efforts where needed to efficiently produce your next best-selling app.

- A brand helps you develop other products outside of iPhone/iPad apps, such as Mac or PC products.

The best way to build a brand is to start before the release of your first app. You can develop your brand by designing the look and feel of your product website. When you have established an identity for your brand, you can include elements of your brand (colors, font styles, graphics, and so on) into each of your apps. The carryover between your website brand and your apps does not need to be 100%, but it should include some elements so that subconsciously buyers link your site to apps they see on the App Store from your company. Figures 13.5 and 13.6 are two examples of companies that have created a brand for their apps and are doing very well on the App Store.

Another way to build your brand is to create a blog and start blogging about iPhone/iPad app development topics. You can build up a following for your brand even before you release any apps to the App Store. Prior to launching your first app, you can generate buzz about your app, allowing you to generate stronger sales when it is released.

Figure 13.5 Smule has built a brand around a number of different successful products. It has received significant funding from venture capital firms to expand its collection of apps.

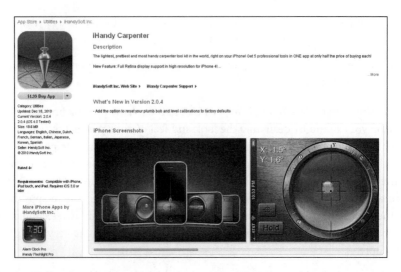

Figure 13.6   iHandy has built their brand around a number of free and paid apps, giving it a strong presence on the App Store.

Reach Out to Apple

Getting chosen for one of the categories like New and Noteworthy, What's Hot, or Staff Picks is a complete mystery for the outside app developer. I'm not sure there really is a system in place for selecting apps for these categories. It may be whatever bubbles up to the top or catches the attention of an Apple reviewer. Sometimes all you have to do is ask, right? It doesn't hurt to approach a reviewer at the App Store and ask her to take a special look at your app. Remember the postcard idea? If you can stand out in the crowd to get someone to look at your app, you have a shot at being selected for one of their special categories. It may sound silly, but doing something like sending a postcard puts you in a class of a handful that do anything beyond submitting apps for approval.

Remember, the Apple reviewers are much like your buyers. They will be interested in an app that has a compelling value proposition with exciting graphics, is easy to understand, has broad audience, and has stickiness. If your app has some of these characteristics, you're more likely to attract the attention of an Apple reviewer, although I have to admit that some of the apps selected for these special categories have not always been the best.

Summary

In this chapter, we have learned about the common elements that are present in an app that breaks into the top 100 for their category. While there is no set formula for a winning app, we know that the winning apps are typically games that are easy to learn, fun to play, and low cost. Increase your chances of breaking into the top 100 or lower by building a free app along with a paid app and making sure that yours is outstanding and not average.

Don't quit after a few weeks of posting your app to the App Store. Sometimes all it takes is the right combination of a great app at the right time with the right exposure. Building a brand is more powerful than building a single app. It takes more time and effort but improves your odds of having that breakout app.

Always seek positive customer and professional reviews. People make purchases based on the positive recommendations of others. The more positive reviews you have, the more your app will be viewed favorably. Don't forget to seek reviews from industry experts outside of the typical iPhone/iPad realm. These experts can give your potential customers a positive recommendation for your apps as well as lots of credibility.

14

Level the Playing Field with a Free App

As long as there are developers creating iPhone/iPad apps, the debate about free apps versus paid apps will probably continue. This is because some people will have success with a paid app, some will utilize the in-app purchase capability, and others will generate ad revenue through their free apps. All of these sales models can work, and often the success depends on the type of app written and the audience to which you are marketing. Some buyers don't mind having ads appear in their free apps and will download lots of free apps and use them for a short period of time or will upgrade to a paid app to get additional features. Others will get tired of the ads and will pay $.99 to get rid of the ads altogether.

Developers should remember that free apps can help them level the playing field and build their brands inexpensively. The current trend is to develop a free app with in-app purchase capability. The customer can download the app for free and play a few levels of a game, for example. But advancing to the next levels requires a purchase, which is made within the app.

When large app developers enter the App Store with a new app, they have the marketing clout and brand recognition that an independent developer does not. They can release paid apps and immediately start to see large downloads because their brands are recognized and trusted. They have already spent perhaps millions of dollars building their brands over many years. They have many followers already. Companies such as Rovio, Electronic Arts, and Chilingo all have strong name recognition as do other large gaming and app companies.

An independent developer does not have that luxury of a well-known brand and must look for other ways to get the word out about his app. If you offer a free app along with an in-app purchase option, you are covering both your bases: building your brand and generating some revenue through in-app purchases. You're allowing users to "try before they buy," which gives them a risk-free opportunity before they buy your additional levels or other features. Even if they don't make an in-app purchase, you are building your brand and gaining recognition in a very competitive field. If they like your app, they will be inclined to tell others about it and will also be inclined to look at what other apps you have for download and sale.

✉ Note

Do not make the mistake of thinking that people are not price sensitive at $0.99! With so many apps to choose from on the App Store, your buyer cannot possibly buy even a fraction of the available apps. So your buyers are selective in what they download for free and especially selective in what they purchase—at any price.

In this chapter I review the different approaches to monetizing apps. Take a close look at the type of app you are marketing. Game apps tend to do very well as a free download with in-app purchase capabilities. Games are generally easier to delineate between free and paid as well. For example, you can limit the levels of play in the free app or the number of weapons in the game. Other nongame apps are more difficult to restrict on features, but it can be done with some careful thought. Each app will be different in terms of where you draw the line from free to paid. An educational app can offer the first set of test questions for free but require an in-app purchase to obtain the entire set of questions, for example.

Table 14.1 illustrates the different app development strategies you can consider when building your app marketing plan. Ultimately you will have to decide which approach works best for you and also what your budget will permit you to accomplish. One other point that's worth mentioning is that you can always start out with a free app and then offer in-app purchase capability later on to generate sales. Many developers have had strong success in building a free app with in-app purchase capability.

Table 14.1   Multiple Development Strategies for Creating Your App Marketing Plan

App Development Approach	Pros	Cons
Paid App— Standalone	Lower costs/faster time to market	Many competing apps, limited brand recognition, slower sales until you build a following
Free App— Standalone	Likely to experience multiple downloads quickly, build your brand	Relying on ad revenue that may or may not result in significant revenue
Free App and Paid App	Build a following, in-app purchase inside free app, achieve ad revenue and paid app revenue simultaneously	More costly to build and support two slightly different versions of your app
Paid App—With Ads	Sell app and gain some ad revenue	Not widely used and unlikely to achieve significant revenue from either side

Build a Paid App—Standalone

Most developers that have been around the App Store for a period of time have built paid versions of their apps first and monitored their sales. Even a year ago, there were far fewer apps competing for your download dollars, and so this strategy could pay off handsomely if you hit the right app. Think of the Tiny Wings app. It started out as a paid app at $.99 and remains at $.99 and was created by an independent developer. If you have a strong brand and a strong following for your apps, you may be able to build a paid app without offering a free version.

For developers of games, this is getting more difficult to achieve. Customers are looking for free first, and then maybe they will buy the full app. Even Ethan Nicholas, the developer of the incredibly successful iShoot game of several years ago, began offering an "iShoot Lite" version after he noticed his sales of the paid version started to slow. Offering the free version allowed his sales to resume their upward growth for a little while. However, this was his only hit, and it shows how difficult it is to hit that grand slam app. Just because a developer creates a blockbuster app does not mean he can do it again.

Perhaps the best opportunity for standalone paid apps is in the more technical and business-oriented apps categories. The reason for this is that often people are looking for an app to solve a particular problem and they are willing to pay for it. In fact, they expect to pay for it. If they can find it for free, great. But if they can't, they are prepared to buy the app. Most app pricing studies show that the buyer is not as price sensitive up to $4.99 for non-game apps.

Build a Free App, Build a Following

There are many reasons to build a free app, most notably so that you can build a following. Perhaps your goal is not to make money right away from your app but to get your name out there in the development world. Building a free app has a number of benefits, including the following, which you should consider as you build your company:

- **Build an app to showcase your development skills**—If your goal is to develop apps for other people, you can use a free app to demonstrate your skills to potential clients. You can create a free app that you can post to the App Store and gain experience building. When a potential client wants to see a sample of your work, you direct them to the App Store to download a copy of your app. An app that has many downloads will help convince a buyer to use you to develop their app.

- **Build a free app for future sales**—Many developers build free apps first with the intention of charging for the app after they have built up a following. However, in certain studies of app sales, a free app that gets changed to a paid app often sees a significant decline in sales after they switch to a paid app. In a fairly well-known example, Tapulous COO and cofounder Andrew Lacy told the press that install rates for one of its free gaming apps dropped 95% overnight when the company started charging $0.99 for it.

  Other studies have indicated that even if the app developer moves the app back to free after trying to charge for it, the damage has been done, and the number of free downloads is still impacted. It appears that the momentum is broken at the point when a free app is altered in any way.

It is probably best to develop a free app and leave it as free and then create another that is a paid app after you monitor the downloads and level of interest around the free version. This allows people to download your free app without risk and then purchase your paid app if they like what they see or want to obtain additional functionality.

- **Build a free app to support other products**—Perhaps you are selling another product that can benefit from building an iPhone/iPad app. You can develop a free app that can either be used to compliment your other product or help you to strengthen your brand. One of the best examples of this is the Bic Concert Lighter. The app shows a picture of a Bic Lighter and looks almost like the real thing. This app has had millions of downloads and has helped Bic to strengthen its brand. The Bic Lighter is shown in Figure 14.1.

Figure 14.1   The Bic Concert Lighter is a free app that is used to strengthen Bic's brand and generate awareness about its product.

- **New to iPhone/iPad app development**—If you are new to developing apps, creating a free app might be the best route to take as you get your feet wet. Building a free app takes the pressure off you to make money right away on the app. But unless you have very deep pockets of cash, build your free app as inexpensively as you can without sacrificing quality. Use this as an opportunity to learn the App Store submittal process and make your mistakes with a free app.

Build a Paid App and a Free App at the Same Time

A number of developers pursue a dual strategy of building a free and a paid app at the same time. Even with in-app purchase capability, there are still a number of free and "lite" apps available on the App Store. This strategy allows you to establish a following for your app from the start, obtaining possibly thousands of downloads of the free version along with sales of the paid version.

Conversion rates from free apps to paid apps are around 1%, according to some developers. Therefore, it takes 1,000 free downloads to generate 10 paid app sales. Keep in mind some apps can achieve hundreds of thousands of free downloads, if not millions, so your free app may be able to generate considerable sales of your paid app.

The more free downloads you get, the closer you are to being shown one of the Top Paid or Top Free download categories on the App Store. Placement of your app in top listings in your specific category (that is, Health and Fitness, Lifestyles, and so on) can catapult your sales of a paid app. Figure 14.2 shows an example of the top 20 paid apps and free apps in the Healthcare and Fitness category. If you open the list entirely, the store shows the top 100 apps in that category for both paid and free.

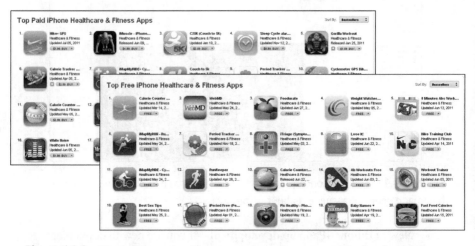

Figure 14.2 Top 20 free and paid apps are shown in two graphics for the Healthcare and Fitness category.

The challenge to creating a free and a paid app is that you may have to maintain two apps for the App Store. This depends on whether you developed the free and paid apps separately over a period of time. If you are going back to develop a free app, you'll have to decide how you want to build your app. Most will take the original paid app and modify the original code to limit its features so that you have a limited function free app. This is probably the easiest and fastest way to come up with a free app when you already have been selling a paid app.

The other option is to develop both a free and paid app at the same time. You develop the app from the ground up with all the features available but disable some of them so the free version is limited. In the free app, you can invite the user to purchase the full app and instantly upgrade them to the full featured app. As shown in Figure 14.3, the developer of this app has created two versions of the app about a month and half apart.

Figure 14.3   This company released a free version and a paid version of the app. Their latest version of both apps were released on the same day.

 Note

Amazingly, a number of free apps on the App Store don't have their own paid apps ad in their free version to prompt the user to upgrade. If you are going to have a free app available, I highly recommend that you prompt the user to upgrade from within your own free app.

Many game developers offer free and paid versions of their games as a matter of course. They update the games at the same time and post to the App Store. Many other developers are taking the in-app purchase route This is becoming the norm as a marketing strategy for game development on the App Store. If you are a game developer, think seriously about offering an in-app purchase version right from the start. Two examples of apps that have in-app purchase capabilities are shown in Figures 14.4 and 14.5.

In-app purchases were allowed by Apple in late 2009. This functionality is a big benefit to developers, allowing them to choose from different business models to meet various types of apps. You can offer your customers additional services and content within your paid app. For example, you can create an educational app that provides a series of lectures or courses. You can request monthly, yearly, or periodic payments fyour users to acquire your content. Apple provides an example on its website of building a general-purpose city travel guide app that lets your customers pick the city guides they want to purchase.

Figure 14.4   Game developers are increasingly offering in-app purchase capability in their apps right from the start.

Figure 14.5   Another example of a free app that has helped cross promoted sales of its paid app.

You can also process payments via the iTunes Store. You can submit items to the store and set their price. If your customer chooses to purchase any item on the iTunes Store, your iPhone/iPad app creates a payment request and sends it to the iTunes Store for processing. The capabilities of in-app purchases have yet to be exploited on a large scale by iPhone/iPad developers. This could be an important area for you to consider when attempting to monetize your apps.

Note

In-app purchase uses the same business terms used for apps sold on the
App Store. You receive 70% of the purchase price of each item you sell
within your app, paid to you on a monthly basis—no credit card fees apply.

Free Apps with Ads

Some developers have found success by building free apps with ads. Their strategy
is to make money by achieving huge downloads for their apps and selling ad space
on their apps. Companies that wish to advertise on the new emerging mobile platform can utilize mobile ad platforms and bid on ad placement just like Google
AdWords. This can be profitable for you as a developer if your apps achieve significant downloads and lots of users click through on ads displayed by your app. Some
apps have achieved considerable success by developing a free app and posting ads
in their apps.

 Note

You will have to do an analysis between what you think ad revenue will generate versus what a paid app will generate. This has been a subject of great
debate among developers; some say there is not revenue in ads for the developer, and others say there is. If you find that your free app is not generating
the ad revenue you thought, don't abandon your free strategy. Keep in mind
the other benefits of offering your app for free go beyond just ad revenue.

A developer can take a number of different routes to pursue ads on his app. These
ad network companies provide a small amount of code to install within an app to
enable ads. There are many ad networks out there competing for your business and
include companies such as Traffic Marketplace, Google, Yahoo!, Videoegg, Mojiva,
Adtini, Jumtap, Quattro Wireless (acquired by Apple), and ValueClick Media, to
name a few. These companies are providing an ad marketplace for app developers
who want to sell space on their iPhone/iPad apps and major companies who want
to sell their products via the mobile platform.

Other companies have created ad exchanges, bringing together competing ad companies for your business and promising 100% fill rates for your app, meaning that
any open time slot while your app is in use will display some sort of ad. The websites of three of the most popular ad exchange companies (Admob [acquired by
Google], Mobclix, and Adwhirl [acquired by Admob]) are shown in Figures 14.6,
14.7, and 14.8.

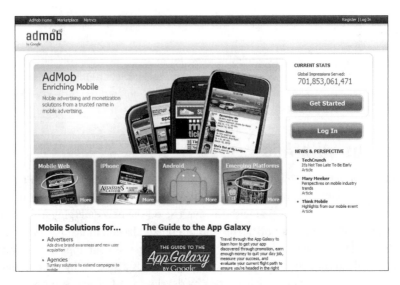

Figure 14.6   AdMob provides developers and advertising a method for mobile advertising.

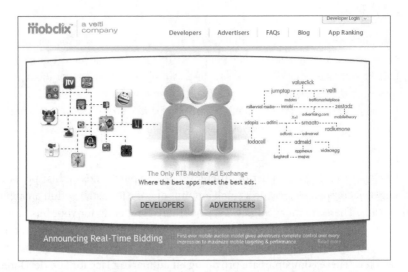

Figure 14.7   Mobclix allows developers and advertisers to provide advertising in their free apps.

AdMob is a mobile advertising marketplace that connects advertisers with mobile publishers. It allows advertisers to create ads, choose landing pages, and target their ads with plenty of detail. Ads can be targeted to locations, carriers, phone platforms, and phone manufacturers.

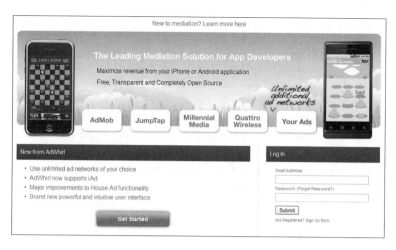

Figure 14.8   Adwhirl is an aggregator of different ad networks and was acquired by Admob in 2009.

Mobclix is an ad exchange provider for iPhone apps. Mobclix targets users based on location and the type of app to maximize the money that iPhone developers can make. Mobclix provides

- 20+ ad networks

- Advanced analytics

- 100% fill rates

Can iAds Help You to Monetize Your App?

As iPhone users await the next release of the iPhone OS 4, most are probably thinking about its multitasking and gaming hub capabilities. But if you're a developer, no doubt you're also thinking about iAd, Apple's new mobile advertising platform, and wondering if it's right for you. Here's a little background info about the iAd and its upcoming rollout.

iAd is Apple's new platform (based on its purchase of Quattro Wireless) to display advertising within iPhone and iPad applications sold on the App Store. According to Steve Jobs, iAd promises to provide a new revenue opportunity for developers and a whole new user experience in viewing ads. For example, ads will show videos and other interactive features. Although the "new user experience" remains to be seen, iAd is definitely going to change the playing field for advertisers and developers. Advertisers reportedly may have to pay upwards of $1 million to leverage the new ad platform, which means Apple will begin by targeting large corporate advertisers. Apple is going to become like the Super Bowl of mobile advertising, with primetime viewing on the iPhone/iPad platform going to the highest bidder.

Apple is also introducing some fairly restrictive policies for third-party mobile ad companies that want to continue using the iPhone/iPad mobile platform. For example, as quoted in Apple's new developer's agreement, Apple is restricting the use of software in an application to collect and send device data to a third party for processing or analysis. This means that a developer using a non-iAd mobile advertising platform won't be able to gather usage data and send that data back to the mobile ad company. It appears that iAd will be the only platform that can allow that kind of capability. If this is the case, Apple will essentially minimize the effectiveness of other mobile ad technologies, while providing its own platform with a key advantage when selling ads. This change also has consequences for developers who want to use analytics to gather usage information from their users to build better apps. Without usage data, some developers fear that they won't know which features need improving on their apps and which features to remove. According to recent reports, Apple will not allow usage data gathered outside of the iAd program under any circumstances.

As a developer, you might be pushed into using iAd for your mobile advertising platform; Apple will offer a clear advantage, as its ads will most likely be sold for a higher price than those of competing mobile ad vendors. You'll have to decide whether you want to get into the action by displaying ads in your applications at all. If you participate in the iAd program, you'll get 60% of the revenue generated, while Apple takes 40%.

Apple plans to roll out the first ads developed internally, working with a few select outside corporations that want to be the first to advertise on this platform. This could be for several reasons:

- Apple likely wants to ensure the quality of the first ads that are displayed with its new technology. Having tight control out of the gate will set the bar for future advertising and help Apple to ensure its success to an audience of millions.

- Apple has decided to utilize HTML5 technology in the development of iAd advertisements. In sharp contrast, nearly every ad agency around the world currently uses Adobe Flash for ad creation. If they're not familiar with mobile ad creation using HTML5, agencies will have to retool to use this new technology. Due to its greater level of experience with HTML5, Apple may be developing the first ads on this technology internally.

Can iAds help you to monetize your app? The answer is yes, but the same old questions remain for you as a developer. Can you make more money selling your app on the App Store, or are you better off creating a free app from which you can generate ad revenue? Some developers have found success by building free apps with ads. Their strategy is to make money by selling ad space on the app and then generating huge download numbers. And I mean huge downloads! You'll need tens of thousands of downloads to generate any sizable revenue from selling ads, regardless of the platform you choose to use.

Companies that want to advertise on this newly emerging mobile platform can utilize mobile ads and bid on ad placement, as with Google AdWords. This approach can be profitable for you as a developer if your apps achieve significant downloads and lots of users click through on ads displayed by your app. Some companies have achieved considerable success by developing a free app and posting ads in the app. You'll have to analyze what you think ad revenue will generate versus what a paid app will generate. This has been a subject of great debate among developers, some saying there is no revenue in ads for the developer and others saying that such revenue exists. Like other mobile ad platforms, Apple may tend to give the best ads to the best app developers. This means that the apps generating the most downloads will get the best ads. The best apps with the best ads will generate the most ad revenue for Apple—and the developer.

We all will have to watch how the iAd show unfolds. It's going to start with large advertisers utilizing the best apps on the App Store. Over time, we're likely to see more and more ads being created, which in turn will open more opportunities for developers to place ads in their apps. You'll still need to decide whether creating a free app is the right approach for you and then measure the success of downloads— as compared to selling your app for a price.

Summary

There are multiple strategies to monetize your iPhone/iPad apps. The first strategy is to create a single app that is completely free with ads. Your strategy is to make money by getting people to click through on the ads displayed with your app. Many users will download the app because it's free, and they don't mind seeing the ads come across their iPhone/iPad every 30 seconds.

The next strategy is to create an iPhone/iPad app that serves ads but also includes an option to upgrade the user to the paid version of your app. If you're going to serve up ads on your app, it makes sense to include an option for the user of your app to make an in-app purchase of your app. Some apps do this, and others don't. I recommend that you include this option.

The last strategy is to create a paid app along with a corresponding free app. This is the best strategy for most developers because you can build your following and attract customers. In the extremely competitive App Store, you must do everything you can to stand out from the crowd. Remember to only give away enough functionality in your free app to interest your user in getting the paid app.

15

The App Pricing Roller Coaster

The average price of an iPhone/iPad app at the time of this writing is $2.26, a drop from $3.13 a year ago. The average price of a game app is $1.04, a drop from $1.30 a year ago. The question that many developers often have after they've posted their apps to the App Store is when should they adjust their pricing? What if the pricing adjustment has no impact on sales? Then what?

As we have said in other chapters, your pricing should depend on what type of app you are selling. Even if you are selling a game app, you need to price it more or less in line with the prices for other games in that particular category. Figure 15.1 shows the range of game prices for May 2011 as reported by Distimo for iPad apps. The highest ranked game apps are between $0.99 and $2.99 on the App Store, as shown in Figure 15.2, also provided by Distimo.

Distimo Publication - May 2011 DISTIMO

HIGHEST RANKED PAID APPLICATIONS
APPLE APP STORE FOR IPAD - UNITED STATES - APRIL 2011

Rank	Application	Category	Price
1	Angry Birds Rio HD by Rovio Mobile Ltd.	Games-Arcade, Games-Puzzle	$2.99
2	GarageBand by Apple®	Music	$4.99
3	Pages by Apple®	Productivity	$9.99
4	Angry Birds HD by Chillingo Ltd	Games-Arcade, Games-Family	$4.99
5	Facebook for iPad with Chat - Pica HD by Dinh Ba Thanh	Social Networking	$1.99
6	Penultimate by Cocoa Box Design LLC	Productivity	$1.99
7	The Masters Tournament by Augusta National, Inc.	Sports	$1.99
8	MLB.com At Bat 11 for iPad by MLB.com	Sports	$14.99

Figure 15.1 Game prices on the iPad vary widely depending on the game type, as reported by Distomo Analytics.

Distimo Publication - May 2011 DISTIMO

HIGHEST RANKED PAID APPLICATIONS
APPLE APP STORE FOR IPHONE - UNITED STATES - APRIL 2011

Rank	Application	Category	Price
1	Angry Birds Rio by Rovio Mobile Ltd.	Games-Arcade, Games-Puzzle	$0.99
2	Angry Birds by Clickgamer.com	Games-Action, Games-Arcade	$0.99
3	Tiny Wings by Andreas Illiger	Games-Action, Games-Arcade	$0.99
4	Air Penguin by GAMEVIL Inc.	Games-Adventure, Games-Arcade	$0.99
5	Fruit Ninja by Halfbrick Studios	Games-Action, Games-Arcade	$0.99
6	Camera+ by tap tap tap	Photography	$0.99 - $1.99
7	Cut the Rope by Chillingo Ltd	Games-Family, Games-Puzzle	$0.99
8	Angry Birds Seasons by Rovio Mobile Ltd.	Games-Action, Games-Arcade	$0.99

Figure 15.2 Highest ranked apps, as reported by Distomo Analytics.

After you have selected a price for your app, you should maintain that price for the first few weeks to a month of sales to get a clear picture of how things are going. Avoid the app pricing roller coaster, where you are constantly raising and lowering the price of your app in an attempt to find the best price. The constant shifting of your price does not give you enough time to see how the price is working out. You will not be able to gather any concrete data unless you wait a few weeks to see how a pricing adjustment impacts sales.

This does not mean you can't do a promotion or two to experiment with temporary price drops, but you should plan to keep prices steady for a while to see how sales go and to get a read on the market.

Raising Your Price

Just like selling almost any software product, it's difficult to raise prices for an iPhone/iPad app. This is because the buyer becomes used to a certain price, and discovering what others have paid for the same or similar product is fairly easy to do in this connected Internet world. So even if you add additional features to your app, you will be hard pressed to raise the price of your current app, even if you are completely justified in doing so. Nongame apps can raise prices more easily than a game can because these types of apps are downloaded less frequently and are not as price-sensitive. Your existing customers will expect you to add more features as you create new versions, and your current customers will get your upgrades at no additional charge anyway.

 Note

Some will argue that new customers won't know if you raise your app's price, but this is not true. People who write reviews of your apps and those who follow your app—like your competition—will know that the price has been raised and may comment on that in reviews or blogs.

There is a way to approach a price increase that can work to your advantage, and that is to create a separate new app altogether with a higher price. It's the same app that you already have for sale, but it has additional features. You can call this version of your app "Pro" for Professional. If you don't already have a free app, you can take your current app and make it a free app with in app purchases. You can call this version App "Lite." Then you can introduce the new higher priced app to the market. The new price cannot be dramatically higher than the previous price of the old app, however—perhaps a dollar or two more. There is almost no other circumstance where you can easily raise the price of your app without negatively impacting sales.

Lowering Your Price

Lowering your app price is easier than raising it. When you first launch your app on the App Store, you need to give it some time to determine if the price is working. If after a few months you are not seeing steady sales or your sales are starting to drop off, you'll want to look at pricing as a possible option to adjust. Be sure to ask yourself the following questions before determining that you want to lower your price:

- Have sales for your app steadily declined over the past two to three weeks?

- Have you checked competitors' prices? Have they dropped their prices?

- Has the leader in your category of apps dropped its price?

- Have your reviews indicated that your price is too high? Figure 15.3 shows a sample of a couple of reviewer comments that indicate an app's price is too high.

- Has an external reviewer from a website indicated he or she likes your app, but it's priced too high?

Figure 15.3   Buyer's feedback will always tell you when the price of your app is too high.

 Note

> You can track price drops through email alerts or RSS feeds by going to sites such as www.148apps.com/price-drops or www.appshopper.com. You can search by categories, free or paid, and most popular with Appshopper.com. A sample of this site is shown in Figure 15.4.

If you have determined that a price cut is in order, then the next step is to determine how much to lower it. This depends on where your price is at. There are some apps that were priced at $49.99 and were dropped to $9.99. That's an astounding

80% drop! However, other apps are priced at $1.99 and are dropped to $0.99. That's obviously a 50% drop but can impact your revenue substantially.

Figure 15.4   Use a website to help you track price drops for apps in your category. This will help you gauge where prices are trending for your type of app.

 Note

Always factor the 30% cut that Apple takes in your pricing decisions. An app that was priced at $4.99 is giving the developer $3.49 after Apple takes its cut. If that same app is priced down to $0.99, Apple pays the developer $0.69 after the price drop. That's an 80% decline in any revenue you might have.

After you have dropped your price, carefully monitor daily sales activity. If your app is priced at the right level, you will see an increase in sales immediately. As you know, there is a great deal of price sensitivity for iPhone/iPad apps. This can be attributed to several things. First, buyers have already spent several hundred dollars on an iPhone and even more on an iPad. So in addition to their monthly phone/Internet bills, they are sensitive about spending more money on additional apps for their devices. Second, the global economy over the past several years has made budgets extremely tight for most typical buyers.

The last piece of advice for pricing is that you have to keep your overall brand strategy in mind. If you intend to build many apps and release them on a fairly frequent basis, your app prices will most likely be on the low end. If you keep prices low and update your app frequently, you can keep the life of your app moving along.

Temporary Price Drops

Temporary price drops do work and can drive traffic to your site. Carefully plan your price drop and make sure you publicize it through your product website and in the App Store verbiage. Follow these three easy steps when planning your temporary price drop:

1. Clearly state the promotion on your site and on the App Store.

2. Include a time frame (offer good until XX date).

3. Provide a clear "call to action" ("Buy Today to Receive Your App Discount!").

You can do a temporary price drop every other month or so depending on the type of app you are selling. If you do promotions too frequently, you'll condition your buyers to simply wait for the next "sale" and then buy the app. See Figure 15.5 for an example of an app that has gone on sale for a limited period of time and got some press out of its price drop.

Figure 15.5 A temporary price drop can breathe new life into the sales of your apps.

Value-Add Sales

As I have discussed in other chapters, some developers are offering their apps for free and then sell advertising as a means to generate revenue from within their apps. Another model that is growing in popularity among game developers is to give away their app for free but attempt to generate revenue through consistent add-on sales. One of the best examples of this happening is demonstrated by Tap Tap Revenge 3, the extremely popular music game. The developers used to charge for this game app, and they were actually quite successful with it as a paid app. But they have recognized that another way to monetize their app is to approach the business model like a razor and razor blades. The seller gives away the razor but sells the customer blades over and over again.

So the developers of Tap Tap Revenge decided to give away their app for free with 100 songs to get the player started. Then within the app, they sell the customer songs from iTunes that can be used with the game. This is a very good approach because it allows the app vendor to sell the customer products over and over again. It is likely that many games will adopt this model in the future if they are serious about gaining strong momentum and achieving repeat sales from the same app buyer. An example of this app is shown in Figure 15.6.

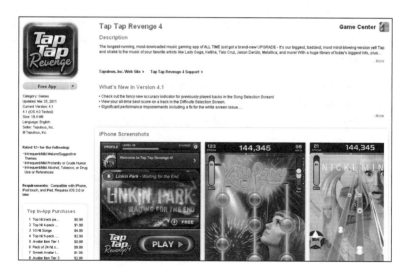

Figure 15.6 Tap Tap Revenge 4 is a free app, but they sell songs to the user and can gain repeat business from the same buyer.

Launch Your App Free for a Limited Time

A number of developers have found success building their brands and gaining exposure for their apps by giving them away for free for a time during the app's launch. You can post a note on the App Store for your app that's states "Free for a Limited Time" or specify that it will be free for a week.

You will see many more downloads while the app is free obviously. When you do change it to a paid app, you'll see the number of daily downloads drop off. Your goal of giving it away for free will help the app gain momentum and get more ratings and reviews.

Summary

If possible, always have a pricing strategy before you post your app for sale. Know exactly where you plan to set your app price. Be sure to research your entire category for app prices. If you are selling a game, be sure to look at the categories of games for your specific prices. Reports by research companies, like Distimo, can be helpful in providing the latest app pricing information.

Keep your price set for the first few weeks or month to allow you to gather sufficient data about how sales are trending. Product reviews will often reveal that your price is right or your price is too high. If your price is too high, then you can do a price drop. A price drop is a reason to issue a press release and make it known on your product website and on the App Store.

Temporary price drops should have an expiration date associated with them to help spur the buyer into action. If a promotion shows that your sales increase dramatically, you may want to consider permanently dropping your price.

16

App Promotions and Cross-Selling

Promotions, plain and simple, provide a marketing strategy to help your customers make buying decisions. Cross-selling is a technique used to sell more products to your existing customers. We're all somewhat familiar with promotions and cross-selling, even if only from buying products such as cars, furniture, clothing, and electronics. In fact, there aren't too many areas where promotions and cross-selling aren't used. Go out to dinner and you are cross-sold to buy an appetizer or soup or salad with your dinner. Even your neighborhood dentist uses these techniques to sell teeth-whitening and other add-on services.

Promotions and cross-selling are so popular because these techniques work! Most consumers like to get a deal on their purchases or win a prize. Many consumers, when prompted, will buy additional products that are complementary to their purchases. Buy a sofa, and you're asked if you want stain-guard protection.

Many will sign up. Buy a TV, and you're asked if you want the extended warranty, and many will sign up. Buy a new suit, and you're asked if you want to buy some shirts and ties to go with it.

In the app world, developers can also use promotions and cross-selling to help sell more iPhone/iPad apps and add-ons to their apps. In the highly competitive App Store, you need every edge you can find to help maximize your revenue. In this chapter, we first look at promotional marketing and how you can apply this technique to selling your iPhone/iPad apps. In the second half, we discuss cross-selling ideas that can help you increase your app sales. Just think about it: If you sell an app for $0.99, and you are able to sell an add-on for an additional $0.99, that's a 100% gain in your sales for that customer.

Promotional Marketing for iPhone/iPad Apps

Promotional marketing attempts to get people to make buying decisions. You can create various incentives to move someone to make an app purchase, including contests, half-off sales, and free downloads. Before you begin an app promotion, review the following questions:

- **What is your reason for the promotion?** Are you just trying to sell more apps, or are you trying to build a following? If you are doing a temporary app price reduction, for example, you are trying to bolster app sales. If you offer the app for free for a limited time, you are trying to build a following. Both are valid reasons for doing a promotion.

- **What is your promotion budget?** If you only have $500 to spend on a promotion, you will plan differently than if you have $5,000 to spend. Don't start a promotion until you know exactly what you can comfortably spend. I give you some ideas in a table at the end of this section on promotions you can execute depending on your budget.

- **How will you measure the success of your app promotion?** You'll need to set some objectives and then measure them. Perhaps you want to capture 500 email addresses and have 350 customers purchase the app through your promotion.

- **What type of promotion do you think will work best for your app?** If it's a creative type of app (photography and so on), you could sponsor a contest for the funniest photo and have an outside panel of judges choose the best use of your app, for example.

Note

Any contests or sweepstakes offered by a company that require a purchase to enter are illegal in the United States. Check your own country or state government agency to make sure your promotion is in compliance with all regulations and laws.

Here are just a few ideas you can employ to increase sales and/or awareness of your app. Keep in mind that you need to choose promotions that are appropriate for your particular app. Some apps may not lend themselves well to doing a contest but might do well if you mark the price to free for a temporary period of time. Other apps are more appropriate for cross-selling, which is discussed later in this chapter.

- **Contests**—Everyone enjoys winning a contest, even though it doesn't happen too often for most of us. Having a contest allows you to acquire new clients and create awareness about your app. For example, at the time of this writing, Threadless, Inc., a merchant that sells custom designed T-shirts and accessories, has created an iPhone app that allows users to create shirt designs. They are currently offering a contest to enter a design of an iPhone case. If you want to enter the contest, you have to download its (free) app so your creative work can be judged. A screen capture of the app page is shown in Figure 16.1. This is not a raffle or drawing; it is a contest where your entry is judged.

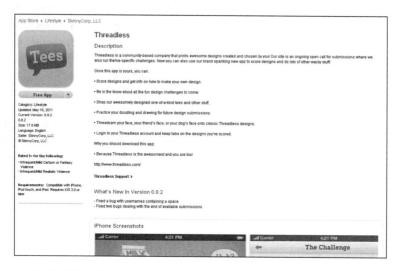

Figure 16.1 Threadless, Inc. has a contest to create the best design for an iPhone case using their app.

- **Periodic giveaways**—You can also create an ongoing promotion where you select certain entries of your app being used in creative situations. Buyers can go to your website and enter their names and email addresses with descriptions of how your app has helped them. You feature the best write-ups on your product home page each week. If a buyer's use of your app is selected, you can send him a T-shirt or small gift for being selected.

- **Half-off sales**—Half-off sales (or a third off or a quarter off, and so on) attract buyers' attention and help spur sales of your app. You can either put the verbiage on your App Store text announcing the sale, or you can post a temporary app icon with the sale announcement. The announcement can go for a few days or a few weeks, depending on the sales results. If you have strong results, you can extend the promotion by saying, "Back by popular demand" or something like that. If sales do not improve fairly quickly, you can set the price back to where it was before the promotion and look to other ideas.

✉ Note

Always set a timeframe for your promotion. You can say things such as, "Ends at midnight, June 15th" or "On Sale This Weekend ONLY." It helps your buyers make a purchase decision more quickly if they know the clock is ticking.

- **Free (for a time)**—Does giving away free samples work? Yes, most definitely! You don't want to give your app away forever, of course, but for a limited time. You can specify in your press release or announcement on the App Store and product website that the app is being given away for free during a limited time. If you have a well-written app, the free users will give you positive word of mouth, which should help your sales.

Table 16.1 provides some recommendations for promotions that you can employ at different budget levels. Again, consider whether your app is appropriate for a promotion such as a contest. These are just a few examples of what you can do in the way of promotions. The sky is the limit. Just make sure you stay within the laws of your state or country.

Table 16.1	App Promotions Vary Depending on Your Budget
Budget Amount	Promotional Recommendations
No money	Offer app free for a limited time or reduce app price for a limited time. See Chapter 15, "The App Pricing Roller Coaster," for more information on raising and lowering prices.
Up to $500.00	**Contest**: Give away an iPad (or an iPod touch) to the winner who makes the most creative use of your app. Contest should run for a couple of months at least. **Contest**: Give away five $100 gift card prizes to the best entries. The gift cards can be for iTunes or another gift card option. You can also change up the amounts, giving a first-place prize of $250, second place of $150, and third place of $100, or any other option. **Contest**: Give away savings bonds that have a maturity value of $250 or $500 for the person who makes the best use of your app, as judged by your expert panel. You can purchase bonds for less than face value, of course. **Giveaways:** Give app-development books, online app-development courses, T-shirts, mugs, caps, and so on to all app users who submit how they've used your app (while supplies last, of course).
Up to $1,000.00	All of the previous options or **Contest**: Macbook ($999) for the person judged to use your app most in the most creative or innovative way as judged by your outside panel.
More than $1,000.00	All of the previous options or **Contest**: Offer a trip to a certain destination, such as an Apple/iPhone/iPad event or to another locale. The trip requires the winner to be published on your website, along with a press release and description of how they used your app to create certain content or solve a problem.

 Note

Whenever you have a contest, you want to require entrants to provide their names, email addresses, and phone numbers to contact the winners. The contest will help you build your company's database of customers for future promotions and app sales.

Cross-Selling

Cross-selling is offering your buyer another product that is complementary to what you are already selling. In the app world, this is offering the app buyer another app or pack to whatever they have already bought. Amazon perfected this approach by displaying other items that similar buyers have purchased along with the item being displayed. This marketing approach has dramatically lifted sales for Amazon across its entire website.

Apple, perhaps taking a cue from Amazon, also includes the icons for similar apps purchased at the bottom of an App's page. The App Store is helping you out by displaying your app along with other apps when someone does a search on the App Store for a particular type of app. Depending on how many similar apps there are, your app could be displayed frequently when someone does a search for the same type of app. An example of a lifestyle app with other recommended/similar apps is shown in Figure 16.2.

Figure 16.2   The App Store helps your app get attention by posting similar apps at the bottom of an app's presentation page.

Every customer is a valuable asset for you. For certain apps, you can create additional add-on packs for your app. For example, Figure 16.3 shows a popular app that has a free and a paid version. In the free version, there is an announcement at the bottom of the app inviting you to purchase and download the paid app instantly through the iPhone/iPad. This is an example of up-selling the app buyer from a less expensive (free) app to the paid version of the app.

Another app that does this quite well is Freeverse's Flick Fishing. Within this app, you are given an option to purchase additional add-ons for other locations to fish. The add-on pack costs an additional $0.99. Because the game is so successful, the creators have the opportunity to capture additional revenue from the add-on pack through an impulse purchase.

A lot of times someone is playing the game and perhaps gets a little bored with the current fishing spots. So the opportunity to buy another set of fishing holes is quite ingenious. I don't know exactly how much revenue has been derived, but it could be 25% to 50% over the base sales. That's no small amount, especially given the app has sold more than 1.8 million copies. An example of the add-on pack advertisement is shown in Figure 16.4.

Figure 16.3   Words with Friends app invites the user to purchase the paid version to avoid further ads.

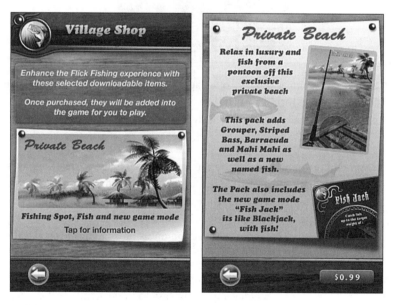

Figure 16.4   Flick Fishing's add-on pack allows buyers to make a purchase from within the app itself.

Another way to cross-sell is to provide a link to purchase other apps from within your own app. You always need to provide a screen with other apps to promote. An example of this approach using the app's menu screen to showcase other apps is shown in Figure 16.5. Some developers have formed consortiums to help each other sell the others' apps. You may also be able to work out revenue-sharing agreements where you promote other developer's apps from within your own app.

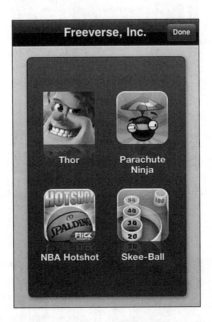

Figure 16.5 This app also shows other apps from the same brand that the buyers can purchase directly from their iPhones/iPads. Never skip an opportunity to showcase your other products, especially when you already have a buyer running one of your apps.

This is something you would have to arrange between fellow developers, as Apple does not provide a means to handle this type of transaction from the App Store payment perspective. However, there are other tracking means that could be employed to track where the purchase originated from. See Chapter 17, "Using iPhone/iPad Analytics," for more information on using analytics to track sales of your apps.

Although not common yet, the iPhone/iPad has made this kind of in-app cross-selling incredibly easy for the developer and easy to understand for the consumer. Don't mistake cross-selling for other forms of advertising on your app, though. You are not posting overt advertisements on your app. You simply create a menu option on your app that allows the consumer to view and purchase other apps from your company. You are not bombarding them with ads at all.

Anywhere that you can post text about your app, you should be thinking about cross-selling opportunities. In other words, you have an opportunity to cross-sell with your product website, the App Store, and the iPhone/iPad. The biggest factors in influencing the success of the cross-sell will be price and reputation. If you are selling an app for $3.99, consider selling the add-on pack for $0.99. It's an easy decision to spend another dollar when they've already spent $3.99.

If your app or brand has established a good reputation, it will also be easier to cross-sell a buyer on additional functionality or add-ons. Always be thinking about how you can market to your existing customer. It's far easier to sell to them than to get a new customer. Here are some other ideas to consider as you cross-sell your app:

- **Cross-sell on your product website and within the App Store**—Use some space on the App Store text to mention your other apps. At the bottom of your verbiage, you can put a note for buyers to check out your other apps as well. Be sure to do the same thing on your website. For each product displayed, be sure to show other app icons to the right or left of the screen displaying the other apps you have for sale.

  The App Store also helps you out with cross-selling by showcasing other apps you have for sale on the lower-left side of your app's display. This is a big advantage that the App Store provides to help you cross-sell or up-sell your customers other apps you have written.

  An example of the App Store showcasing a paid app is shown in Figure 16.6, along with the other apps this same company/developer has for sale. Keep in mind that if a buyer clicks on a paid app, and a free app is also offered from the same company/developer, the free app is also shown at the bottom of the page.

- **Cross-sell to build your brand**—If you are looking for way to build your brand, you can always sell other items on your website such as mugs, caps, or T-shirts with your company's logo or app icon. Are you going to make tons of money doing this? No! But you will help build a following for your apps and establish your brand more firmly with your buyers and site visitors.

Up-Selling

The definition of up-selling is moving someone from a less expensive product to a more expensive one. Auto dealers will advertise a less expensive car to get people to visit their showrooms. When buyers are at the dealer, the dealer shows them multiple models of cars, knowing that the chances of them buying the original car that brought them in are slim.

Figure 16.6   An app is displayed on the main screen while other apps are shown below as additional options for the buyer.

The most common example of up-selling with an iPhone/iPad app is when a user downloads a free app and then converts to the same paid app as mentioned earlier. Your marketing messaging must invite the user to upgrade to your paid app. Do not assume that just because you have a free version of your app that customers will instinctively upgrade to the paid version. They need to be prompted, prodded, coerced, coached, cajoled, and invited to move over to the paid app. You can do this in the following ways:

- Prompt them within a menu screen of your free app.

- Invite them to upgrade at the bottom or top of your free app.

- Tell them that they will no longer have ads if they buy the paid app.

- Explain to them how many more features they will get with the paid app.

- Prompt them periodically within the free app to give the paid app a try.

Note

Do not annoy the customers by bombarding them constantly with invitations to buy your paid app. Just remember to push your paid app where appropriate in the menu page, with an icon they can click to get more information, or at the bottom of the first screen of the free app.

Summary

Promotions and cross-selling should be a part of your overall app marketing plan. You can't afford not to explore these approaches when the competition for apps is so strong. Promotions, when done right, can help you increase your profits and raise your brand awareness. Another benefit of doing promotions is that they can be repeated multiple times, especially if you find success with one type of promotion over another.

Contests can be done as promotions, even on a limited budget. You can sponsor a contest where users of your app demonstrate how they have used your app in the most creative way. You can give away cash prizes, hardware, software, T-shirts, hats, mugs, and other items. Contests will drive awareness and downloads for your app.

Cross-selling and up-selling are effective marketing approaches. You can cross-sell add-on packs for your apps or subscriptions that generate additional or recurring revenue for you. Always attempt to up-sell your buyer from a free version of your app to the paid version. Do not assume that if you have a free app that your user will automatically move to a paid app. They must be invited to do so.

17

Using iPhone/iPad Analytics

Don't let the word "analytics" scare you off. From an iPhone/iPad marketing perspective, being able to gather information about how your buyers are using your apps is extremely helpful in making adjustments to your marketing plan. Marketing is a dynamic activity. You'll find that some strategies work better to market your app than others. Analytics data helps you make better decisions about what's working for your particular circumstances and what's not. App Analytics is simply a small block of code available from the analytics provider that you insert into your iPhone/iPad application and enables you to collect information about user actions. The information is gathered periodically on the local smartphone, and then it's transmitted to the company who has licensed the code to you. You can then view the results for your individual app or in aggregate for multiple similar apps on the analytics website. If a connection on the smartphone is not available at the time of transmission, the analytics software will try again when a connection is established.

Analytics data enables you to make better marketing decisions because you know who is using your app, when they are using it, and how frequently it gets opened. You can develop more targeted ad campaigns, focus on refining specific features, or identify certain user groups for your app. As long as the information you are gathering is not intrusive to the end user and you are not violating any privacy laws, you'll find this type of data to give you a competitive edge you need in the app world.

 Note

Apps that have access to location data must have the user's consent. The user must opt in for location tracking. Clearly explain this in your terms of service of your app. See the privacy section at the end of this chapter for more information about protecting privacy and complying with the law.

Analytics Components

Analytics can provide you scores of different views. Some of the more popular data points are listed here. Keep in mind that analytics code must be inserted into your iPhone/iPad app prior to submitting your app for review. Each time you wish to change what you're tracking in the app, resubmitting your app to Apple for review will be required.

There are also many custom data points that you can configure into your app using analytics. You can get very creative as far as the type of data you want to track within your app because the code is flexible and customizable.

Track Your App's Sales

From a pricing perspective, analytics can help you assess how your app is being used in the market. For nongame apps, you can measure the frequency of use for your app over time and see if it makes sense to drop your price or give your app away for free and pursue an ad revenue model. Analytics are another data point to help you make a better pricing decision.

Track Your App's Location

Another helpful feature of most analytics software is that you can track your app's use by location. This requires the user to "opt in" to allow this data to be tracked and does not give a complete picture of usage because not all users will permit it. But it will give you a general idea of where your app is being used in different parts of the world. This can help you make more informed advertising and product decisions. For example, if you see that your app is doing really well in the United Kingdom, you can dig a little deeper to discover why that's the case. You may want to look at making adjustments to your app.

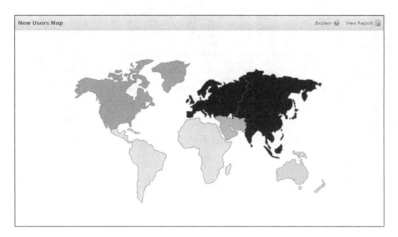

Figure 17.1   Location map from the Flurry Analytics software for the iPhone/iPad.

If you are able to determine where your app is being run and which features are being used, you can tailor your advertising efforts either to that geography or to other geographies that might respond in similar fashion to the same type of marketing.

Track Your App's Usage

A developer can also discover how many times an app is opened during the day. You can identify if your app is used frequently such as several times a day, or infrequently, such as once a week or once a month. For example, a game app being used several times a day is a good sign that it has the winning formula that everyone's looking for. A game that is downloaded and then never used is a sure indication that it doesn't have the staying power needed to become a hit. It may cause you, as a developer, to make adjustments to improve the app to drive future success.

The graph in Figure 17.2 shows how many new users have downloaded the app on a weekly basis. Figure 17.3 shows the average amount of time the app is being used. Both of these data points provide you with very useful information.

Tracking average time used for you app can also help you determine if your app is going to have longevity in the market. If you feel that the average time used on your app should be 20 minutes, and you're seeing it used only 7–10, you can do further research to figure out why this is happening. It could be an indication that your app is not easily understood or someone is getting bored with it too quickly. Both cases are cause for concern and can be addressed when you have this information. Without analytics, you'll never really know why someone is abandoning your app.

Detailed View

Explain Download CSV

Zoom: days | weeks | months

Date	New Users	% of New Users
Jul 04	1,549	2.1%
Jun 27	6,926	9.2%
Jun 20	7,799	10.3%
Jun 13	9,006	11.9%
Jun 06	10,112	13.4%
May 30	11,573	15.3%
May 23	13,507	17.9%
May 16	14,897	19.8%
May 09	12	<0.1%
May 02	3	<0.1%
Apr 25	3	<0.1%
Apr 18	8	<0.1%
Apr 11	2	<0.1%
Apr 04	0	0.0%
Mar 28	2	<0.1%
Mar 21	1	<0.1%
Mar 14	0	0.0%
Mar 07	4	<0.1%

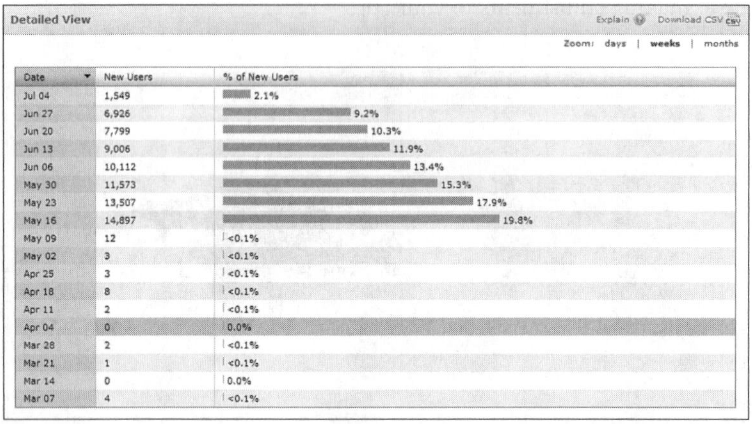

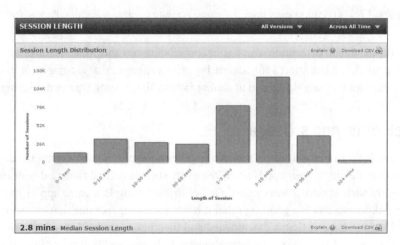

Figure 17.2 Sample graph from the Flurry Analytics software for the iPhone/iPad.

Figure 17.3 Sample analytics from the Flurry Analytics software for the iPhone/iPad.

Analytics help you track your sales and the number of users for each app. You can then look at how frequently your app is being used and which features are getting the most use. This can be a big benefit for a game developer who wants to know which features are being used the most and which are used the least. For example, you may discover that users are quitting your app during a particularly difficult part of your game. With this information, you could offer them an in-app purchase at this point in your game that will give them more ammo or "power" to get over the hurdle. Of course, you may decide to make the game a little easier at certain points.

This information can inform future development decisions and help determine the focus for subsequent revisions. Some features that don't get much use could be eliminated altogether or replaced with new features. Other features that get used somewhat more frequently could be enhanced. You are essentially gathering product-use data that you're not going to get any other way.

Track Specific App Events

Events are almost anything that occurs during the operation of your app. Events can be tracked for frequency, duration, or a combination of factors. A developer can track a feature being used, a button being pressed, or the time to complete a task. If you are selling an educational app, you might want to get some information on how long it takes typical users to complete an exercise or how long it takes them to take a quiz.

Developers can also gather valuable information on how long a certain process or task takes users. For example, an app that handles your finances might track how long it takes typical users to balance their checkbooks. Understanding this information allows developers to modify their code, focusing on improving the most-used features.

Event tracking is like having a user panel give you feedback about your app. Rather than a live user panel reviewing your app and providing input, you are gathering the data electronically. Precision apps such as games benefit from gathering analytic data on how the game is being used. Levels of play can be analyzed to see if the player is moving through the game in a normal manner or if some adjustments need to be made. You want your game to be more challenging at each level but not so much that it's impossible to win. Analytics help you gather crucial data to make just the right adjustments for a game.

A byproduct of installing analytics is that you will be able to tell generally when your app is being reviewed by Apple. This assumes that you don't have a lot of people using the app while it's being approved. When Apple gives you a message that your app is in review, you can then watch for daily activity of your app. If nobody else is using your app during that time period, you can tell exactly when Apple reviewers are looking at and approving your app.

Measure App Interface Patterns

Developers can also use analytics data to improve and test user interfaces for their iPhone/iPad apps. For example, you can measure how many times a certain menu page is opened or how many times a particular button is pressed. This data gives you a picture of how your app's interface is being used. Perhaps you find that your user is going to a particular screen out of sequence, contrary to what you have programmed. This could prompt you to make changes to the screen flow of your app.

Utilizing analytics also allows you to claim, rightfully, that you are in touch with your customers and willing to listen to their product suggestions. Other than reviews, which are often limited in the information they provide, this is one of the best ways to gather accurate product use data without employing a costly user panel to review and test the product.

Utilize Paid Ad Campaigns

Another benefit of installing analytics is that you can participate in the analytics vendor's paid install or ad programs to help you drive downloads. Flurry's App Circle, for example, provides the following benefits:

- Make money each time your app is recommended and sold from within another app.

- Make money each time another application is recommended and sold from within *your* app.

- Open up a new revenue stream from within your app without disrupting your user experience.

- Set up with no hassles and start solving application discovery challenges today.

Mobclix offers an analytics driven ad exchange. Through their program, you make your app available for displaying ads. You will have access to unlimited ad networks as these networks bid for your inventory. The Mobclix auction algorithms automatically select the highest paying ads for your app across multiple ad networks. They guarantee 100% fill rates.

Top Analytics Vendors

There are many iPhone/iPad analytics vendors with quality products. For brevity, here are a few of the more popular vendors. These vendors offer free analytics to the developer community; some feature enhancements can be purchased.

Flurry

Flurry and Pinch Media merged about a year and a half ago. The new company is simply known as Flurry. Both companies provided analytics software for the iPhone/iPad with some similar and some differing features. They merged the feature set together and delivered enhancements to the combined solution as they have stated in the FAQs of their press release:

"While Flurry and Pinch Media analytics services shares many similarities in terms of what is tracked, there are meaningful differences between each service. We are currently evaluating the feature set of each standalone service, and will be combining them into a 'super set' of features for all to use in the new, unified service. So whether customers come from the Pinch side or the Flurry side, they will each have access to new features. For example, Flurry uniquely provides support for other platforms like Android as well as a unique click-stream tracking feature called 'User Paths.' Pinch Media offers unique features including jailbroken phone detection and the ability to evaluate data by cohorts vs. absolute date. In addition to this, the new, unified Flurry service will add more new features, delivering the largest set of relevant features requested by our customer base."

Flurry Analytics Features

Cost: Analytics are free to developers; other optional (cost) solutions are coming.

Benefits:

- Increase revenue by satisfying users and increasing retention rates
- Save time and money, focusing on features users care about most
- Improve decisions—know exactly how, where, when, and by whom an application is used
- Increase coverage by identifying problem handsets

A screen with some of the dashboard analytics and graphs that Flurry provides is shown in Figures 17.4. and 17.5 shows an example of the active users analytics screen.

Mobclix

Mobclix is a mobile application platform that, as part of its solution, delivers analytics data for the iPhone/iPad along with its ad network. Mobclix is one of the largest mobile ad exchange networks and gives developers a sound technology if they decide to pursue an ad-generated business model.

Figure 17.4   Sample analytics dashboard from the Flurry Analytics software for the iPhone/iPad.

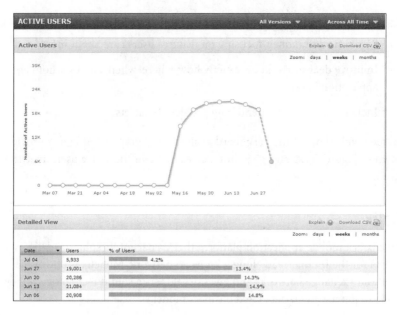

Figure 17.5   Sample analytics from Flurry's analytics software for the iPhone/iPad shows active users.

Mobclix Analytics Features

Cost: Analytics are free to developers.

Benefits:

- Determine how much time someone spends in your app

- Determine whether users are on WiFi or carrier

- Determine whether users are using an iPhone or an iPod touch and identify the version

- Track the health of your app

- Find out how often the app fails

- Full event tracking

- Pop-up request to gather data, additional opt-out button

- Get feedback directly from your users with comment plug-ins

Figure 17.6 shows a section of the Mobclix website that allows you to download their software development kit (SDK) and implement their analytics along with their ad-revenue software. The SDK installs in under 15 minutes, so it's quite easy for any developer to implement and realize its benefits.

Figure 17.6   Mobclix Analytics can be installed into your app with a simple download of their SDK.

Analytics and Privacy

Although mobile analytics offer a great mechanism for gathering valuable user data, you do have to be aware of privacy laws and make sure you follow all Apple guidelines when gathering data. Apple does require that a user agrees before certain information is gathered and transmitted by your app. Always explain in your app what data you will be gathering and how you intend to use the data.

You can explain this information in a Terms of Service (TOS) document, which should be displayed within your app in English. The user should be required to read and accept the terms of service by checking a box or clicking OK. Always state your intent for gathering such information and how it will be used.

Managing a User's Privacy Expectations

Although some users may be concerned about their privacy, all data is gathered anonymously. On Flurry's own website, they state that when Flurry is installed within an application, the following information is sent back on each application run:

- A hardware identifier not connectable to any personal information
- The model of your phone (3G, 3GS, and so on) and operating system (2.2, 3.0, 3.0.1, and so on)
- The application's name and version
- The result of a check to see if the device has been jailbroken
- The result of a check to see if the application has been stolen and the developer hasn't been paid
- The length of time the application was run
- If the user explicitly agrees to share it, the user's location
- If the application uses Facebook Connect, the gender and age of the user

None of this information can identify any individual. No names, phone numbers, emails, or anything else considered personally identifiable information is ever collected. When it arrives at the servers, the information sent from applications is quickly converted to aggregated reports—unprocessed data is processed as quickly as possible. The aggregated reports show counts and averages, not anything user-specific. For instance, a developer can see the following information:

- The number of distinct users who've accessed the application
- The average length of time the application was used
- The percentage of phones using each operating system

- The percentage of each model of phone (3G, 3GS, and so on)

- A breakdown of user locations by country, state, and major metropolitan area (for example, 20,000 in USA, 700 in New York state, 500 in New York City)

- The percentage of users of each gender

- The percentage of users by "age bucket" (21–29, 30–39, and so on)

Summary

Implementing the code for analytics is not difficult, does not cause latency in your app, and is free for the developer. Analytics providers show aggregate data and never divulge any personal IDs or other information about a specific user. However, be sure to inform your users that you are using analytics and seek their consent before transmitting data.

Developers can benefit significantly from using analytics software in their apps; it can undoubtedly help you produce a better app for your customer, make adjustments to marketing and pricing, and plan for future enhancements. I believe all apps are good candidates for using analytics. The benefits far outweigh a little extra time and effort to insert analytics.

IV

Implement a Marketing Plan/Launch Your App

18 Why Have a Marketing Plan? 249

19 Components of an App Marketing Plan 257

20 Marketing Essentials and the Right Mix 269

21 25 Essential iPhone/iPad Marketing Activities 275

22 Implementing Your Plan 287

23 iPhone/iPad Apps for Corporate Marketing 295

18

Why Have a Marketing Plan?

Some app developers not as familiar with marketing may ask why anyone should spend time developing a marketing plan. The thought of creating a plan conjures up ideas that a marketing plan must be huge, painful, and lengthy. This is simply not true. A marketing plan needs to be long enough to define a strategy and the components that will give your app a good chance of sales success. It does not need to be binders full of lengthy information. In Chapter 19, "Components of an App Marketing Plan," we discuss the components you need. Don't worry about the length of your plan. Rather, make sure that your plan defines how you are going to achieve success selling your app.

Some developers can cite all kinds of examples of successful apps that don't or didn't have any kind of marketing plan. This is true, but they are the standout apps that got a lucky break when the App Store was in its infancy.

A marketing plan is going to improve your chances of getting that lucky break. Remember what Thomas Jefferson said about being lucky? "I find that the harder I work the more luck I seem to have."

The first point to understand about a marketing plan is that there is a difference between a marketing strategy and a marketing plan. A marketing strategy can be defined as a summary of your company's apps and their position as they relate to your competition. For example, if you are a developer of game apps, you could define your marketing strategy as geared to a male, teenage audience in the category of racing games. Marketing plans are the specific actions you intend to take to meet the goals of your marketing strategy. Your marketing plan might include releasing a new racing game app every three months so that you have four apps within the first year of business.

Another marketing strategy could consist of someone developing the best financial iPhone/iPad app on the market in your category on the App Store. The marketing plan then spells out how you intend to make the strategy a reality, such as partnering with a major bank or other financial institution to distribute the app to realize thousands of downloads.

A good marketing plan will help you to improve your odds against more experienced competitors on the App Store (EA and Sega come to mind) as well as newly emerging ones. The marketing plan enables you to recognize and take action on any trends that other app developers may have overlooked and to develop and expand your own select group of loyal customers now and into the future.

The plan also means that you have carefully considered how to produce an app that is innovative, unique, and marketable, improving your chances of stable sales and profits and providing incentive for customers to stick with you for the next release or new app. So following the popular Top 10 List format, here are the top 10 reasons you should create a marketing plan along with some explanation for each item.

Top 10 Reasons Why You Should Have an App Marketing Plan

1. Brings your target market into focus

2. Allocates scarce marketing funds

3. Measures your progress

4. Provides a roadmap for growth

5. Helps you obtain funding

6. Coordinates your app launches

7. Sets realistic sales targets

8. Evaluates your app against competitors

9. Sets prices and defines promotions

10. Helps define a strong value proposition

Brings Your Target Market into Focus

Having a marketing plan helps you focus on your target market and identify any gaps in the market that could provide new or unique opportunities for you. Many developers have ideas for an apps in their heads, and they think they've got it all figured out without taking any time to assess their markets. Does the app idea in your head address a few thousand people, or does it address hundreds of thousands? Is the idea going to appeal only to a small group of hobbyists, or can the idea be global? "Just build an app, and they will come" is often what developers think. A marketing plan will cause you to carefully outline your target market and help you make the decision whether to proceed with your idea.

Without a marketing plan, your app may turn out entirely different from where it started. This could be okay if you produce a better app, but in most cases the app ends up being somewhat disjointed and unfocused without a plan. Your customers will immediately recognize this, and the reviews will not be favorable. Start out with a clear idea of who you are developing the app for and what benefits they will gain from using it. Having a written record of this will help you gain a competitive advantage in the app market.

Allocates Scarce Marketing Funds

A marketing plan helps you identify the most cost-effective ways of reaching your target audience and performing the functions needed to reach that audience. For example, banner ads might work well to advertise your app after you have done some research on how they work and what sites might be the best to take your message to the right audience.

You also save money by cutting out unnecessary expenses and avoiding marketing ideas that aren't going to yield you any results. So many developers approach marketing with a scattered approach, trying one thing and then another without too much success. They end up wasting a lot of money on programs that could have been avoided if they had spent a little time on a marketing plan. A good plan allocates funds appropriate for your budget and will also keep your activities and budgets on track.

Measures Your Progress

You've heard the saying, "You can't track what you can't measure." To see results from your marketing efforts, you have to be able to measure your progress. Now, some marketing efforts are more difficult to measure than others. You can measure how many people open emails or how many click through to your website based on a particular campaign. But measuring brand awareness is a lot more difficult. You know you've made progress with brand awareness when bloggers are talking about your apps and you're seeing multiple reviews come through.

A marketing plan can help you track your progress from initial development of your app through product launch along with the various marketing campaigns that you employ to sell your iPhone/iPad app. Much of the measurement aspect of a marketing plan will include budgets. You'll set a budget for your app development costs, and you'll set budgets for marketing campaigns. You should measure the amount you spend on a campaign and the number of sales derived from that campaign. Although you won't be able to pinpoint exact sales, your campaigns should yield a noticeable uptick on app sales. If you don't see that uptick in sales after implementing an ad campaign, email campaign, promotional campaign, or other campaign, then you need to make adjustments to your marketing activities to create better results.

Provides a Roadmap for Growth

If you intend to create multiple apps and build a brand, having a marketing plan is a must. With a marketing plan you can create a roadmap (timeline) for when you plan to release each app into the App Store. Your plan can include a launch calendar, and you can strategically launch each app in succession. Without a calendar to track all your development and launch activities, you will experience confusion building your brand.

A number of companies that provide serial types of apps benefit by having a plan. A serial app could be an app that identifies other apps for purchase on the App Store. For example, you develop an app that identifies the latest medical apps and gives you that list inside of that app. You may build an app that aggregates the best finance apps into your app. Your marketing plan will also define marketing approaches that you want to take with each app that is released. Your strategy for your first app may be to release it as a free app to gain brand awareness and followers. The next app you release may be a paid app that is a follow on to the free app. Your entire strategy can be outlined in your marketing plan.

Helps You Obtain Funding

Perhaps you have not given much thought to funding your app endeavors, but there are some developers who want to build a formidable company around selling apps on the App Store and on other mobile phone platforms. One of the key requirements for any businessperson seeking funding is developing a solid business plan, which includes a marketing plan. A marketing plan is going to help your investors understand the type of apps you are going to develop, who your competitors are, and how you intend to bring your app to market.

The marketing plan provides your outside financiers with the confidence that you know your market and that you know how to achieve your objectives. The key to obtaining funding is demonstrating that you have a solid market for your apps and that you have a clearly defined strategy to meet your sales goals. Having a great idea for an app will not be enough. You'll have to demonstrate that you have the experience and vision to make your apps successful in a very competitive market.

Coordinates Your App Launches

A marketing plan helps you keep track of all the pieces of your product launch. From your marketing calendar you can track the following:

- The date your app was submitted for review

- The date (approximately) that your app will be released

- Reviewers and bloggers you have contacted to review your app

- The date(s) for your press release(s)

- Articles you have lined up with magazines, newspapers, and other outlets

- Promotions you have planned to launch your app

With your plan, you can coordinate the timing of a press release to coincide roughly with the release and posting of your app on the App Store. If you have a press release that has been correctly written with the right key words and a few reviews in place, you will see a strong pick-up in the news about your app, and your website will see a bump in traffic, which will lead to stronger initial sales.

Sets Realistic Sales Targets

A marketing plan helps you set realistic sales goals. After you have done a thorough analysis of the scope of your market and your competitors, you are in a position to do more accurate sales forecasting based on your intended promotions. You need to be able to visualize your sales goal in an easy-to-track spreadsheet. Apple provides daily, weekly, and monthly sales reports for you to track your progress. These reports can be easily downloaded into an Excel spreadsheet for viewing.

There are other companies out there that provide tracking services if you want to get very detailed metrics on sales progress for multiple apps. One of the companies is Tap Metrics (www.tapmetrics.com). It provides analytics and sales trend graphs and information. It charges a monthly fee for its services, but it also offers a free version of its tool (TapMini), which can be downloaded from the home page. TapMini automatically downloads and organizes your sales reports from iTunes Connect, shows you maps of where sales are occurring, and updates you on user comments and blog posts or twitter comments about your app. You don't need a TapMetrics account to use it, just your iTunes Connect login and Mac OS X10.5 or 10.6. You can use the free version to track up to three apps at no charge. The Tap Metrics home page is shown in Figure 18.1.

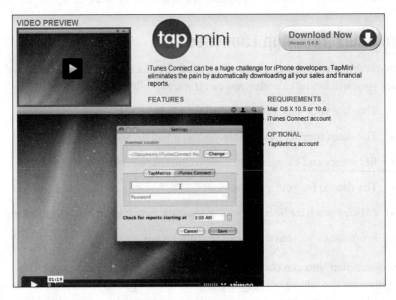

Figure 18.1 TapMini from Tap Metrics allows you to track your App Store sales—free up to three apps.

Evaluates Your App Against Competitors

Your marketing plan should have a section with information on key competitors to your app. Competitive information is crucial to develop a better app and to remain competitive in your category. If you have your competitors clearly in focus with a marketing plan, you're more likely to stay up-to-date on when they release updates and what new features they have added to their apps.

There a number of websites you can utilize to monitor when new apps are released into a category where you have an app. These websites include App Figures (www. appfigures.com), which allows you to create your own app list. You won't be able to track competitor's downloads, but you can see rankings for all apps in any category. This is a great tool for automating (to some degree) the tracking of your competitors. The home page of this website is shown in Figure 18.2.

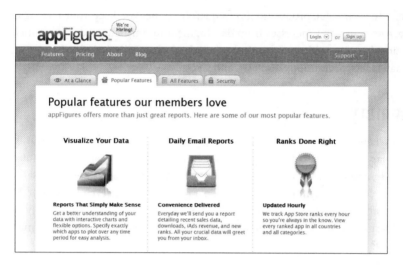

Figure 18.2   App Figures allows you to track new apps and changes, reviews, and so on to existing apps on the App Store

Sets Prices and Defines Promotions

Pricing is a big part of marketing an iPhone/iPad app, and you'll want to spend some time writing down some detailed notes about how you arrived at your price and what you intend to do over time when making adjustments to your app pricing. Your pricing information should include competitor's pricing and other notes as to why you believe your app will sell for a certain price.

Your marketing plan should also include promotions that you intend to have during the next 12 months. You may offer a launch special, half off to the first 500 customers or for a limited amount of time. You may want to offer a contest announcing your app and give away an iPad to the person who wins your contest. Apple has just included guidelines for contests, which can be found in your contract information on iTunes Connect.

Helps Define a Strong Value Proposition

Your marketing plan should include a definition of your app's value proposition or key values. Remember this information is what you use to develop your App Store and website copy and describes what your app does and why it's valuable to the customer. A strong value proposition takes some time and effort to develop. You want to make sure you have this written down as a key point in your marketing plan.

Refer to your value proposition(s) frequently so that you keep your messaging on track as your app progresses from development to finished product to launch. Use your value propositions to support your advertising. This includes banner ads, email blasts, promotions, contests, and so on.

Summary

A marketing plan is essential to growing your iPhone/iPad app business. A marketing plan forces you to carefully consider how to produce an app that is innovative, unique, and marketable. This is going to improve your chances of stable sales and profits considerably. Take the time to do a marketing plan, even if it's brief. You may discover after doing some research that the app you intended to build may not be the best investment of your time and money. Who doesn't want to save time and money?

A good marketing plan is your blueprint for action. Build your marketing plan with an end goal in mind to develop your brand and grow app sales. Follow the steps in your plan much like a carpenter follows a set of house plans when building a home. A marketing plan is a more successful route to gaining App Store success than just trying to wing it without any real idea of how you intend to achieve success.

19

Components of an App Marketing Plan

A marketing plan is your personal roadmap of how you intend to make your app produce a profit after it's released on the App Store. An iPhone/iPad app marketing plan has some basic components that you should attempt to include in your plan. Not all of these components, however, will apply to your plan based on the type of iPhone/iPad app you are developing. A game app, for example, may have fewer components to its plan than a personal finance app.

Your marketing plan can be simple or extensive depending on your audience (for example, venture funding, angel investors, and so on), If the audience is only you (solo developer), then the plan can be quite simple, a couple of pages perhaps. If you are a small firm with a few employees or maybe you have a few investors, then you need to create a more comprehensive marketing plan. All marketing plans should have the basics, including the sections described in this chapter. These sections should be created in Word and printed so that they can easily be reviewed by your team.

Note

A marketing plan is a strategic summary that demonstrates your understanding of your product, audience, message, and value. A marketing plan can be an indicator of how successful your app will be when launched to the App Store.

Table 19.1 shows the key components of an app marketing plan. The length of the plan is not important. The information covered in the plan is what counts. After reviewing the table, this chapter discusses each component in more detail.

Table 19.1   Typical iPhone/iPad App Marketing Plan Components

App Marketing Plan Component	Description (Possible Ideas)
Marketing Goals & Objectives	Overall objective for your app; build a brand.
Sales Objectives	Gain market share; achieve huge downloads?
Profit Objectives	Break even in 1 month and so on, generate $X in the first 3 mos. and so on.
Pricing Objectives	Price high; reduce price later?
Product Objectives	Create game app based on PC version.
Market Analysis	How large is my market?
Demographics	Who is my market? Teens? Elderly?
Competition	Who are my top three competitors in this app category?
Consumer Analysis	How much does a typical consumer spend on this type of app? How often do they buy?
SWOT Analysis	What are the strengths, weaknesses, opportunities, and threats to building such an app?
App Functionality	What special features will my app have that will blow away the competition?
Promotions	What are the promotions I intend to use to market my app, generate awareness, and increase sales?
Pricing	What is my pricing strategy?
Financials	How much will this app cost to develop and market? What are the dangers to developing this app? What if development time takes longer? Include key metrics here, such as breakeven charts, revenue projections, and so on.
Calendar	What are my development, launch, and promotion timelines?

Note

The sample plan shows tables and graphics that will help you visualize many of financial areas that are discussed in this chapter.

To see a nice sample marketing plan for iPhone/iPad apps, go to http:/ /www.morebusiness.com/templates_worksheets/bplans/printpre.brc.

Marketing Goals and Objectives

To introduce your marketing plan, provide a brief "mission statement" of your business. A mission statement is simple but clearly communicates your goals to your customers and potential customers. For example, "Develop the best productivity app for pharmaceutical sales reps" or "Develop the most innovative air combat game ever created." After you have a written mission statement, you can move on to determining your objectives for product, sales, profit, and pricing.

Product Objectives

In this section of your marketing plan you can list the goals you have for this app from a product perspective:

- Much like what you would be doing for your pricing objectives, focus on the wants, needs, and perceptions of your app consumers.

- Show how you will attract more buyers of your app. Determine the decision criteria of customer preference toward your app like price, or number of features, and so on.

- Indicate the goals you may have for resolving customer complaints with your app or fixing bugs.

Your iPhone/iPad App Sales Objectives

- Compare your chances for future sales with either past performance or a general estimate of new sales through "guesstimates," as was covered in Part III, "Pricing Your iPhone/iPad App." You'll never get it exact, but you should have a forecast of potential revenue.

- Identify industry-wide challenges and create strategies to overcome them. This also demonstrates that you have the necessary foresight to allow you to recognize future problems. For example, the fact that so many apps are priced at $0.99 is an industry-wide problem. What can you do to overcome this low price point?

- Create a goal for how many downloads you would like to achieve on a daily basis. One hundred? Five hundred? One thousand per day? Write down this goal.

Profit Objectives

- Include your predictions for profit for each of the apps you have written for the next year. Relate this profit assumption based on the estimated costs to develop your iPhone app.

- Indicate how you will reinvest some of your profit margin in specific areas of app development, including future releases and marketing activities you might employ.

Pricing Objectives

- Focus on the weaknesses of your competitors by offering better quality at a competitive price. Remember what your own attitudes are toward apps you are familiar with. Remember how you react to low or high prices for poor or marginal quality apps.

- Justifying your prices for your app while thinking like a customer will give you an advantage. Keep in mind that it's easier to come down in price than go up.

- Survey a sampling of your potential customer group and ask them directly how they feel about competitor's apps and any areas for improvement.

Market Analysis

After completing the objectives section of your plan, create a section for market analysis. This is where you spend some time identifying your market, your competitors, and your chances for success. Going through this exercise helps you evaluate from a more analytical perspective how successful your app might be in the real world.

- Examine whether your app has the potential for growth. Be honest with yourself.

- If the market for your app is declining, identify the problems that exist and change the ones you can. Show how you can adapt to changes that you may not control. Think of the iShoot example in which the author offered a free "Lite" version of his game and set his sales on fire!

- In a newly emerging and growing market (the best scenario), differentiate yourself from new competitors. Show how you expect to become a dominant game vendor, for example, utilizing the latest technology. Think about the new features coming in version 3 of the iPhone. Ascertain what new development frontiers open to you.

- Look for ways to prolong the "life" of your app if you recognize that the market you're getting into is threatened by newly emerging apps. Advancing your app in the highly competitive App Store means finding your niche or creating one of your own.

- In your market analysis, your focus should be on key areas like industry-wide sales performance of iPhone and iPad apps. Pinpoint why sales (as a whole) may be declining and then carefully consider if you have pricing flexibility with your particular app.

Business Environment

The business environment area of your marketing plan provides information on the demographics for your app. You need to have a clear understanding of your audience so that you can create age/gender appropriate marketing campaigns. You'll spend your marketing funds more wisely, and you'll be more accurate in reaching your target audience if you have this information.

Demographics

- Describe the population base that exists to support your app sales. Identify the market size for your app and the people that make up your app's consumer group; for example, teenagers, young adults, children, females, males.

- Describe the expected response to your advertising and how this will boost sales. Indicate what overall market trends you will be following to stay current and "in touch" with your app buyers. What special techniques will you employ to match consumer demands? For example, are you employing social media to drive interest and demand?

Competition

- Identify your direct competition by naming their apps, describing their capabilities, identifying their share of the market (if you can find it), and reviewing the weaknesses of their marketing approaches. Perhaps they have done limited marketing, and you feel you might have an advantage through better and more consistent marketing.

Consumer Analysis

- Identify your target market, describing how your app will meet the needs of the buyer better than the competition. List the expectations buyers have for your type of app.

- Identify the segment of the market that will benefit from your app as well as your approach to selling your app to that audience.

- Predict the sales potential that may be realized by tapping into and holding onto your target market and attracting others through different strategies and approaches. These different approaches can be done at the same time or can be more incremental—obtaining a core audience for your app first and then expanding into the rest of your potential market. Identify the sales potential for each of these target groups.

Strengths, Weaknesses, Opportunities, and Threats Analysis

A SWOT analysis is commonly used in all kinds of marketing, not just software. A SWOT analysis gives companies a more complete view of their products and how they're positioned in the marketplace. A SWOT analysis (Strength, Weaknesses, Opportunities, and Threats) will help you hone your marketing efforts and spend your limited marketing funds in the best possible areas for maximum sales impact.

Building an app that clearly fills a need for a particular audience allows you to deliver a concise message to an audience that understands your app's value from the beginning. Not having to convince buyers they need your app is 80% of the battle.

Strengths

- List the strengths of your app, such as number of features, quality of graphics, ease of use, and so on.

- List other assets of your app such as

  - Innovativeness

  - Camera support

- Email support

- Ability to connect to other apps

- Upload/download data

- Sound quality

- iPhone technology (Accelerometer)

- Use of other iPhone/iPad graphics capabilities

Weaknesses

- Describe any areas of weakness in your app, such as a large number of competitors, a difficult app to differentiate, and so on.

- List the costs to develop product that may require a higher price and possibly hinder your sales.

- Recognize the limited impact of a new app on the market—its lack of recognition may be attributed to your inexperience in promoting.

- Recognize that poor performance will mean lower-than-expected profits—which will result in a lot of the money going to reduce your debts rather than contributing to your profitability.

Opportunities

- Examine how proper timing and other factors such as your app's innovativeness may improve your chances of success.

- Use analytics tools in your app to determine usage patterns for your app (see Flurry.Com and Pinch Media).

- Relate your app's focus to a segment of the present market that is being overlooked.

Threats

- List the external threats to your app's success, such as existing and newly emerging competitors, performance of the overall economy, and your dependency on driving traffic to your personal website and the App Store.

Marketing Focus

In this section, list the key areas your app will focus on. This type of information includes the basic functions of your app, the type of promotions you intend to use to sell it, and pricing considerations. In other words, if you intend to sell a higher priced app, your marketing focus should be on greater functionality for the buyer. Someone else may be developing an app that is in the $2.99 range but will have periodic price promotions (discounts) to attract attention and drive sales volume.

If you are selling a game, then you can list the category/subcategory you intend to place this app into and the age range for its use. For example, a children's reading game can be described as being placed in the games/adventure category if that's the most logical place for it.

Your App's Functionality

- Identify your app by what it is, who will buy it, how much they will pay for it and how much it will cost for you to produce it, why a consumer demand exists for your app, and where your app sits in comparison to similar apps now available.

- Describe the marketplace rationale for the differences between your app and a competitor's. Look at quality, price, new ideas/approaches, and how your app appeals to a specific customer base—both existing customers and new customers you hope to attract to the market.

- Be specific about how your app improves upon those apps that already exist on the App Store.

Promotions

- Describe the type of promotional methods you will use to spread the word about your app. Identify techniques such as word of mouth, social media, and Internet ads.

- For newspapers and other print mediums, mention if you will be obtaining reviews for your app and in what mediums (trade magazines, professional, recreational, cultural, hobby, special interest, and so on), how often, and the timing of such reviews (seasonal, special issues, and so on).

- Create a list tradeshows or other forums that might work to showcase your app to your buying audience.

- Explain your use of mediums, such as television and radio, to conduct interviews where you can discuss your app.

- List promotions through social networks including Facebook, Myspace, Twitter, and others.

Price

- The price of your app should reflect your overall marketing strategy. Pricing should be competitive as well as a reflection of the quality, costs, and profit margin. Again, I am of the opinion that you should start out higher than $0.99 for most apps.

- List the features of the app to help justify the price, such as six levels of games, complex graphics, and charting capabilities, and so on.

- List the strategies you plan to use, such as providing a discount at times to spur sales and generate some buzz.

Financial Information

In this section, you identify the levels of sales you hope to achieve with your apps and how you plan to break even on your apps.

- Show the predicted level of sales with and without the strategies you have outlined in the marketing plan. Show a baseline level of sales and then show the expected increase in sales as they relate to specific marketing techniques you will use.

- Show the market share you will hope to attain, based on "high," "medium," and "low" estimates for the success of your marketing strategy.

- Forecast the breakeven point for selling your app in the number of sales in dollars. This will demonstrate your need to realize a certain amount of sales to cover your expected costs for the next year. You should forecast for at least one year in advance and at least two years if you are producing multiple apps with your brand.

Marketing Calendar

A marketing calendar will be a crucial part of your marketing plan as you plan the development and marketing aspects of your app because it will keep you focused and driving toward specific dates. Your marketing calendar should answer questions like the following: How long do you expect your app to take for development? Are there special graphics that you need to have developed that might take extra time? What other things might contribute to possible delays in the launch of your app?

You also want to look for opportunities to promote you app around various events during the year, such as complementary product launches, trade shows, or conferences. You first begin by reviewing a 12-month calendar so that you have a picture of the coming year. Start by considering holidays—do any lend themselves to being promotional opportunities for your app sales? You can use these holidays as promotional opportunities on your personal website. Here is a list of holidays and promotions to consider:

- **New Year's Day**—Almost all apps can leverage something around New Year's Day, such as getting organized, fresh start, resolutions, and so on.

- **Valentine's Day**—Great time to promote lifestyle apps.

- **St. Patrick's Day**—Fun holiday to promote "green" apps.

- **Memorial Day**—Traditional start of summer travel and vacations. Does your app have a play here?

- **Independence Day/4th of July**—Promote patriotic-themed apps or other activities related to the holiday.

- **Labor Day**—Traditional end-of-summer travel and vacations. Travel apps could fit in here.

- **Halloween**—Fun holiday for game apps.

- **Veteran's Day**—Great holiday to support the troops! Offer a percentage of daily app profits as a donation to a veteran's organization.

- **Thanksgiving**—Family, giving thanks, or big meal-themed promotions.

- **Christmas/Hanukkah**—Holiday-related apps and scheduling and appointment-setting apps may fit in here nicely.

Many other holidays may be relevant for your app sales—Easter, Martin Luther King Day, President's Day, Secretary's Day, Grandparent's Day, and on and on. Again, carefully review the calendar and think through the holidays that you could leverage to create a unique promotion for your app. After you've reviewed the holidays and determined which ones would be good promotional tie-ins for your app, take another look through the calendar annual events that are not necessarily holidays but are certainly traditions. The following is a list of annual events to consider:

- **Super Bowl**—Guaranteed football parties and an especially great event if your local NFL team is in the Super Bowl. (Equally, the playoffs leading up to the Super Bowl are great for promotions of local NFL teams.) Is your app football-related?

- **Mardi Gras**—A fun party-themed promotion. You can even donate a portion of the app proceeds toward New Orleans rebuilding efforts.

- **March Madness**—Celebrate college basketball's greatest tournament. Especially fun to offer promotions if your app is in any way related to college football.

- **Tax Day**—Great way to promote a discount for your tax calculator app. No one really likes tax day, so you might as well create a promotion to help lift the burden.

- **World Series**—Similar to Super Bowl promotions. Extremely effective if your app is in any way related to baseball; offer discounts to your app or offer a drawing on your website for a free pair of baseball tickets to one of the world series games.

- **Earth Day**—Great day to offer "green" and Earth-friendly promotions for your app.

- **Seasons or solstices/equinoxes**—Spring, summer, fall, and winter are great themes for a marketing campaign, as are the summer and winter solstice or vernal and autumnal equinoxes. You might have a nature-related app that would work in this category.

- **Mother's Day**—Celebrate mothers by offering a discount or something for mothers; maybe it's a short-term discount on your app.

- **Father's Day**—Celebrate fathers by offering a discount on your app for fathers.

- **Time change**—Spring forward or fall back: or whatever your area's time change ritual is, your app may find something relevant to promote around the changing times.

Summary

A marketing plan is a valuable tool to help you align your development and marketing efforts into a single, cohesive plan. Most app developers do not consider a marketing plan to be necessary, but it can make the difference between a mediocre app and best-selling one. It does not need to be lengthy, but it must include the necessary components to fully cover the app's purpose, development efforts, target audience, launch plans, and financial objectives. If you want to become a big player in the App Store, spend some time getting organized and create a marketing plan.

A marketing plan will also help you have a strategy to selling your app. If one type of marketing does not work well, you have a plan for trying other promotions or activities that will help you achieve your results.

20

Marketing Essentials and the Right Mix

Striking a balance between how much you should spend on marketing and anticipated revenue is a challenge for any product developer. It's especially a challenge for iPhone/iPad app developers because of the low price point of their app and the fact that the Apple App Store takes a 30% share from all sales including in-app purchases. So the question often asked is how much marketing is needed for profits to be realized?

Think of marketing in terms of driving visitors to two locations to learn about your app: the App Store and your app product website. Ultimately they have to visit the App Store to purchase your app, but they may visit your website first and then click over to the App Store. You will spend most of your time optimizing your product website, just like any other web-based business. But you should always look for opportunities to update your content on the App Store as well even though you may not think it will have a big impact. Every bit of marketing helps the cause. If you have had a certain event occur for your app, you can post this information on the main page for your app on the App Store. You never know who will be reading about your app.

Keep Your App Store Content New and Exciting

The following events are reasons for you to update the content for your app on the App Store:

- **New review posted by external source**—Include the highlights of the review on the App Store in the top section of text. Keep in mind that you can edit your content anytime you want on the App Store. It usually takes a few hours for your edits to take effect after you save them.

- **New icon for your app**—A new icon can change the levels of interest for many buyers. A new icon can catch the eye of a previously uninterested buyer.

- **Download milestone reached**—Include specifics such as "more than 100,000 copies downloaded," or "best rated" app for the second year in a row, and so on.

- **Additional app added to your portfolio**—Introduce your new app in your app verbiage. You can say something like, "If you've enjoyed this app, please take a look at our newest game app called XYZ."

- **When your app is added to any App Store category on the first page of the App Store**—For example, your app has been added to "New and Noteworthy," "Staff Picks," "What's Hot," and so on. You can post a note at the top of your page saying that you were selected for one of these categories.

Of course, whenever you have updates that are newsworthy, you should also post them to your product website as well. The business of online selling (of any kind) requires your content to be ever changing and exciting. If you let the content on the App Store or on your product website become stale, you will find your customers start to lose interest in your apps.

It takes effort to keep the content updated and active, but people want to see that your app is vibrant and active. A number of buyers are turned off when they notice that an app has not been updated for a year or two. This is usually an indication that the app hasn't sold too well or is experiencing declining sales.

How Much Should I Spend?

Determining how much to spend is always a difficult question. Spend nothing, and you might end up with nothing in terms of sales. Spend a lot, and you might end up with strong sales if you have a well-written app. The best advice I can give is to carefully choose which marketing activities you will use for your type of app. When you've selected a marketing activity, you can test the waters to see what the results are before spending more money than you should.

For example, let's assume you have created an app that helps singers train their voices to sing on key. You have decided to do a press release, and you're going to do an email blast to musicians and music stores across the United States and Canada. Before spending perhaps thousands of dollars on an email blast, consider doing a much smaller test to see what the results are going to be. You'll be able to get an idea from a smaller sample as to how the list will perform.

In another example, you are trying to sell a game. This game is geared to 10 to 15-year-old children. You've decided to incorporate paid installs into the app, meaning you've included code that will allow your app to be displayed by other apps around the world. When someone downloads and installs your app through this program, you are charged an installation fee by a provider such as Tapjoy or Flurry. You can do a small test run by limiting the total number of installs to whatever budget you can afford. So if you're willing to pay $.25 per install and you cannot afford over $25.00 per day, you can limit the total number of installs per day to 100. If you start to see positive results in that your app is moving up in the rankings or you're having a lot of organic growth, you can ramp up the daily budget.

A general rule of thumb is not to spend more than 20% on marketing for the total cost of your app. Therefore, if your app is selling for $.99, you'll want to keep the marketing costs at 20% of $.99 or 20 cents. This means that when you negotiate for an install price, you're not willing to pay over 20 cents per install.

Email campaigns and banner ads are much more difficult to quantify on a per-install basis. You don't know if your email blast to 10,000 people will result in 2%, 3%, or 5% of app sales. So you'll have to do the math and make some projects based on the sample email blast that I recommend you do.

Striking a Balance

To strike a balance in your marketing activities, it helps to think in terms of the different phases of your app's progression. You will do some marketing activities prior to its launch. Then you will do some more activities during the app's launch, and finally, you'll follow it up with ongoing activities to help you maintain app sales. Tables 20.1, 20.2, and 20.3 provide recommendations on essential marketing activities during each stage of your app sales cycle.

Table 20.1 Essential Marketing Activities Prior to App Launch

Marketing Activity	Estimated Cost of Activity
App product website creation.	$500–$2,000
SEO activities for your site including keywords, site submissions, external links.	Usually free—can take several months for search engines to pick your site up and start to establish your page rank
App and brand blog.	Free—does require consistency and time
Press release draft.	$250–400 (if written professionally)
Identify blog sites and post comments.	Free—does require consistency and time
Identify app reviewers and offer them early access to your app.	Free—does require consistency and time
Identify companies with whom you can partner that are complimentary, not competitive.	Free—requires your time
Contact news media about preannouncing your app to your audience.	Free—requires your time
Determine any promotions you want to have when app is launched.	Free—planning stage
Develop a free version of your app.	Costs money and time for you to either develop a free version of your app or to hire someone else to develop it

Table 20.2 Essential Marketing Activities During App Launch

Marketing Activity	Estimated Cost of Activity
Issue press release.	Free on some sites; $20 with PRMac and $80–$360 with PRWeb
Contact review sites and distribute promo codes when requested.	Free—but takes lots of time
Contact bloggers and online publications about your app.	Free—but takes lots of time
Advertising.	Free (news stories) to unlimited (banner ads and so on will cost)
Promotions.	Contests with prizes can cost from $100–$10,000 depending on the prizes given to the winners of your contest

Table 20.2   Essential Marketing Activities During App Launch

Marketing Activity	Estimated Cost of Activity
Email campaign.	Free (if you have a list already)—email cost 0.10–0.18 cents per recipient if you have to rent a list. Possible cost to use an email service to send out the emails. Many services offer 30–60 day free trials, so use that option first before signing up for a monthly fee. See www.constantcontact.com for a free 60-day trial of their email solution.
Create blog post about your new app.	Free
Use Twitter to send out announcements about your new app.	Free
SEO activities for your site including keywords, site submissions, external links.	Usually free—can take several months for search engines to pick your site up and start to establish your page rank

Table 20.3   Essential Marketing Activities After Launch

Marketing Activity	Estimated Cost of Activity
Monitor pricing and downloads of your app.	Free
Determine if a temporary price adjustment is needed.	Free
Make temporary pricing adjustments.	Free to change but will impact your revenues, hopefully in a positive way
Keep reviewers looking at your app by seeking new reviews.	Free—requires your time
Introduce promotions to punch up sales.	Free but can cost money, depending on the promotions you utilize
Continue working on SEO for your product web page.	Free—requires your time
Advertise your app to increase sales.	Costs money (banner ads, product review sites, and so on)
Drop price permanently for your app.	Free to change price but may impact your revenue and profits either positively or negatively
Develop free version of your app.	Costs money and time for you to either develop a free version of your app or to hire someone else to develop your app

Table 20.3   Essential Marketing Activities After Launch

Marketing Activity	Estimated Cost of Activity
SEO activities for your site including keywords, site submissions, external links.	Usually free—can take several months for search engines to pick your site up and start to establish your page rank

The best way to determine how much to spend on your marketing is to do a small trial before launching an all-out marketing campaign. If you plan to do an email campaign about your app, then send out 100 emails first to see what the response is before sending out a blast to 10,000 addresses. You'll save money and time by testing what works before wasting a lot of money.

Summary

Achieving the right marketing balance of activities and cost requires a bit of trial and error. It helps to first break out your marketing activities in prelaunch, launch, and post launch categories. Many of the marketing activities do not cost money but will cost in terms of time. The activities that cost you money should be approached by using a small trial first to measure the results.

For example, place a small banner ad on a popular app game site if you are trying to sell your game app. Then measure the results to see whether this marketing method is effective for your app. If it does help you increase sales, then look to expand the ad's coverage and search out other sites on which you might also advertise.

Marketing requires a constant effort. You have to be consistent to make people aware of your apps and to download them. Some marketing activities work better for one type of app than another. Only you can determine the best marketing mix for your app. Use the marketing activity tables provided in this chapter to help you get started.

21

25 Essential iPhone/iPad Marketing Activities

You can use numerous marketing activities to gain exposure and sales for your app. Because the App Store and iPhone/iPad apps are relatively new in the world of commerce, you face a learning curve to understand what works and what doesn't for marketing apps through the store and from your own product website.

In this chapter, we discuss 25 iPhone/iPad marketing activities that we consider essential to your sales success. Some of these activities we have discussed in more detail in other chapters, but we've brought them all together into a single list for easy reference. As you create your marketing plan, you can review this list to ensure that all these activities are being performed at different points in your plan; from prelaunch to postlaunch and during your ongoing marketing campaigns.

These marketing activities are grouped by marketing activity categories and not in any specific order.

Delivering Your iPhone/iPad App to the World

The following tips will help you get your app to a strong start. The more you can do before the launch, the more success you'll have getting downloads. An app usually shows promise within the first few days of launch so it's vital that you prepare.

Seek Reviews from Any Review Site That Matches Your App's Category

Submit your app for review in as many places as you can. It's a numbers game to get reviews for your app. Submit it to at least 30 sites as soon as your app is launched on the App Store. Keep an ongoing list (or spreadsheet) of sites and the date you have submitted your review request. This way, you can track who you've sent requests to and when. It is difficult to get attention on review sites because so many app developers are requesting reviews, but you should still submit to them. The more you submit your app for review, the more likely you'll find a reviewer. It doesn't hurt to know people at these sites too. Start to establish relationships with review sites by submitting comments, offer to write a review for another app, and so on. Get out there and get noticed.

Be sure to provide a promo code so the editorial staff can review your app at no cost. Here are some of the leading app review sites: www.macrumors.com, www.arstechnica.com, www.macworld.com, www.ilounge.com, www.148apps.com, www.touchpodium.com, www.theiphoneblog.com, www.appstoreapps.com, www.maclife.com, www.gizmodo.com, and www.appcraver.com.

Search on Google and Yahoo! for online magazines and other review sites and publications that would be interested in giving your app a review. You should also ask industry-specific magazines for reviews. For example, if you have developed a financial app, look for financial publications that might be interested in giving your app a write-up. See Chapter 6, "Electronic Word of Mouth," for more information.

Showcase Your App on the App Store

Prospective customers often browse within the top apps categories listed in the App Store categories, such as "What's Hot" and "New and Noteworthy," using their computer or directly from their iPhone. Your app's ranking is determined by the number of downloads; the more downloads, the more likely you are to get into the Top 100 categories. It does take several thousand downloads per day to take a spot in the Top 100 category.

As I've mentioned before, select a clever and unique app name so that buyers will remember the name and pass it along to others. Having a unique app name for games is crucial to your success, while having an easy-to-remember name for nongame apps will help you when people search for apps via Google or Yahoo!. You should routinely check the App Store to determine what others are doing in terms of their positioning and messaging. For more information, see Chapter 5, "Building Your App's Total Message."

Use Press Releases Consistently

Use press releases to announce the launch of your app and to broadcast any other timely and relevant information to the iPhone/iPad audience. Many developers feel that once they do a single press release, that's that. Think instead in terms of your press releases being a steady drum beat of messaging about your app. The most effective means is through online PR agencies, which can distribute your press release to all media agencies, including Internet, blogs, newspapers, and industry trade publications. You should also contact directly editors, news analysts, and other professionals to review your app.

If possible, have a blogger or reviewer post comments at the same time you issue a press release for your app. The more total exposure you can give your app at the same time, the more likely people will notice and take a look at the app on your product website or on the App Store. See Chapter 9, "Getting the Word Out About Your App," for more information about writing a press release.

Market Through Email

Send out an email campaign to potential app buyers. The best list is your own list if you have developed one for other products or apps. You can also purchase lists from list brokers, such as InfoUSA.com, which allow you to filter to specific categories, including contacts by industry, Standard Industrial Classification (SIC), size, job titles, spending, location, and more. You can also purchase millions of consumer email contacts by location, age, income levels, hobbies and interests, ethnicity, religion, household occupant info, and so on. As I have said before, use caution buying email lists and be sure to test a small subset of a list because this marketing approach can eat into your profits, especially on a low-priced app.

Many other agencies (chamber of commerce, business communities located around airparks and in most towns, and so on) have databases of subscriber email addresses and will usually let you have access to their lists if you join their groups. Again, be sure to evaluate what type of list you are getting. Just sending emails to anyone in a list is not going to help you. Sometimes there are costs to join, so make sure you spend your money wisely on groups that match your demographic for your app.

Choose online or printed publications whose audience matches your targeted customers. For example, if you are selling an aviation app, you can look at targeting flying websites or publications that cater to pilots. See Chapter 6 for more information.

Use Word of Mouth

Good old-fashioned word of mouth can help you spread the word about your app. Tell everyone about your new app, including family, coworkers, friends, and other developers. Tell everyone using Twitter and Facebook as well. Electronic word of mouth is the most powerful form of advertising you have.

You can also send an email message out to all those people in your address books announcing your new app. If you attend any events, such as luncheons, seminars, or forums, be sure to talk about your app to all who will listen.

Look into attending weekly app meet ups. These are meetings that are held in many large cities across the U.S. and Canada that discuss iPhone/iPad app development and share ideas with each other. It's a great way to make new contacts and get ideas on how others are successfully marketing their apps. You can leave behind your business card or a small product flyer that describes your app. See Chapter 6 for more information.

Use Targeted Advertising

Advertising is another way to get the word out about your app. There has not been too much advertising by developers because they are concerned about the cost, but you can find local television and radio stations that might be interested in discussing your app on a show, and you'll get free advertising. Keep in mind that not all apps are well suited to TV or radio advertising. Your app must have broad appeal, such as a game, shopping tool, or weather or navigation tool, and so on.

For example, an app that provides train schedules for the Phoenix light rail system should focus on the ridership for that rail system. It makes sense to look at poster advertising at train stations and in local publications that discuss the trains or are distributed at the stations.

Banner ads should also be considered. They can be targeted somewhat closely to your app-buying audience. A banner can direct people to either your website or directly to the App Store to review your app. See Chapter 6 for more information.

Use Analytics for Your Apps

You should look at employing analytics to measure the success of your apps. Analytics tools help you measure how many apps are being sold, how people are using your apps, and where in the world your apps are being used. Analytics is an important marketing tool because it can help you make adjustments to your marketing campaigns or add and enhance features that your buyers are interested in.

Analytics can be downloaded and used for free from most analytics firms, including Admob and Flurry/Pinch Media. They also have monetization platforms that can help your app generate revenue from the placement of ads on your free apps. See Chapter 17, "Using iPhone/iPad Analytics," for more information.

Analytics are also the precursor to using paid install programs from Tapjoy, Flurry, and others. The paid install programs allow your app to be displayed on "app walls" of other apps. Users of those apps can then view your app, click on it, and download it. If they download your app you are charged a fee such as $.25 to $.40 depending on what you have bid as an acceptable payment.

iPhone/iPad Pricing and Promotions

Pricing and promotions are another important area of marketing where you can make an impact on your sales. Always be thinking about how pricing adjustments can help your sales. Promotions are also a great way to get your sales moving.

Develop a Pricing Strategy

You must have a pricing strategy to find success on the App Store. Look at other developers and companies to see how they have successfully priced their apps or have done a promotion that has generated large sales for them. Some companies have found that by doing a three-day promotion over a long weekend, they have been able to significantly increase their app sales.

Other developers start out by offering their apps for free to build up their install base, get favorable reviews, and drive awareness. You can offer your app for free in the first week of its availability and then change the price, for example. For more information on promotion see Chapter 16, "App Promotions and Cross-Selling."

Promote from Ads Within Other Apps

You can promote your app using interactive ads contained within other iPhone apps that you purchase. There are many ways to engage a customer using ads, such as a click-to-call ad, click-to-video ad, or click to the App Store. You can test different types of ads to see which ones might work the best for you. There are also many ad networks that provide in-app advertising options with very specific audience targeting including age, gender, geography, category, carrier, device, and handset that you can also experiment with different ads. For more information, see Chapter 14, "Level the Playing Field with a Free App."

App Product Website

Your product website is an important vehicle to help sell your app. You want to work to have a common look and feel between your website and your product page on the App Store.

Increase Your Website SEO

Create a product website to showcase your apps. Always include screen shots and describe the features and benefits of your app. Just like any website, you want to optimize the website content with keywords and make sure that you build a following of other sites that link back to your website. This improves your search rankings for your site. Always have a Buy Now button to link to your app within the iPhone App Store. Promote your app throughout every page on your product website.

Getting your app noticed also means getting your app product website noticed. If you have just created a new website, you can get your site listed in free online directories, such as DMOZ (www.dmoz.com), the open directory project. As stated by their own site, the DMOZ powers core directory services for some of the most popular portals and search engines on the Web, including AOL Search, Netscape Search, Google, Lycos, HotBot, and hundreds of others.

Use the Google AdWords keyword tool; research search terms that are most relevant to your app audience and populate your app description with those terms. Don't go overboard with the use of terms but make sure you have the relevant terms on every page of your site. Also use the search terms in all your marketing efforts, including social media activities such as blogs, email campaigns, and promotional efforts. See Chapter 5 for more information on creating your product website.

Let Visitors Market Your Site

Having a high page rank for your personal website is, in part, about getting external links back to your app product website. You do this by getting visitors to post comments about your site and app on blog posts and on their own websites. Blogging is a great way to help your site get noticed and keep visitors coming to it. Be sure to utilize the Add This button on your site to promote your apps and website. The Add This button can be installed on your blog or website pages, and it allows visitors to share your content with their friends and coworkers who use Facebook, LinkedIn, MySpace, Digg, TypePad, Blogger, WordPress, and other social media sites.

Be sure to use a Follow Us note on your homepage as well. Beneath the Follow Us, you can post links to Facebook, Twitter, YouTube, and other social media sites that link directly to your content on those sites. This will keep your visitors engaged with your apps and development activities. For more information, see Chapter 5.

Social Media Marketing

Social media marketing is very important to help impact your app sales. Keep in mind social media activities take time. The sooner you start social media activities before the release of your app, the more downloads you'll get when your app is launched.

Promote Through YouTube

Create a YouTube video describing and demonstrating your new app. You can set up an YouTube account for free in a matter of seconds. In your video, highlight the use of your app and how its features and benefits make it worthwhile. Videos are powerful because people tend to watch a video over reading about something. So when you post a video on YouTube, you can have literally thousands of views in a short period of time. People can comment on the video and your app just like on the App Store. But you can also comment back when someone posts a comment. This interaction will help you establish a community of followers to your apps and brand.

You can also create YouTube ads for your app using a Google AdWords account. As we recommend in this book, use this approach sparingly and go slowly before spending too much money. Gauge if your ads are going to work or not before committing too much money to it. For more information, see Chapter 7, "Using Social Media in Your App Marketing."

Promote Through LinkedIn

LinkedIn can be another great way to reach an audience of developers and buyers for your app, especially if you have written a business-related app that is geared to working professionals. You can join up to 50 LinkedIn groups based on your own target audience. A search of groups will reveal perhaps hundreds of groups that you can contact. Be sure to find groups that have many members so that your communication efforts are not in vain. There is a news category where you can let the group know about your app.

If you haven't created your own LinkedIn profile, you need to do that to post to these groups. But having a profile showcasing your development skills is a huge benefit. You can post announcements on your profile about your app's availability, and you can update your contacts about updates and other news about your brand. See Chapter 7 for more information about LinkedIn.

Promote Through Blogs

As discussed in Chapter 7, you want to post an announcement about your new app to your blog. You can create a blog if you don't already have one, but remember blogging is a commitment, and you must post comments at least weekly to be followed with any regularity. You can use WordPress or Blogger, and they're free and simple to use. There are so many ways to link and use your blog posts to spread the word about your app. For example, you post your blogs to your LinkedIn profile. You can send a Twitter message (Tweet) with a link to your blog post.

Create a Facebook Fan Page

Create a Facebook fan page to showcase your new app and develop your brand. A number of popular games apps are using Facebook fan pages, and they have generated huge followings. Facebook fan pages are easy to set up and don't cost you a dime. Your app page can be found in the search engines as well, which is going to help people find you. Additionally, when a visitor joins your fan page, the updates are broadcast to all members of that person's group, and they are helping you to spread the word about your app. For more information on creating a Facebook fan page, refer to Chapter 7.

Create Digg Articles and Videos

You can spread the word about your app article or video online at Digg.com. Digg will post your submission immediately in "Upcoming Stories," where other Digg members can find it. If the readers like your article, they will "Digg" it, meaning they will give it their approval. When a submission reaches a large number of Diggs, your post can become one of the most read, and it jumps to the home page in its category, where even more people will read it. Be prepared to post many articles to this site before one of them takes off. It's a lot of work but could be well worth it when your app get noticed in a big way. See Chapter 7 to learn more social media techniques.

Visit Forums and Post Comments

Many developers are already members of forums and discussion groups where they can post comments about iPhone/iPad development topics. You can also identify new forums that meet your target audience criteria for your app and start a dialogue about apps in your category and other relevant topics. You can participate in discussions and talk about your apps as appropriate when you have established yourself as a regular. Be sure to follow each forum's protocol, as we have discussed in earlier chapters. This helps you build awareness for your brand and for your app. See Chapter 6 for more details.

Other App Marketing Activities

There are many ways to gain exposure for your app, and here are a few more ideas to help you improve your downloads. Your success starts with a great app, but these other activities will only help to increase your success.

Create Trial and Paid App Versions

Offer a free trial version with an option to have more functionality enabled in the paid version as discussed in previous chapters. A free app is going to drive downloads and awareness for your brand and app. The biggest challenge for your success is developing enough functionality in your free app to be compelling, yet not so much that your audience doesn't feel the need to purchase your paid app. For more information on developing a free version of your app, see Chapter 14.

Secure App Launch Sponsorships

Secure a launch sponsor and co-promote. Examples include Fram Oil utilizing the Gas Cubby app to co-promote their brand. Within your prelaunch marketing materials, promote and provide clear instructions for those who might be interested in being a launch sponsor. Explain the benefits they'll receive in terms of publicity exposure, placement within the app, and other perks. See Chapter 13, "Breaking into the App Store Top 100," to learn more.

Continuously Improve Features

Add new features to your app frequently, such as every couple of months. Just reposting your app will energize sales for a time. Feature upgrades allow you to do another press release and garner fresh interest on the App Store. Along with feature improvements, you should monitor your app's review on the store and act upon insightful new feature requests to keep customers coming back and lure new ones into the fold.

When your app is developed, utilize mobile analytics so that you can learn about how your app is used, referring sources and app performance characteristics. Within your app, you can request that your users send feedback to your company's private email address. Also encourage your users to post positive review on the App Store if they like the app. For more information on mobile analytics see Chapter 17 and Chapter 2, "What Makes a Winning iPhone/iPad App?"

Collaborate with Other People

There are many ways to collaborate with other vendors. Try to find companies and entrepreneurs who would be willing to talk about your app in their product pitches, meetings, and sales conferences. For example, look for industry conferences where your app might be appropriate to that audience and contact speakers who might be willing to mention your app.

Some developers are teaming together to create a consortium and a brand. If you are a small independent developer with limited time to create multiple apps, you can look into finding other developers who are interested in building a brand. iPhone/iPad meet ups are great place to locate other developers who are interested in cobranding and comarketing their apps.

Seek Non-App Review Sites for Your App

Seek out other venues to get reviews of your app. For example, if you have an app that helps people learn how to garden, look for web and print publications that are focused on gardening, and make a few inquiries to see if they would be interested in reviewing your app for an article. You'll be surprised how many publications will be interested in doing such a story. The reason is simple. Publications are always looking for topics that would be of interest to their readers. The iPhone still carries the "cool factor," and for those readers outside of the traditional tech world, the iPhone/iPad and apps that are germane to their interests carry strong interest. You will probably have to arrange a call to demo the app for the editor or writer of the publication if they don't have an iPhone, but it is well worth the effort, and you circumvent the long lines at the traditional review sites.

Exchange Ad Space

You can use a download exchange such as Admob to exchange ad space with other apps. Admob handles all the placement of your ad within other apps ads. In return, you exchange ad space on your app. This implies that you are building a free app. This functionality allows new users to discover your app from inside hundreds of other apps, which helps drive downloads and hopefully sales of your paid app. For more information on this process, see Chapter 14.

Create an Icon Worth Remembering

Carefully evaluate your app's icon to ensure that the graphic describes your app and conveys its value. This is easier than it sounds and requires you to spend some serious time on the creation of this key graphic. If you are concerned that your logo may not convey what your app does, you might want to consider developing another graphic or adding text to the graphic that gives the app's name. Seek the advice of friends who can review the icon and give you some honest feedback.

Determine Your App's Unique Value

In the iPhone/iPad app world, you have to identify the unique functionality of your app and communicate that value to your audience. The trick to creating a powerful unique selling proposition is to boil down in a few words an identifying point that embodies your app's unique value. Your unique selling proposition must answer the question as to why anyone should buy your app over all the other similar apps in the App Store that they have to choose from. For more information, refer to Chapter 3, "Identifying Your App's Unique Value."

Summary

Use the preceding material to help you formulate your prelaunch and postlaunch marketing activities for your iPhone/iPad apps. These activities are some of the most important marketing activities you can perform to get your app off to a solid start when it's posted to the App Store. As you develop your marketing plan, group your activities into prelaunch, postlaunch, and ongoing marketing activities. Many of these recommended activities are free or inexpensive, costing you only in time to develop them.

Keep in mind that some of these activities take time to be effective. Doing something once and expecting results may be disappointing for you. The more consistent you are in doing marketing, the more consistent results you're going to see. Letting up on marketing usually results in a slowdown of app sales.

22

Implementing Your Plan

Perhaps one of the most challenging aspects of marketing an iPhone/iPad app on the App Store is that you must implement your marketing plan with a sustained effort over a period of time to realize positive results. The most effective marketing campaign is an integrated one that combines multiple marketing touch points that leverage your carefully developed, consistent app message.

You can achieve greater results by including many different methods to reach your audience—social media, word of mouth, email, product reviews, paid installs, and so on. The following steps will help you to implement your marketing campaign.

Determine Goals for the Marketing Campaign—What Results Do You Hope to Achieve?

Before you launch an app campaign, it is important to determine what your overall goals are so that as the plan is implemented, you can measure the results and make adjustments where needed. Here are just a few objectives that you might pursue with your marketing campaigns. Although the goal of implementing a campaign is to increase sales, some campaigns might approach this indirectly:

- **Direct traffic to your app's product website**—Keep in mind that you have all the control over your product website in terms of search engine optimization, look and feel, and content. You can develop search engine optimization programs to drive traffic to your website. You can utilize banner ads and email campaigns to direct traffic to you product web pages. You can post YouTube videos to your site to showcase your app. You have much more flexibility in what you can post to your own web-site than you do on the App Store. Always have the Apple App Store logo prominently displayed on your site so that visitors can click through to your app on the App Store.

- **Increase app sales on the App Store**—This is obvious, but you want to have a goal to increase sales by a certain amount so that you have something to measure and track against. If you are only seeing 10 downloads a day, then set a goal to realize 20 downloads a day and so on. Also you should measure which campaigns are helping you to increase your sales. Keep in mind that if you do too many campaigns at once, you'll have a difficult time determining which campaigns are producing increased sales.

- **Establish a brand**—Establishing a brand takes time and effort but is necessary and important to building long-term success on the App Store. Even the most successful app developers (think Rovio: Angry Birds) have spent a long time building their brands and producing a lot of not-so-successful apps. You establish a brand by being in front of your target audience for an extended period of time. This is done by developing a common look for your apps and icons and developing a website that also carries the same look of your brand. Measuring brand awareness is more difficult, but your initial goal should be to simply establish your brand and be recognized by iPhone/iPad app users.

- **Bring back old customers to look at your newest app**—Although you don't know who your customers actually are from App Store sales, unless you've persuaded them to register on your product site, you can conduct campaigns that will bring some of them back to your new app.

This can be done through banner ads, email campaigns, and blog posts. You can mention that you are the creator of the best-selling app that they used to enjoy.

Your campaign goals can vary from meeting basic expectations to very lofty revenue aspirations. The key behind setting goals is to be realistic, based on your overall budget and your time frame. You will only set yourself up for disappointment if you set a goal to be achieved in two days that realistically could take more than two months to produce the results you have in mind. You will be equally disappointed if you expect huge sales but have a very limited marketing budget. Here are some sample goals that you might pursue with your marketing campaigns:

- Establish your app as the hottest new entrant in the App Store Lifestyle category.

- Increase online ordering conversion rates from your personal website.

- Increase overall leads while minimizing cost to obtain new leads.

- Successfully cross-sell to your existing app customer base.

 Note

Always have a clearly defined goal in mind prior to launching a campaign. Not all campaigns have the same purpose. Your overall goal is to drive app sales, but in some cases you are also trying to build awareness for your brand and attempting to get your name recognized in the App Store.

Establish Measurement Criteria

The next step is to determine how you will measure your desired goals. If your goal is to increase iPhone/iPad app sales, you will measure the success by reviewing the number of sales coming in after each campaign. Measure sales before you start the campaign and then during the campaign to compare the difference. It's easy to measure sales on a daily basis through iTunes Connect. There are also a number of sites that will track and graph your daily app sales. Sites such as App Annie will show you daily sales, reviews, and rankings on a global basis for all or your own apps.

Flurry also provides very good data on usage of your app, how many sessions are currently open, how many users are using the app from each country and so on. These tools are invaluable to help you measure results of your marketing campaigns.

You'll most likely want to associate these measurements to a specific campaign so that you can determine the pieces of the overall plan that were most effective in reaching a set goal. This allows you to refine the marketing plan over time to make it as successful as possible. Here are some examples of measurements that you'll want to evaluate for your own iPhone/iPad apps:

- Number of app sales on the App Store over a daily, weekly, and monthly basis.

- Strong lead response to your app messaging—ensure success of all lead generation programs.

- Review revenue associated by campaign to determine if sales increase can be attributed to certain areas of your marketing plan.

Gather Prospects to Target for Campaign

Perform a thorough review of your target audience. Do you have a database with customers that have purchased an app from you previously? As I have mentioned before, always include a registration option on your product website so that visitors can be notified by email of your latest apps and upgrades. Unfortunately there is no way to track who buys your app from the App Store. The only way to gather this type of information is through your website. Your Facebook fan page can also redirect buyers of your app to your website to register. You can also offer a weekly drawing for something like a Starbucks Gift Card for those who submit their names and email addresses on your site.

Other developers have email databases from previous products launched. Maybe you have a PC game that you are now launching as an iPhone app. If you've sold to a PC audience, you should notify them of the availability of your new iPhone app. Always look for ways to cross-promote your app if you have another list of customers for other non-iPhone/iPad apps. Gather all of the leads that should be targeted for the campaign and use a clean email list, meaning the names have been scrubbed for duplicates and invalid addresses.

Tracking Results—Measuring Marketing ROI

One of the most important tasks is tracking the successes and failures for each marketing initiative, campaign, and so on. You will better understand the most effective ways to promote your app to your audience, therefore allowing you to maximize your marketing dollars. Learn how to track results:

- Build tracking mechanisms into your marketing pieces if possible. If you have users registering on your product website, have them use a particular "coupon code" or "tracking code" that they enter on your registration page. This will allow you to determine if a certain campaign is generating results.

- Send users to a landing page on your website and track hits using Google Analytics.

- Add mechanisms to your product website to track unique hits for each page and links within your site—understand where website traffic is coming from and what people are viewing when they get to your site.

- Analyze leads and sources by revenue.

- Track sales by lead source.

- Compare total app sales from Apple's stats to conversions from your product website.

- You will be able to identify if your website is producing more sales than the App Store by itself.

- If your website is converting less than the App Store on its own, you need to work to improve your website hits and conversion rates.

 Note

You can't improve what you can't measure. Always gather data on the success of each campaign so that you can fine-tune going forward.

Managing Your App Marketing Activities

First, I need to reiterate that you need to manage your marketing activities. Use your marketing plan to write down what you want to accomplish and when. Your marketing plan will help you to chart and track your initiatives. You can also use your marketing plan as a tool to review how many marketing projects you've implemented and their levels of success. You could also use a checklist to keep track of what you need to do and by when to implement an iPhone/iPad marketing activity.

You should also set up an accountability system. This can be part of your app marketing plan where you keep track of initiatives. Or you can set up a simple Excel spreadsheet that lists the app name, date, action, cost, target completion date, date completed. and results. By managing your app marketing activities and being accountable for them, you'll be well on your way to actually putting the marketing strategies in motion. An example of such an accountability system is shown in Table 22.1.

Table 22.1 Marketing Campaign Tracking Spreadsheet

App Name	Date	Action	Cost	Target Completion	Completion Date	Results
MyFirstApp	2/27/10	Banner Ad	$179.99	4/27/10	4/30/10	Sales increased to 125 downloads/day
MySecondApp						

Successfully implementing an iPhone/iPad marketing activity requires you to do the following:

- **Focus**—On the marketing task at hand and the end results (more downloads of your app!).

- **Implement**—Make sure you do everything that is planned for your app and leave nothing out of your plan.

- **Manage**—Make sure all who are involved in the campaign are working to accomplish all tasks.

- **Delegate**—Do what you know how to do best and outsource the rest. If you are not skilled in writing email copy and doing a campaign, then hire someone to do it.

Implementation is the key to your app marketing success. Implement some kind of marketing effort every day, no matter how small, and you'll be that much closer than your competitor to getting that app sale. To properly implement your marketing plan, you must do the following:

- **Always check your progress**—Know what's working in your campaigns and what isn't. If you do a status check every day, it will help you stay on top of programs that need work and those that are working.

- **Always try new things**—Never sit on your hands when your app sales are not picking up. The App Store and the app market is always changing and so should you.

- **Don't jump ship too soon**—Give your plan time to work. So many developers give up after a month or so. If it's not working, don't give up. Work with your development team and marketing consultant and let them help you succeed.

- **Ask for feedback**—Ask your customers to comment on your apps and how you are doing solving their challenges. Ask team members if they are pleased with how the "plan" is going and how it may be improved.

Summary

Implementing your marketing campaigns is where the real proof of your efforts will be seen. Use your marketing plan and marketing calendar to track and measure your app campaign progress. Set some goals that you want to accomplish for each campaign.

Measure your app sales prior to your campaign and then after the campaign has been implemented. Be sure to give the campaign sufficient time to achieve the desired outcome. If you are not seeing the desired results, make some adjustments to the campaign and try it again.

23

iPhone/iPad Apps for Corporate Marketing

Developers of other products outside the iPhone/iPad world are looking at mobile platforms as a way to reach millions of tech savvy users with their product messages. There are several ways that companies are using mobile technology. One is advertising through mobile marketing. This is usually done through SMS text messages. A company can create a text message ad and utilize a mobile marketing platform that charges a fraction of a penny for each text message sent. A company can reach literally millions of potential customers relatively cheaply. It has proven to be an effective method to advertise many products.

Another way that companies are using mobile technology is creating apps for smartphones and tablets that help extend or establish their brands. Companies that are looking to extend their brands will typically provide a free app. A free app might be used to help facilitate product sales such as an order processing app. For example, a restaurant can use an app to help customers view a menu and order food. Chipotle has developed a very successful app that allows customers to place orders and then go in and pick them up later.

Companies are also using iPhone/iPad apps to reignite their brands or to extend functionality from an existing cloud-based app to the mobile platform. Some companies are seeing a resurgence of their brands through the use of iPhone/iPad apps. Vans, the shoe company, for example, has successfully launched an app called Vans: House of Vans. The app provides a news feed, store locator, and other comments from "sneaker freaks" all around the world. This app has helped Vans to keep its brand alive with the "cool" crowd of iPhone/iPad users. The app is free and has seen tens of thousands of downloads.

Bic and Zippo lighters are great examples of companies that have been successful promoting their fake lighter apps to millions of users. The apps do nothing more than show a virtual flame on the screen from a Bic or Zippo lighter. But more importantly they get people to remember their brand in a powerful manner whenever they take their iPhonse to a concert.

Another option for corporations is to use an app as an extension to their existing web products. Banks, for example, create a home banking app that is complementary to their web-based banking access. The iPhone/iPad app may not have all the functionality of the web-based access but will provide the most common features, such as the ability to check your account balances or transfer funds from one account to another. In these examples, companies are offering the app as an additional customer service option. Brokerages and bill payment systems are also racing to develop apps for the iPhone/iPad to help facilitate use of their products through mobile devices.

✉ Note

Some companies charge for their extended apps, whereas most give ithem away for free with the idea that only existing subscribers or account holders of their products will use the apps. Kraft Foods has seen tremendous success with its iFood Assistant app, which currently sells for $0.99 on the App Store. The app provides more than 7,000 recipes (with Kraft ingredients of course) and a store locator.

Other apps taking advantage of the mobile platform, but not necessarily charging for them, include commerce apps like eBay and Amazon, email apps like Constant

Contact, social networking apps like Facebook and MySpace, travel apps like Tripit and Hotels.com, and many others. Here are some other reasons why your company should look at the iPhone/iPad platform as a new way to reach your audience:

- The iPhone/iPad mobile platforms provide new and exciting ways to interact with your brands and reach an untapped audience.

- The mobile platform lets users connect and interact with their favorite content in their own way and in their timeframe. When they're connected to your app, you have a huge advantage over your competitors. Apps help create brand loyalty quite effectively because the app provides the means for the end user to interact with your brand daily. There has never been a more powerful and personal way to connect users with brands than through mobile devices.

- Companies can leverage their brands to create new interactive experiences that utilize the power of the iPhone/iPad technologies, such as a camera, GPS, and the accelerometer.

Is an iPhone/iPad App Right for Your Company?

I would argue that most companies are a good fit for creating an iPhone/iPad app to either promote their brands or extend existing services to their customers. However, this advice comes with a few caveats. It's more a question of if a company has the resources and wherewithal to keep the app relevant and significant in the eyes of the customer.

 Note

Using an iPhone/iPad as a branding tool has had mixed results for some companies as they have launched their apps. Using the app as a customer acquisition tool has seen limited success. Using the app as a way to reinforce your brand has seen much better results. It also does take some clever thinking to identify ways to make an app relevant for your brand, which is a crucial part of app success. Your company must produce an app that goes beyond the simple "store locator" functionality that many apps only provide.

For example, a company selling paint might devise a color palette that shows pictures of rooms and walls with any paint color that you select. The paint samples could include an entire inventory of the company's paints and color recommendations. Sherwin William Paint Co. has a similar app (ColorSnap) on the App Store that allows you to snap a photo of something and compare the color to their inventory of paint colors. Not to be outdone, Benjamin Moore also has the same type of app available on the App Store for free.

Building an app is a long-term commitment, and companies need to evaluate carefully if they have the internal resources to maintain the app and support it along with the usual customer issues. Providing an app is a big endeavor, requiring a dedicated internal team to ensure the project's success. The following points should be considered before you embark on app creation:

- What is your demographic of users? Do you have a way to poll your users to identify how many of them are currently using an iPhone or iPad? Recent reports show that about 9% of the U.S. mobile user community has an iPhone.

- Do you understand how your customers are using mobile devices? The iPhone/iPad has more features and capabilities than a lot of other mobile devices. How will your corporate app take advantage of those features?

- How will you measure the success of your app? Do you intend to implement analytics into your app to measure beyond downloads so you can understand which features are being used the most?

- What is your budget for this project? Designing and building a free corporate app can easily cost $50,000, if not much more, when you factor in a small team to design, code, and support the app. Do you have ongoing plans to support and update the app on a regular basis?

- What is your timeframe for releasing the app? Will it coincide with other marketing campaigns you are rolling out?

- How will you promote your app and make its availability known?

Build an App to Extend/Reignite the Brand

Some companies are looking at iPhone/iPad apps to help them improve their brand reputation. What better tool than an iPhone or an iPad to promote your brand? The reason is clear. What other medium can you think of that has such a powerful adoption by their users? The iPhone demographic has their iPhones with them almost constantly. Young people are online more hours every day than they watch TV. If you can get someone to download your app and use it on a regular basis, you are able to reinforce your brand consistently. An iPhone/iPad app is typically used for about three to seven minutes each time it is accessed. No other medium has had this type of reach before.

Rather than attempting to generate a revenue stream, these brands are using apps to create branded mobile experiences that drive usage of the app. This usage helps reinforce the brand and indirectly drive sales. The intention is not to generate income from the app but awareness. There are very few brands that can't benefit from an iPhone/iPad app if it's done properly. Even a grocery store such as Whole Foods was able to create a recipe and grocery list app that helps reinforce their brand, as shown in Figure 23.1. The app does not facilitate sales of their products but builds a strong link between the user and their stores. The user might be more likely to shop at Whole Foods Stores than go elsewhere.

Figure 23.1   Whole Foods has an app that provides recipes and a shopping list feature that helps reinforce their brand.

Another company that has created a free app that provides some useful functionality is Walgreens. The Walgreens App allows you to fill prescriptions and order photos and view the latest sale items; a great combination of features. So in addition to building brand awareness, they are providing some useful functionality at the same time. Their app is shown in Figure 23.2.

The granddaddy of branding using an app has been Zippo. Zippo, the lighter company, developed a virtual lighter that allows users to customize the look of their lighter and simulate an actual flame when the iPhone is moved around. Zippo has had more than three million downloads of their app, making it one of the most downloaded free apps in the history of the App Store. The most popular branded apps for 2009 are shown in Table 23.1. This list will give you a feel for the variety of branded apps that have achieved success and perhaps prompt a few ideas of your own. Figure 23.3 shows the infamous app.

Figure 23.2 The Walgreens App helps them build brand awareness while providing the customer with the ability to fill prescriptions and order photos.

Table 23.1 The Top 10 Most Popular Branded Apps for 2011

App Name	App Function
Zipcar	Zipcar members can find and book a Zipcar, honk the horn, even lock and unlock the doors—all from their iPhone.
Starbucks Mobile Card	Just enter your Starbucks Card number and your iPhone "becomes" your Starbucks Card.
Pizza Hut	Use your iPhone to order your favorite Pizza Hut pizza, pasta, and wings.
Nationwide Mobile	The first iPhone car insurance app, Nationwide Mobile provides an Accident Toolkit that guides you through the steps to take after an accident.
AAMCO, iGUAAGE	iGAAUGE provides a car's maintenance schedule, troubleshoots car issues, provides traffic updates, locates the nearest gas station, contacts roadside assistance, and connects users to the nearest AAMCO.
Kraft iFood Assistant 2.0	iFood Assistant powered by Kraft brings simple food ideas, anytime and anywhere you go. Provides more than 7,000 recipes.
Sherwin-Williams ColorSnap	Find a color you like; snap the photo and receive the matching Sherwin-Williams paint color and coordinating palette.
Barnes and Noble Bookstore	Search millions of books, CDs, and DVDs with your iPhone. Find and reserve products in your local store. Browse recommendations, new releases, and read reviews.
App Name	Make your favorite Chipotle order, assign it to a store location of your choice, and securely pay for food right from your iPhone.
Weber on the Grill	Features 250 classic Weber recipes plus 40 recipes for rubs, marinades, and sauces.

Figure 23.3   The Zippo app has seen more than four million downloads.

Apps to Extend a Web-based Product's Use

Another option companies can use is developing an app that is an extension of existing products or services. These types of apps typically provide a scaled down service of the main web-based app. They often lack all the features of the original app because the app is new or because the original web app is much more complex than an iPhone/iPad app can support. In the case of the recently released app from Fidelity Investments, they offer a lot of the functionality for traders but not all of it. Complex option trades are currently not available in the mobile app, but features that the majority of their audience needs are included. Other apps do not lend themselves well to the smaller iPhone screen. The iPad will eliminate this issue for a lot of these types of apps.

Any company that offers computing on the Web where users access their site for account information, placement of orders, or other online tasks will want to look carefully at extending their functionality to an iPhone/iPad app. It will become vital to provide these apps as more and more users move to mobile technology to accomplish their daily activities. Companies that fail to recognize this trend in mobile technology will find themselves behind the curve and could be at a disadvantage from a competitive standpoint.

Providing a mobile app to extend your web-based technology is also about customer service. Your customers will be pleased when you provide technology that meets their needs and makes their lives easier. Your app can help you retain customers who might move to another bank, broker, or tool because you don't have an iPhone/iPad app available. You can bet your competitors will tout their apps as being better solutions than yours.

Some of the most popular apps that help extend functionality are discussed in the next sections. These are just a few examples of some of the most popular apps. Each of these apps requires a user to already have a login and password for their existing accounts. The apps are of no value to someone who doesn't already use this company's products.

 Note

> As you evaluate the following apps, look for how your product might benefit from an iPhone/iPad app. An app helps you extend access to your existing web-based tools. Your first version can provide just the essentials from your web-based app. Identify the key features that you believe must be in the iPhone/iPad app and determine if the cost of development is acceptable and the need is there for such an app. Be thinking about how your app can benefit customers and noncustomers alike.

NetSuite

NetSuite for iPhone/iPad provides mobile access to NetSuite's integrated business management suite. Included in the app are real-time dashboards, as well as financial and customer data and task management capabilities. The benefit of this app is that it provides CRM access for iPhone/iPad users who are on the road or can't get to their laptops. An example of this app is shown in Figure 23.4.

Fidelity Investments

This app allows you to access your Fidelity brokerage accounts online, place trades, and do stock research. The nice thing about this tool is that even noncustomers can download and use it to watch the markets, do research, or create a watch list. Fidelity has done a nice job with their first entry into the iPhone/iPad app world. Figure 23.5 shows an example of this app available on the App Store.

Figure 23.4   The NetSuite for iPhone/iPad app provides functionality similar to their web-based tools. It requires a user to use their login/password for their existing NetSuite account.

Figure 23.5   Fidelity's app allows customers to access their accounts and place trades. Noncustomers can also use the app to track stocks, do research, and read news.

Woodforest Mobile Banking

Many smaller companies such as regional banks are getting into the iPhone/iPad app game as well. These companies are providing smart customer service options to their loyal customers. The Woodforest Mobile Banking app was designed by an outside development company xcelMe.com and allows customers to check their balances, transfer funds from one account to another, and locate bank branches in the south and southeastern U.S. These apps allow a bank to deliver value to their customers and keep them in the fold and perhaps avoid losing them to a bigger bank with a similar app. Figure 23.6 shows this app and some of the capabilities provided for their customers.

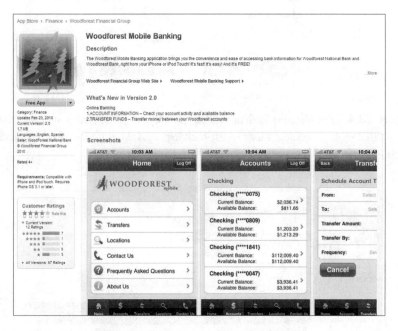

Figure 23.6   Woodforest Mobile Banking app is an example of a regional bank that provides an extension to their online branch service to their Southern and Southeastern customers.

Chipotle

Finally, let's look at one last example of an app that is an extension of a product in the restaurant business. Chipotle has done a very nice job developing their iPhone/iPad app, which allows you to view a menu, locate a restaurant, and place an order securely through their ordering system. You can then go in and pick up your food and avoid the long lines. Figure 23.7 shows an example of this app and its capabilities.

Figure 23.7   Chipotle has been successful providing an app that allows you to place orders at any of their restaurants. This app has seen tremendous success.

Summary

Companies across the globe are realizing that they need to take their product message to their users, wherever they are. As their users are moving toward mobile platforms, smart marketers are looking for ways to leverage this new and exciting technology. iPhone/iPad users provide an "always connected" opportunity where they invite certain forms of advertising; advertising that is clever and at the same time useful.

Many companies are finding that building iPhone/iPad apps can help them extend their brand reach, increase customer interaction, and increase loyalty. They usually don't charge for the app as they can obtain tens of thousands of downloads for free apps and keep their names in front of users. Companies are shifting some of their ad budgets to build iPhone/iPad apps instead of spending it elsewhere.

Other companies are using mobile technology to extend the usefulness of existing web-based tools. These apps are used in banking, commerce, social networking, and many other areas to create extensions of existing services to the mobile platform. It's almost a necessity to provide a mobile-based app as part of your regular online access. Companies that embrace mobile technology will experience greater customer satisfaction and retention than those who wait to implement an app. In the not too distant future having a mobile app will be a prerequisite for many customers when choosing a vendor.

Index

Numbers

148apps.com/price-drops website, 218
20MB size limit, 35

A

AAMCO, 300
ad exchanges, 209-211, 284
ad network companies, 209
Add This button, 280
addictive apps, 35
AdMob, 104-105, 209-210, 284
Adobe After Effects, 124
advertising, 100
  ad exchanges, 209-211, 284
  ad network companies, 209
  communities, building, 108-109
  cross-promotion, 194
  goals, setting, 288-289
  in free apps, 209-211
  iAds, 211-213
  in-app advertising, 279

mobile ad providers, 103-104
  AdMob, 104-105
  Mobclix, 105
  pay per install, 105
newspaper advertising, 100-102
online advertising, 107-108
paid ad campaigns, 240
paid placement programs, 106-107
radio and TV advertising, 102-103
targeted advertising, 278
Adwhirl, 209-211
AdWords, 280
allocating marketing funds, 251
analytics
  app interface patterns, measuring, 239-240
  event tracking, 239
  explained, 235-236
  Flurry, 240-241
  importance of, 278-279

location tracking, 236-237
Mobclix, 241-243
paid ad campaigns, 240
privacy, 244-245
sales tracking, 236
usage tracking, 237-239
Angry Birds, 17
App Annie, 289
App Figures, 255
App Store. *See also* apps
  achieving success on, 13-14
  App Store text
    building total message, 77-79
    optimizing web copy, 196
    updating, 270
  categories
    explained, 11-12
    selecting for your app, 59-60
  New and Noteworthy, 198
  number of apps on, 10-11
  searching, 13
  showcase apps on, 276-277
  Staff Picks, 198

top 100, breaking into,
189-190
app integration with
other apps, 195
app price, 195
app quality, 190-192
app size, 194
Apple reviews, 198
building brand, 196-197
cross-promotion, 194
networking, 192-193
testing and feedback, 192
web and App Store copy,
196
What's Hot, 198
Apple reviews, 198
apps. See also specific apps
app buying cycles, 126-128
Big Win apps
benefits/drawbacks, 22
characteristics of, 14-18
buying cycles, 126-128
characteristics of winning
apps
20MB size limit, 35
addictiveness, 35
new features, 28-29
seasonal and holiday
apps, 32-33
social networking-related
apps, 32-34
trendiness, 30-31
uniqueness, 26-28
collaborating with other
vendors, 284
competition
competing against free
apps, 155-158
definition of, 40
direct versus indirect
competitors, 42-44
evaluating apps against,
254-255
explained, 40-42
identifying, 42-44
learning from, 45-47

corporate apps
advantages of, 295-297
extending
products/services with,
301-305
extending/reigniting
brands with, 298-301
when to use, 297-298
creating from other
platforms, 33-34
customer service, 157-158
documentation, 157
free apps
ads, 209-211
advantages of, 204-205,
283
building paid apps and
free apps at same time,
206-209
iAds, 211-213
as marketing tool,
201-204
functionality, 264
graphics, 156-157
icons, 80-81, 284-285
identifying your app's
unique value, 37-39
app benefits, 48-49
key features, 47-48
questions to ask, 39-40
unique qualities of app,
50-51
in-app purchases, 65, 208
intuitive design, 156
launching
coordinating app
launches, 253
launch sponsors, 283
timing, 131-132
winning strategies,
129-131
naming, 70-77
brainstorming for app
names, 68-76
educational apps, 71-72
games, 72-73

Google and Yahoo
searches, 76-77
guidelines, 74-75
seasonal apps, 72-74
synonyms, 76
testing names, 77
No Win apps, 20-21
pricing, 167-168, 195
average price, 215-217
breakeven analysis,
161-164, 175-176
competing against free
apps, 155-158
cost/benefit analysis,
168-175
factors to consider,
153-155
"free for limited time"
offers, 222
lowering price, 218-220
misconceptions, 158-160
offering free versions,
160
price sensitivity, 181
price strategy in
marketing plans, 265
pricing objectives, 260
raising price, 217
setting price, 160-165,
255
strategies, 161-162, 279
temporary price drops,
220
value-add sales, 221
productivity apps, 184
recommender apps, 129
sales objectives, 259-260
seasonal apps, 127
showcasing on App Store,
276-277
size of, 35, 194
Steady Win apps
benefits/drawbacks, 22
characteristics of, 18-19
submitting for review,
131-132

target audience,
identifying, 55-57
*picking your market
segment, 62-63*
refining audience, 57
*segmenting market,
57-62*
targeting market, 63-65
technical support, 157
"total message," building,
67-70
app icons, 80-81
app name, 70-77
App Store text, 77-79
graphics, 79
product websites, 82-84
reviews, 85-86
updates, importance of, 15,
28-29, 283
value. *See* value
AppsForAll Healthful Apps, 93
appshopper.com, 218
audiences. *See* target audience,
identifying
average app price, 215-217

B

balancing marketing activities,
271-274
BarMaxCA, 184
Barnes and Noble, 300
Base Hit apps
benefits/drawbacks, 22
characteristics of, 18-19
belief and value systems, 58
benefits of apps
identifying, 48-49
quantifying, 172-174. *See
also* cost/benefit analysis
Benjamin Moore, 298
beta testers, 192
Bic Concert Lighter, 205, 296
Big Win apps
benefits/drawbacks, 22
characteristics of, 14-18
BigNerdRanch, 171

Blanks, 296
Blogger, 121
blogs, marketing with,
120-121, 282
body copy (press releases),
144-145
brainstorming for app names,
68-76
brands
building, 196-197
extending/reigniting with
corporate apps, 298-301
breakeven analysis, 161-164,
175-176
budgeting for marketing,
270-271
business environment, 261-262
buyers
app reviews
importance of, 85-86
*positive external reviews,
92-94*
*reading competitors'
reviews, 61*
communities, building,
108-109
privacy expectations,
244-245
reaching interested
buyers, 96
buying cycles (apps), 126-128

C

calendar (marketing), 265-267
categories (App Store)
explained, 11-12
selecting for your app,
59-60
challenges of app marketing,
9-10
Chipotle, 296, 300, 304-305
Clancy, Tom, 16
Coin Dozer, 65
collaborating with other
vendors, 284
ColorSnap, 298, 300

communities, building,
108-109
competition, 261-262
competing against free
apps, 155-158
definition of, 40
direct versus indirect
competitors, 42-44
evaluating apps against,
254-255
explained, 40-42
identifying, 42-44
learning from, 45-47
Constant Contact, 297
consumer analysis, 262
contests, 225
coordinating
app launches, 253
marketing efforts, 94-95
corporate apps. *See also*
specific apps
advantages of, 295-297
extending or reigniting
brands with, 298-301
extending products or
services with, 301-305
when to use, 297-298
cost/benefit analysis, 168-175
marketing costs, 270-271
performing cost/benefit
comparison, 174-175
quantifying app
development costs,
169-172
quantifying benefits,
172-174
cross-promotion, 194
cross-selling
advantages of, 223-224
recommendations, 227-231
up-selling, 231-233
customer reviews. *See* reviews
customer service, 157-158
customers. *See* buyers

D

Daily App Show, 193
delegating tasks, 292
delivery methods, choosing, 96-97
demand, generating, 95-96
demographics, 58, 261
development costs, quantifying, 169-172
Digg.com, 282
digital signatures for press releases, 147-148
direct competition, 42-44
direct mail, 97-98
direct marketing
  direct mail, 97-98
  email, 99-100, 276-278
distributing press releases, 148-150
DMOZ, 280
documentation, 157
Doodle Jump, 17

E

eating healthy apps, 30
educational apps, naming, 71-72
eldergadget.com, 93
electronic word of mouth
  coordinated marketing efforts, 94-95
  delivery methods, 96-97
  generating demand, 95-96
  importance of, 89-92
  positive external reviews, 92-94
  reaching interested buyers, 96
email, direct marketing with, 99-100, 276-278
embedded links in press releases, 145-146
essential marketing activities
  after app launch, 273-274
  during app launch, 273
  prior to app launch, 271-272

evaluating apps against competition, 254-255
events, tracking, 239
extending
  brands with corporate apps, 298-301
  products/services with corporate apps, 301-305
external reviews, 92-94

F

Facebook, marketing with, 115-117, 282
fashion apps, 30-31
feedback, soliciting, 192
Fidelity Investments, 302-303
Final Cut Pro, 124
financial information in marketing plans, 265
Flick Fishing, 228-229
Flurry, 160, 289
  analytics, 240-241
  pay per install programs, 105
focus, 292
Follow Us notes, 281
forums, 282-283
Fram Oil, 283
free apps
  ads, 209-211
  advantages of, 204-205, 283
  building paid apps and free apps at same time, 206-209
  competing against, 155-158
  "free for limited time" offers, 222, 226
  iAds, 211-213
  as marketing tool, 201-204
  offering, 160
"free for limited time" offers, 222, 226
Freeverse Flick Fishing, 228-229
Fruit Ninja, 17
funding, obtaining, 253

G

games, naming, 72-74. *See also* specific games
Garmin, 183
Gas Cubby, 129-130, 283
generating demand, 95-96
Giuliani, Rudi, 14
giveaways, 226
goals, setting, 288-289
Google
  AdMob, 104-105
  AdWords, 280
  searching for app name ideas, 76-77
GPS apps, 182-183
Grand Slam apps
  benefits/drawbacks, 22
  characteristics of, 14-18
graphics, 156-157
  app icons, 80-81
  importance of, 79
green apps, 30
growth, planning for, 252

H

half-off sales, 226
headlines, writing for press releases, 142-143
Healthful Apps app, 93
healthy eating apps, 30
hiring writers, 138-139
holiday apps, 32-33, 72-74
holiday promotions, 265-267
home decor apps, 31
The Hunt for Red October (Clancy), 16

I

I Am T-Pain, 191
iAds, 211-213
icons, 80-81, 284-285
iFood Assistant, 296, 300
iGUAAGE, 300
iHandy, 198

Illiger, Andreas, 15
implementing marketing
 plans. *See* marketing plans
in-app advertising, 279
in-app cross-selling, 230
in-app purchases, 65, 208
indirect competition, 42-44
interested buyers, reaching, 96
interface patterns, measuring,
 239-240
intuitive design, 156
iPhone simulator, 124
iShoot, 204
iTunes App Store. *See* App
 Store
iTunes Connect, 289

J-K

Jefferson, Thomas, 250
Jobs, Steve, 211

key features, identifying, 48-49
Kraft Foods iFood Assistant,
 296, 300

L

Lacy, Andrew, 204
launch sponsors, 283
launching
 apps
  coordinating app
   launches, 253
  launch sponsors, 283
  timing, 131-132
  winning strategies,
   129-131
 press releases, 149-150
learning from competition,
 45-47
life stage, 58
lifestyle, 58
LinkedIn, 121-122, 281
links, embedding in press
 releases, 145-146
location, tracking, 236-237
lowering app price, 218-220

M

Mac applications, developing
 iPhone apps from, 33-34
managing marketing activities,
 291-292
market
 market analysis, 260-261
 picking your market
  segment, 62-63
 segmenting, 57-62
 targeting, 63-65
marketing
 advertising, 100
  ad exchanges, 284
  communities, building,
   108-109
  goals, setting, 288-289
  in-app advertising, 279
  mobile ad providers,
   103-105
  newspaper advertising,
   100-102
  online advertising,
   107-108
  paid placement
   programs, 106-107
  radio and TV
   advertising, 102-103
  targeted advertising, 278
 analytics
  app interface patterns,
   measuring, 239-240
  event tracking, 239
  explained, 235-236
  Flurry, 240-241
  importance of, 278-279
  location tracking,
   236-237
  Mobclix, 241-243
  paid ad campaigns, 240
  privacy, 244-245
  sales tracking, 236
  usage tracking, 237-239
 App Store text. *See* App
  Store

balance of marketing
 activities, 271-274
breaking into top 100,
 189-190
 app integration with
  other apps, 195
 app price, 195
 app quality, 190-192
 app size, 194
 Apple reviews, 198
 building brand, 196-197
 cross-promotion, 194
 networking, 192-193
 testing and feedback, 192
 web and App Store copy,
  196
budgeting for, 269-271
calendar, 265-267
challenges of, 9-10
collaborating with other
 vendors, 284
competition
 definition of, 40
 direct versus indirect
  competitors, 42-44
 explained, 40-42
 identifying, 42-44
 learning from, 45-47
corporate apps, 301-302
 advantages of, 295-297
 extending
  products/services with,
  301-305
 extending/reigniting
  brands with, 298-301
 when to use, 297-298
cross-selling
 advantages of, 223-224
 recommendations,
  227-231
 up-selling, 231-233
direct marketing
 direct mail, 97-98
 email, 99-100, 276-278
electronic word of mouth
 coordinated marketing
  efforts, 94-95

delivery methods, 96-97
generating demand,
  95-96
importance of, 89-92
positive external reviews,
  92-94
reaching interested
  buyers, 96
essential activities
  during app launch, 273
  after app launch,
    273-274
  prior to app launch,
    271-272
free apps
  ads, 209-211
  advantages of, 204-205,
    283
  building paid apps and
    free apps at same time,
    206-209
  offering, 160, 201-204
identifying your app's
unique value, 37-39
  app benefits, 48-49
  key features, 47-48
  questions to ask, 39-40
  unique qualities of app,
    50-51
marketing plans
  advantages of, 250-256
  app sales objectives,
    259-260
  business environment,
    261-262
  explained, 249-250
  financial information,
    265
  goals, setting, 288-289
  managing marketing
    activities, 291-292
  market analysis, 260-261
  marketing calendar,
    265-267
  marketing focus,
    264-265

  measuring progress,
    289-290
  pricing objectives, 260
  product objectives, 259
  profit objectives, 260
  ROI (return on
    investment),
    measuring, 290-291
  SWOT analysis, 262-263
  table of components,
    257-259
  target audience,
    identifying, 290
press releases, 135-136
  body copy, 144-145
  embedded links, 145-146
  headlines, 142-143
  hiring a writer versus
    writing it yourself,
    138-139
  multimedia, 146-147
  publishing and
    distributing, 148-150
  signatures, 147-148
  structure of, 139-142
  summary copy, 143-144
  when to use, 277
  when to write, 136-138
pricing. See pricing apps
promotions
  advantages of, 223-224
  contests, 225
  defining, 255
  describing in marketing
    plans, 264-265
  "free for limited time"
    offers, 226
  half-off sales, 226
  holiday promotions,
    265-267
  periodic giveaways, 226
  questions to ask, 224
  recommendations,
    226-227
recommender apps, 129
reviews, soliciting, 276, 284

selling value, 179-182
  price sensitivity, 181
  quality, 182-183
  return on investment,
    184-185
  tips and
    recommendations,
    186-187
  usefulness, 183-185
social media, 111-115
  blogs, 120-121, 282
  Digg.com, 282
  Facebook, 115-117, 282
  forums, 282-283
  LinkedIn, 121-122, 281
  marketing tips, 112-114
  RSS feeds, 121
  Twitter, 118-119
  YouTube, 123-124, 281
sponsorships, 129-130, 283
target audience,
  identifying, 55-57
  picking your market
    segment, 62-63
  refining audience, 57
  segmenting market,
    57-62
  targeting market, 63-65
timing marketing activities,
  125-126
  app buying cycles,
    126-128
  app launches, 131-132
  press release launches,
    148-149
  winning strategies,
    129-131
"total message," building,
  67-70
  app icons, 80-81
  app name, 70-77
  App Store text, 77-79
  graphics, 79
  product websites, 82-84
viral marketing, 158
word of mouth, 278

marketing plans
  advantages of, 250-256
  app sales objectives,
    259-260
  business environment,
    261-262
  explained, 249-250
  financial information, 265
  goals, setting, 288-289
  managing marketing
    activities, 291-292
  market analysis, 260-261
  marketing calendar,
    265-267
  marketing focus, 264-265
  measuring progress,
    289-290
  pricing objectives, 260
  product objectives, 259
  profit objectives, 260
  ROI (return on
    investment), measuring,
    290-291
  SWOT analysis, 262-263
  table of components,
    257-259
  target audience,
    identifying, 290
measuring
  app interface patterns,
    239-240
  progress, 252, 289-290
  ROI (return on
    investment), 290-291
misconceptions of app pricing,
  158-160
MLB.Com app, 19
Mobclix, 105, 209-211, 240,
  241-243
mobile ad providers, 103-104
  AdMob, 104-105
  Mobclix, 105
  pay per install, 105
mobile GPS apps, 182-183
MovableType, 121
multimedia, attaching to press
  releases, 146-147

N

naming apps, 70-77
  brainstorming for app
    names, 68-76
  educational apps, 71-72
  games, 72-73
  Google and Yahoo
    searches, 76-77
  guidelines, 74-75
  seasonal apps, 72-74
  synonyms, 76
  testing names, 77
Nationwide Mobile, 300
NetSuite, 302-303
networking, 192-193
New and Noteworthy
  category, 198
new features, 28-29
news, tying apps into, 30-31
newspaper advertising,
  100-102
Nicholas, Ethan, 204
No Win apps, 20-21

O

objectives
  app sales objectives,
    259-260
  pricing objectives, 260
  product objectives, 259
  profit objectives, 260
obtaining funding, 253
online advertising, 107-108
opportunities, analyzing, 263
optimizing web and App Store
  copy, 196

P

paid ad campaigns, 240
paid placement programs,
  106-107
paid search, 106-107
pay per install programs, 105
PC applications, developing
  iPhone apps from, 33-34

periodic giveaways, 226
Pinch Media, 160, 240-241
Pizza Hut, 300
plans (marketing)
  advantages of, 250-256
  app sales objectives,
    259-260
  explained, 249-250
  goals, setting, 288-289
  managing marketing
    activities, 291-292
  measuring progress,
    289-290
  product objectives, 259
  profit objectives, 260
  ROI (return on
    investment), measuring,
    290-291
  table of components,
    257-259
  target audience,
    identifying, 290
Pocket God, 15
posting on YouTube, 123-124
press releases, 135-136
  body copy, 144-145
  embedded links, 145-146
  headlines, 142-143
  hiring a writer versus
    writing it yourself,
    138-139
  multimedia, 146-147
  publishing and
    distributing, 148-150
  signatures, 147-148
  structure of, 139-142
  summary copy, 143-144
  when to use, 277
  when to write, 136-138
pricing apps, 167-168, 195. *See
  also* selling value
  average price, 215-217
  breakeven analysis,
    161-164, 175-176
  competing against free
    apps, 155-158

cost/benefit analysis,
168-175
*performing cost/benefit
comparison, 174-175*
*quantifying app
development costs,
169-172*
*quantifying benefits,
172-174*
factors to consider, 153-155
"free for limited time"
offers, 222
lowering price, 218-220
misconceptions, 158-160
offering free versions, 160
price sensitivity, 181
price strategy in marketing
plans, 265
pricing objectives, 260
pricing pressure, 10
raising price, 217
setting price, 160-165, 255
strategies, 161-162, 279
temporary price drops, 220
value-add sales, 221
privacy, analytics and, 244-245
PRMac, 148-149
product objectives, 259
product websites, 82-84
promoting, 280-281
SEO (search engine
optimization), 280
web content guidelines, 84
web copy, 82-83
productivity apps, 184
products, extending with
corporate apps, 301-305
profit objectives, 260
progress, measuring, 252,
289-290
promotions
advantages of, 223-224
contests, 225
defining, 255
describing in marketing
plans, 264-265

"free for limited time"
offers, 226
half-off sales, 226
holiday promotions, 265-
267
periodic giveaways, 226
questions to ask, 224
recommendations, 226-227
PRWeb, 148-149
publishing press releases,
148-150

Q

quality, selling, 182-183
quantifying
app development costs,
169-172
benefits, 172-174

R

radio advertising, 102-103
raising price, 217
reading competitors' reviews,
61
Reagan, Ronald, 16
Real Simple Syndication
(RSS), 121
recommender apps, 129
refining audience, 57
reigniting brands with
corporate apps, 298-301
results, tracking, 290-291
return on investment (ROI)
measuring, 290-291
selling, 184-185
reviews
Apple reviews, 198
importance of, 85-86
positive external reviews,
92-94
reading competitors'
reviews, 61
soliciting, 192-193, 276, 284
submitting apps for,
131-132

roadmap for growth, 252
ROI (return on investment),
measuring, 290-291
RSS feeds, marketing with, 121

S

sales, tracking, 236
sales objectives, 259-260
sales targets, 253-254
Save Benjis, 19
search engine optimization
(SEO), 280
searching
for app name ideas, 76-77
App Store, 13
paid search programs,
106-107
seasonal apps, 32-33, 72-74,
127
segmenting market, 57-62
selling value, 179-182
price sensitivity, 181
quality, 182-183
return on investment,
184-185
tips and recommendations,
186-187
usefulness, 183-185
SEO (search engine
optimization), 280
services, extending with
corporate apps, 301-305
Sherwin Williams Paint Co.,
298, 300
showcasing apps on App Store,
276-277
signatures for press releases,
147-148
size of apps, 35, 194
Smule, 197
Snapz Pro X, 124
social media, 111-115
blogs, 120-121, 282
Digg.com, 282
Facebook, 115-117, 282
forums, 282-283

LinkedIn, 121-122, 281
  marketing tips, 112-114
  RSS feeds, 121
  Twitter, 118-119
  YouTube, 123-124, 281
social networking-related
  apps, 32-34
soliciting
  feedback, 192
  reviews, 276, 284
sponsorships, 129-130
Staff Picks category, 198
Starbucks Mobile Card, 300
Steady Win apps
  benefits/drawbacks, 22
  characteristics of, 18-19
strengths, analyzing, 262-263
Strikeout apps, 20-21
submitting apps for review,
  131-132
summary copy (press
  releases), 143-144
Survey Monkey, 192
surveys, 192
SWOT analysis, 262-263
synonyms, 76

T

Tap Metrics, 254
Tap Tap Revenge, 221
Tapjoy, 105
TapMini, 254
Tapulous, 204
target audience, identifying,
  55-57, 251, 290
  picking your market
    segment, 62-63
  refining audience, 57
  segmenting market, 57-62
  targeting market, 63-65
targeted advertising, 278
technical support, 157
temporary price drops, 220
Terms of Service (TOS)
  document, 244
testing app names, 77

Threadless, Inc., 225
threats, analyzing, 263
timing marketing activities,
  125-126
  app buying cycles, 126-128
  app launches, 131-132
  press release launches,
    148-149
  winning strategies, 129-131
Tiny Wings, 15-16, 35, 203
top 100, breaking into, 189-190
  app integration with other
    apps, 195
  app price, 195
  app quality, 190-192
  app size, 194
  Apple reviews, 198
  building brand, 196-197
  cross-promotion, 194
  networking, 192-193
  testing and feedback, 192
  web and App Store copy,
    196
TOS (Terms of Service)
  document, 244
"total message," building, 67-70
  app icons, 80-81
  app name, 70-77
  App Store text, 77-79
  graphics, 79
  product websites, 82-84
  reviews, 85-86
tracking
  app's usage, 237-239
  app's use by location,
    236-237
  results, 290-291
  sales, 236
  specific app events, 239
trends, tying apps into, 30-31
trial versions. *See* free apps
TV advertising, 102-103
tweets, marketing with,
  118-119
Twitter, marketing with,
  118-119
Typepad, 121

U

uniqueness
  identifying your app's
    unique value, 37-39
    app benefits, 48-49
    key features, 47-48
    questions to ask, 39-40
    unique qualities of app,
      50-51
  importance of, 26-28
updates, importance of, 28-29
updating
  App Store text, 270
  apps, 15, 283
up-selling, 231-233
usefulness, selling, 183-185

V

value, 186-187, 218-220
  defining app's value
    proposition, 256
  identifying, 37-40, 284-285
    key features, 47-48
    unique qualities of app,
      50-51
  selling, 179-182
    price sensitivity, 181
    quality, 182-183
    return on investment,
      184-185
    tips and
      recommendations,
      186-187
    usefulness, 183-185
value-add sales, 221
Vans: House of Vans, 296
videos, posting on YouTube,
  123-124
viral marketing, 158

W

Walgreens App, 299
weaknesses, analyzing, 263
web content guidelines, 84
Weber on the Grill, 300

websites, 82-84
  optimizing web copy, 196
  promoting, 280-281
  SEO (search engine
    optimization), 280
  web content guidelines, 84
  web copy, 82-83
What's Hot category, 198
Whole Foods, 299
Woodforest Mobile Banking,
  304
word of mouth, 278
  coordinated marketing
    efforts, 94-95
  delivery methods, 96-97
  generating demand, 95-96
  importance of, 89-92
  positive external reviews,
    92-94
  reaching interested
    buyers, 96
WordPress, 121
Words with Friends app, 229
writing press releases, 135-136
  body copy, 144-145
  embedded links, 145-146

  headlines, 142-143
  hiring a writer versus
    writing it yourself,
    138-139
  multimedia, 146-147
  publishing and
    distributing, 148-150
  signatures, 147-148
  structure of, 139-142
  summary copy, 143-144
  when to write, 136-138

X-Z

xcelMe.com, 304

Yahoo, searching for app name
  ideas, 76-77
YouTube, marketing with,
  123-124, 281

Zipcar, 300
Zippo, 296, 299

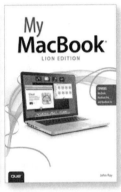

iPhone & iPad Apps MARKETING

Secrets to Selling Your iPhone and iPad Apps

JEFFREY HUGHES

FREE Online Edition

Your purchase of *iPhone and iPad Apps Marketing* includes access to a free online edition for 45 days through the Safari Books Online subscription service. Nearly every Que book is available online through Safari Books Online, along with more than 5,000 other technical books and videos from publishers such as Addison-Wesley Professional, Cisco Press, Exam Cram, IBM Press, O'Reilly, Prentice Hall, and Sams.

SAFARI BOOKS ONLINE allows you to search for a specific answer, cut and paste code, download chapters, and stay current with emerging technologies.

Activate your FREE Online Edition at
www.informit.com/safarifree

> **STEP 1:** Enter the coupon code: SVSZKCB.

> **STEP 2:** New Safari users, complete the brief registration form. Safari subscribers, just log in.

If you have difficulty registering on Safari or accessing the online edition, please e-mail customer-service@safaribooksonline.com